Dream On, America

A History of Faith and Practice

Volume I

Frederick Gentles

Melvin Steinfield

San Diego Mesa College

 Canfield Press
San Francisco

A Department of Harper & Row, Publishers, Inc.

New York • Evanston • London

". . . one nation under God, indivisible,
with liberty and justice for all."

DREAM ON, AMERICA: A History of Faith and Practice, Vol. I
    Copyright © 1971 by Frederick Gentles and Melvin Steinfield

Standard Book Number: 06—382777—8

Library of Congress Catalog Card Number: 72—151347

Cover and Interior Illustrations by Robert Bausch

Contents

Preface   vii

1   Origins of the American Dream

Essay:
It's Only a Dream   3
Frederick Gentles

Readings:
The Politics   14
Aristotle

The Unnaturalness of Doing Wrong   17
Cicero

Urban Institutions and Law   21
Henri Pirenne

The Magna Carta   27

The Need for Discipline Within Freedom   32
Jack Perry

What's Right With America   36
Norman Thomas

Questions   40

2   Puritan Truths and the American Dream

Essay:
True Believers in the Promised Land   45
Frederick Gentles

Readings:
The Way to Wealth   50
Benjamin Franklin

On Puritans   58
Charles A. Beard

Errand Into the Wilderness   63
Perry Miller

BYU—A Campus of Peace and Patriotism   67
John Dart

Rituals—The Revolt Against the Fixed Smile   74
Melvin Maddocks

The True Believer   80
Eric Hoffer

Questions   81

3   The Declaration of Independence as Dream and Reality

Essay:
Dissecting the Declaration of Independence   85
Melvin Steinfield

Readings:
Hedging on Slavery   94
Thomas Jefferson

The Myth of the Savage Indian   95
Ashley Montagu

The Literary Qualities of the Declaration   98
Carl Becker

The Promise of Equality   104
William Lloyd Garrison

Is Freedom Dying in America?   106
Henry Steele Commager

Equality of Educational Opportunity   117
Andrew Billingsley, Douglas Davidson, Theresa Loya

Questions   127

4   The Dream of "One Nation, Indivisible"

Essay:
Challenges to the Federal System   131
Melvin Steinfield

Readings:
The Articles of Confederation   140

The Nullification Crisis   144
John A. Garraty

The Union Above All   150
Abraham Lincoln

A More Perfect Union   152
D. W. Brogan

Federalism in 1970   155
Henry Brandon

The Federal Role in Education   158
Clark Kerr

Questions   164

5   Ethnic Minorities and the American Dream

Essay:
The Myth of the Melting Pot   167
Melvin Steinfield

Readings:
Anti-Chinese Riots   176
Betty Lee Sung

Contents

Ethnic Groups and the Melting Pot   181
Nathan Glazer and Daniel P. Moynihan

The American Irish   188
William Shannon

Recent Trends in Anti-Semitism   195
Howard M. Sacher

Today's Ghettos   201
Paul Jacobs and Saul Landau

Questions   203

6   The Dream of Westward Expansion in the Nineteenth Century

Essay:
Rationalizations for Territorial Acquisition   207
Melvin Steinfield

Readings:
Not Counting Mexicans   213
Carey McWilliams

Racial Oppression   220
Walton Bean

The Traps of Expansionism   231
Frederick Merk

Will the Indians Get Whitey?   239
John Greenway

America's Obligations   250
William Jennings Bryan

The Frontier That No Longer Exists   254
Walter Allen

Questions   256

7   Civil War, Hot and Cold

Essay:
The House Is Divided, Mr. Lincoln   259
Frederick Gentles

Readings:
Lincoln's House Divided Speech   265
Abraham Lincoln

South Carolina Declaration of Causes of Secession   266
South Carolina Convention

The Emancipation Proclamation   270
John Hope Franklin

The Radicals and Lincoln   275
David Donald

Contents

The Negro in American life: 1865–1918   279
    C. Vann Woodward

Report of the National Advisory Commission
on Civil Disorders   287
    Otto Kerner, Chairman

The Black Nation   292
    James Burnham

Questions   294

Preface

Classic expressions of the American Dream vary from official documents such as the Declaration of Independence, to presidential speeches such as the Gettysburg Address, to popular literary images such as the Horatio Alger myth of success. The American Dream is many things to many people, but it includes the ideals of liberty, equality, individual rights, rugged individualism, unlimited opportunity, democracy, education, change, progress, and the Christian ethic of love and charity.

What could be more relevant to concerned students today than a fresh examination of the successes and failures of the American Dream? In this book, we have attempted to assess the gap between the *promises* and the *practices* of American history. Our approach has been to compare traditional goals and ideals—the basis of the American Dream—with the realities of the past and present. We have not hesitated to cite praiseworthy achievements of the American experience, nor have we shied from reporting shocking failures. By "telling it like it is"—and was—we seek to involve students in judging the historical performance of their country. Pride mingled with shame will undoubtedly be the emotional reactions to the topics discussed in this text.

The book consists of seven chapters, each centering around a different theme, starting with the European background and Puritan experience and progressing to the Civil War and Reconstruction. The emphasis is on ideas and concepts, not facts; on understanding, not memorizing; on connecting past to present to show that our history is alive, vivid, meaningful. Primarily, we hope that *Dream On, America* will provide the impetus for discussion and written expression in class, as well as encourage outside assignments involving further research in history, political science, and man's behavior—particularly that of American man—as he responds and reacts to his ideals.

It is impossible to acknowledge every individual who assisted in the development of this book, but a few names do stand out for the magnitude of their contribution. Special thanks go to Gracia Alkema, whom we consider a co-author because of her creative contributions as copyeditor and production editor in taking *Dream On, America* from manuscript to book. The rest of the Canfield Press staff—especially Joseph Dana, Brian Williams, and Ann Wehrlen—offered expert assistance in many ways. Of course, the authors assume responsibility for all interpretations in their essays and any errors that might appear in the book.

Frederick Gentles

Melvin Steinfield

1

Origins
of the American Dream

Essay

It's Only a Dream
Frederick Gentles

Readings

The Politics
Aristotle

The Unnaturalness of Doing Wrong
Cicero

Urban Institutions and Law
Henri Pirenne

The Magna Carta

The Need for Discipline Within Freedom
Jack Perry

What's Right With America
Norman Thomas

The American Dream is not uniquely American. It has been dreamed
by other peoples at other times on African, Asian, and European continents.
But though there have been times when the vision of democracy and
freedom has been realized here and there, the dream—as dreams so
often do—flickered like an old movie and then went out.
"Dream On, America" has been developed in the hope that the ideals
and goals which are the basis of that Dream will be better understood
and will finally come true—with liberty and justice for all.

It's Only a Dream

Frederick Gentles

The mystique of the American Dream has captured the imagination of the world, for it has created a glamour and a dynamism that
make this country stand in vivid contrast to less vital societies. The
aura surrounding the Dream is complex and not easily described. It is
like a beautiful impressionistic painting contrasted with one of stark
reality, though the Dream has its share of realism, too. The Dream
has what John F. Kennedy had, and what Calvin Coolidge did not—
soul—but this is not to say that it excludes the "straight" man. The
Dream encompasses the schoolroom and the barroom down the
street, sedate Southern gentleman and rowdy Western cowpoke, Wall
Street and Beal Street, church steeple and bank vault—impressions
are manifold of the amazing Dream that has excited the world.

The Dream is not 100 percent American. It evolved from a light in
the mind of a Golden Age Greek, and later from a down-to-earth
Roman, and still later from a liberty-minded Englishman of the
Middle Ages. It evolved from the minds of several Frenchmen of
early modern times, including John Calvin, Montesquieu, Jean Jacques
Rousseau, and Voltaire. It developed vaguely in Germany through
the nationalism of Herder, Hegel, and Wagner, and it came on strong
in Britain with John Locke, Adam Smith, Charles Darwin, and Herbert
Spencer. Part of the Dream comes from the English Bill of Rights of
1689 and the Declaration of the Rights of Man proclaimed during the
French Revolution one hundred years later. The Dream is a mixture
of economic, religious, democratic, national, and social elements woven
together in a complex fabric.

Economics and the Dream

One aspect of the American Dream has its roots in the very beginnings of civilization. Historians have suggested that man learned to read and write, at least in part, as a result of trade in and between the first towns of the lower Tigris and Euphrates valleys (Mesopotamia), where goods were labeled with seals and then with more detailed descriptions to identify and keep records of them. Ninety percent of the cuneiform tablets found in this most ancient of lands are business records of transactions engaged in by individuals and city or temple governments. From these records, says the Sumerian scholar Samuel Noah Kramer, one sees the genesis of a commercialism that was to vitalize and at the same time disturb society way into the twentieth century.

The commercial spirit was not as profound in ancient Israel or Greece as it later was in Rome where great emphasis was placed on trade, engineering, and the acquisition of worldly goods. Roads, aqueducts, markets, multistoryed apartments, and large cities testify to a lively economy. It has been said that America more closely resembles Rome at its height than it does Israel or Greece—that it is oriented more to the practical (material) side of life than to the spiritual or intellectual. Businessmen and soldiers dominated the Roman governmental establishment during its heyday.

During most of the Middle Ages, people were dedicated to the Church and to life on the manor, but toward the end of that era commercialism—with its attendant emphasis on materialism—came again to the fore with cities dedicated to trade and industry. The medieval city, inspired by a desire for spices, stones, and silks that had been discovered by the Crusaders in the East, was a bustling mecca of artisans, merchants, bankers, and professionals of various sorts who linked their given names to their livelihood or to some other distinctive feature; hence, John the Smith, William the Carpenter, Charles the Tailor, Joseph the Mason, Tom Brown or Small or Young or Wise, and John's son or Tom's son or Peter's son. Freedom from the dull and often oppressive manor life and opportunities of enterprise were the attractions of the city. A vigorous economy, characterized by controls on wages, prices, and profits, evolved. Imagine a system with no inflation. Professor Henri Pirenne writes:

> The city economy was worthy of the Gothic architecture with which it was contemporary. It created with complete thoroughness—and, it may well be said, it created *ex nihilo*—a social legislation more complete than that of any other period in history, including our own. In doing away with the middleman

4

between buyer and seller, it assured to the burgher the benefit of a low cost of living; it ruthlessly pursued fraud, protected the worker from competition and exploitation, regulated his labor and his wage, watched over his health, provided for apprenticeship, forbade woman- and child-labor, and at the same time succeeded in keeping in its own hands the monopoly of furnishing the neighboring country with its products and in opening up distant markets for its trade.[1]

Sounds a bit like America evolving after the dream of Franklin D. Roosevelt's New Deal of social security measures, and a bit like Richard M. Nixon's proposal for a guaranteed annual income. In writing about the late Middle Ages, Pirenne also speaks of compulsory taxation, with everyone contributing according to his means. Studies of the era indicate that the medieval burgher was quite content in his egalitarian society which provided for schools, aid to the poor, pensions of sorts for the aged, public works, and control of business in the interest of the public good.

The commercial spirit dominated western civilization as it moved from the late Middle Ages into the Renaissance and early modern times. The materialistic drives of Spanish, Portuguese, French, Dutch, and English founded colonies in the New World. The dream of wealth has become a major part of the overall Dream in which Americans worship not always God, but the wonder man has wrought.

Religion and the Dream

God has played a part in the Dream nevertheless. The God of Christianity goes back to the Old Testament people of ancient Israel. The experiences of these early people have had a substantial influence on American life. The Ten Commandments form the moral base for western and American civilizations, although the parts about killing and coveting have been modified to comply with economic and nationalistic aspects of modern civilization. The Hebrews felt they were the Chosen People of the ancient world. Many Americans dream they are the Chosen People of the modern world. It is more than a dream, say enthusiastic Americans enamored with their upholstered lives; it is a fact.

The "Chosen People" dream was not unique to the Hebrews. To some degree at least, people of all the major religions have considered themselves the specifically chosen favorites of their deity. The great faiths have all had the conviction of what Aldous Huxley calls

Does he think this is in essence of Xtianity? Does he equate this with idea of a chosen people

the Perennial Philosophy; that is, there is a spark of the divine in each man testifying to his oneness with God. The beautiful idea of brotherly love and doing well unto others is found among Hindus, Buddhists, Jews, Muslims, and Christians; only the *means* of attaining the eternal beauty vary from faith to faith. But the means have divided man and led to bitterness and violence between one Chosen People and another; they have even fought among themselves.

The violence that can result when one religion tries to convert others to its beliefs, or to protect followers living in "infidel" lands, was probably never more strikingly apparent than in the Middle Ages. There were Christian crusades against infidel Muslims and Jews as there were Muslim crusades against infidel Christians and Jews. Infidel killing infidel, each in the name of God.

Religious conflict characterized much of western history. There were long and bitter wars between the Holy Roman Emperor and other dynastic rulers and the forces backing the Roman Catholic Pope. The growth of Protestantism led to more strife: as America was being founded in the seventeenth century, Christians in Europe were bringing to an end over one hundred years of religious wars among themselves. Cardinal Richelieu of France helped turn the last of these wars, the Thirty Years' War, from a primarily religious struggle into a dynastic one. "Render unto God that which is God's" gave way to "Render unto Caesar that which is Caesar's." The dream of Christian unity in Europe dissolved into the disunity of national and partisan Christian loyalties. A person's first loyalty to the Pope or to God was displaced by loyalty to the state.

Not the issue! Pope had become a sovereign.

America was settled rapidly by Puritans from England, Presbyterians from Scotland, Dutch Reformers from the Netherlands, Lutherans from Germany, Huguenots from France, and Catholics and Jews from everywhere in Europe, all flocking to the new land in search of freedom, opportunity, and the right to worship God as they pleased. The settlers wanted to escape from the European heritage of religious persecution and wars. There was still some intolerance, of course, but because people of so many faiths had to live among each other, and because of the pioneering work toward religious tolerance by Roger Williams, the Maryland Act of Toleration in 1649, and later the Northwest Ordinance of 1787, Americans learned to live at peace with their neighbors. They all had one God in common, after all, and this God became a vital part of the American Dream. Churches were built everywhere and money was stamped in God's trust. God, the wealth of the country, democracy, freedom, and other ingredients were mixed in such a way that many looked upon their new land as the Chosen one. "One nation under God. . . ."

stupid, unconnected

6

Democracy and the Dream

The democratic idea was born in Greece with the people's assembly, the Council of 500, and the archon elected for a year at a time. Since then it has come to be a major part of the Dream—especially for those who have found themselves at the lower end of the political, economic, and social scale—for it provides a governmental structure which makes legislators responsive to their electorates. Many of the legislative procedures of this country have antecedents in ancient Greece; the Sherman Anti-Trust Act of 1890, for example, had as a predecessor an anti-trust act of 594 B.C. when the archon Solon pushed through a reform act breaking up large estates so that more people could share in the wealth of the state.

Economic considerations have always played a large part in the structure and functions of democracies. Nearly one hundred years after Solon's reform act, Cleisthenes divided the ten tribes around Athens into a C.C.C.—demes of the Coast, Countryside, and City—so that instead of being pulled in ten different directions by selfish tribal loyalties, there would only be three economic interests competing for favors. Later, the internal politics of western nations have divided generally along these lines, with legislators voting the selfish interest of their constituents, many times at the expense of the larger national unity. Democracy, as well as being the standard-bearer for progress and freedom, has been a fountainhead for factions and conflict.

Freedom of thought and speech are just as important to the success of democracies as elected political representatives, but the guarantee of such freedoms evolved slowly. Socrates tested the democratic spirit by urging youth to question Establishment values and institutions. But Establishments, even democratic ones, do not often like to be questioned, and an un-Athenian Activities Committee brought Socrates to trial before a court of 500 that convicted him of leading youth astray. Socrates refused the chance to escape to a nearby city, saying, "Rather I die than Athens." Law and order were important to Socrates, says Plato in his writings on the trial and death of Socrates. The fact that he was convicted by the democratic process was accepted by him even though a minority believed him innocent of the charge.

Plato's *Republic* aimed at a socialistic system run by an elite, but Aristotle's *Politics* contained wise counsel which Americans have often followed in realizing the democratic aspect of the Dream. It is important, said Aristotle, that governments provide as much political and economic equality as possible to prevent internal warfare. Democracies are less likely to fall because of their larger base of power: "Where a larger number have equal shares, they are more content. . . ." Particularly from the New Deal onward, American administrations have been engaged in programs to provide greater economic and political equality to insure liberty and justice for all.

The political structure of ancient Greece provides us with examples of both democratic and totalitarian complexes, with Athens representing the democratic ideal and Sparta representing the highly disciplined military state dedicated to law, order, and conformity. The historian Plutarch describes the Spartan aversion to the corruption of luxury with the common dining table, a fixed allowance of food, and education to insure obedience, endurance, and the winning of battles. The state imposed equality on its citizens in place of a previous condition of great inequality that had enabled a few rich to dominate the many who were in dire poverty. But an equality maintained by totalitarian methods has never been the ideal of the Dream.

Lycurgus, the founder of the Spartan military state, would not permit citizens to leave the country to tour other lands because they might pick up strange ideas from the unregulated lives of other people. He also banned all strangers from Sparta because they might impart foreign ideas which would cause citizens to question established ways. In other words, the Spartans were afraid of ideas, just as the Commissars in the Kremlin are afraid when they restrict freedom of speech, press, and travel. But some Athenians were afraid of ideas too. Remember Socrates? And to what extent are we in the United States afraid of the freedoms guaranteed in the First Amendment?

Athens, with its democratic ideals, came close to realizing the Dream. But the Athenian Dream failed because of a paranoia—Athenians feared the totalitarian Sparta and so they embraced war as a means of controlling their neighbors. They were also ambitious and greedy, says the Athenian citizen Thucydides, historian of the Peloponnesian War, who spoke of a domino thesis sponsored by those who favored armed conflict: "And Syracuse once taken, the whole of Sicily is in their hands, and Italy will follow at once." The war was immoral and unjust, maintained Thucydides, and Athens violated her great name as a bastion of freedom by treating the Melians (of the nearby island of Melos) tyrannically in forcing them to comply to her will. The Melians had been friendly to Athens but stood firm in maintaining neutrality in the great war between Athens and Sparta. After a siege, Melian males were massacred and women and children were taken by the Athenians as slaves in an atrocity long remembered. Thucydides suggested that power and wealth corrupted the Athenian Dream of justice to all.

The Roman Republic offered, as many believe the American Republic now offers, hope to the world. At the beginning of the Republic in 509 B.C., there were significant differences between rich and poor, the privileged Patricians and the lesser Plebeians, but through protest and some violence, the Plebeians threatened the Patrician Establishment so that equality was eventually attained. In their quest for more representative government, the Plebs learned that simple requests were not very effective in soliciting change. Requests often had to be put in the form of demands, and if the demands were not met, then some show of force—such as a strike or barricades in the streets —usually "encouraged" the Establishment to reform the unequal laws. Abolitionists, labor unionists, suffragettes, and, more recently, blacks, Chicanos, and Indians have rediscovered this fact of life. Those in power want to keep power and sometimes respond to change only by threat. But herein lies the genius of both the Roman and the American republics: both Establishments and minority groups have been willing to compromise their differences in order to preserve the system.

The democratic-republican idea slumbered during the greater part of the Middle Ages, but it emerged again in 1215 with the Magna Carta. This document delivered the first major blow to the theory of the divine right of kings, a theory which ended in western civilization only with the demise of tsar and kaiser in Russia and Germany after World War I. The Great Council which Edward I convened in 1295 gradually evolved into the English Parliament with its divisions of a House of Lords and a House of Commons. This bicameral political structure emerged because the burgesses and knights of the shires found that they had more in common and could work better with each other than with the king and greater lords. Along with the English Common Law, the bicameral system developed to provide greater justice for all.

Much of America's political heritage is the result of Engand's experience. American legal structure is patterned after the British system, not the Roman, and the English Bill of Rights set the precedent for the American Constitution one hundred years before that document was written. Also based on the English model, the Bill of Rights appended to the American Constitution guarantees freedom of speech, press, and assembly—a substantial part of the American Dream, though it is qualified now and then.

Nationalism and the Dream

The concept of nationalism is a complex one because it is just an *idea,* a state of mind for the individual and the mass living within some arbitrarily defined borders. It is inextricably mixed in with the economic, religious, and democratic institutions described above, and it is woven into the very fabric of societies around the world in the twentieth century—and nowhere greater than in America, it would seem, with its ubiquitous symbols.

The national idea is an old one. It can be seen in the old Sumerian towns of five thousand years ago when temple gods were adopted as "protectors" of the newly formed city-states and people first went out to die for "god and country." As one city conquered other cities, the boundaries of god and country were enlarged, and when the boundaries transcended cultures, empires were formed to command the people's loyalty.

Egypt developed around provinces called *nomes,* each ruled by a governor, or *nomarch.* There were about twenty-two nomes each in Upper and Lower Egypt, and the history of that land is one of conflict between those wanting centralization and those wanting local states' rights. Upper and Lower Egypt were first unified as two separate kingdoms; then, around 3100 B.C., the two were brought together under one king, or pharaoh. The political loyalties of the people were divided between at least three entities: the nome, Upper or Lower Nile cultures, and Egypt's king. For the better part of 2000 years loyalty to "king-power" prevailed, largely because the pharaoh was considered a god, but also because he had priests, police, and military might to maintain his law and order.

Other peoples, such as the Hebrews and the Greeks, were held together by cultural bonds but could not realize a larger national unity because of petty tribal and city-state jealousies. Had they been able to rise above their narrow views, perhaps the universalism and unity of mankind preached by some leading Hebrews and Greeks would have become reality.

The Roman Empire, unlike the Roman Republic, does not readily relate to the American Dream, though Americans by the twenty-first century might be conditioned for a dream realized by the Romans, the *Pax Romana*—a two-hundred-year period of peace in the Mediterranean world imposed by a central government. Stoics of both the Roman Republic and Empire adhered to the idea that we all spring from the same source and should be integrated in a single body politic. But in *The Idea of Nationalism* Hans Kohn states:

> The decline and fall of the Roman Empire was caused by the fact that the ideas of the Stoics were only imperfectly realized. For two reasons the Empire did not live up to its professed goal of a world-state based upon equality. While it was on the one hand not large enough, it was in another respect too large. It did not include and civilize the barbarians at its frontiers, and it

Part Point on nationalism very vague. If every or many nations had it why is it & how is it specifically part of the Amer. dream.

therefore suffered from their incursions. Nor did it integrate and really civilize the masses within the Roman Empire.[2]

Nationalism does not appear again as a significant force in western history until modern European states started to take shape during the latter part of the Middle Ages. Dante dreamt of a *universal* state in the fourteenth century, but John Wycliffe and John Hus suggested national states for England and Bohemia (part of modern Czechoslovakia) in protesting against the universalism of the Church of Rome. And that remarkable heretic, Joan of Arc, led the French against the English to help round out France's boundaries during the Hundred Years' War. One of the reasons she was sent to the stake was because she opted for the narrow idea of the royal state as opposed to the universal brotherhood of man as taught by the Church. In effect, the struggles for national identity nationalized the Christian Church, as various countries embarked on crusades (both territorial and religious) under the banner "God is on our side." Even today we continue to "nationalize" God with such slogans as "God Bless America." And "Praise the Lord and Pass the Ammunition" was a popular ditty of World War II—in the national interest, of course.

Society and the Dream

Class systems in society, which have always had the effect of making some people superior to others, have posed a real obstacle to realization of the Dream. To the victor belong the spoils, and the victors have typically been those with wealth, power, and ingenuity, not necessarily those with superior brains. Aristotle, though he saw a need for dissimilarity in the make-up of the state, maintained that inequality was the basis for internal warfare: "Those who see others honored and themselves degraded soon become revolution-minded."[3] But even Aristotle went along with the major institutions of his time, including slavery and the belief in the inferiority of women. Only Sparta, relying on totalitarian means, achieved any degree of social equality among its citizens.

Ancient Rome also faced problems of social inequality, with the Plebeians being made to feel inferior to the Patricians. The historian Livy described the feeling of dignity which was denied the lower classes about 450 B.C.—long before Aristotle avowed that this condition was a cause of revolution. The tribune Canuleius is defending his proposed reforms:

"Men of Rome," he said, "the violence with which the Senate has been opposing our programme of reform has made me realize more vividly than ever before the depth of the contempt in

11

which you are held by the aristocracy. I have often suspected it, but now I know; they think you are unworthy of living with them within the walls of the same town. Yet what is the object of our proposals? It is merely to point out that we are their fellow citizens—that we have the same country as they, even though we have less money. We seek the right of inter-marriage. . . ."[4]

From the other side of the social conflict, a conservative Senator lamented the protest and violence of the Plebeians and made a heart-rending speech describing the sacrifices Patricians had made in agreeing to reforms:

The truth is that our communal life is poisoned by the political discord and party strife, and it was that which raised his [the enemy's] hopes of destroying us, seeing as he did your lust for liberty in perpetual conflict with our lust for power, and each party's loathing of the representative magistracies of the other. What in God's name do you want now? Once it was tribunes, and to preserve the peace we let you have them, then it was *decemvirs* and we permitted their appointment. . . . You have your tribunes to protect you, your right of appeal to the people, your popular decrees made binding on the Senate, while in the empty name of justice all our privileges are trampled under foot: all this we have borne, and are still bearing. How is it to end? Will the time ever come when we can have a united city, a united country?[5]

The Plebeians continued to gain more rights—including the right to marry into Patrician families—as the Republic continued on through the years, because the system was flexible enough to provide change. But eventually a new aristocracy of leading Patricians and Plebeian families came to rule Rome, and the earlier promise of the Republic to provide a legislature responsive to the needs of the people gave way to the tyranny of the new elite and of a legislature and executive responsive only to its special needs. There was to be liberty and justice only for those who had made it, not for all.

The example of Rome with its contending factions of privileged and underprivileged has been repeated again and again throughout history. Like the Patrician, the upper class has repeatedly asked, "What more do you want?" And the lower class, like the Plebeian, has always had an answer: greater justice and equality on all levels—social, political, economic, religious.

The upper class Patrician asked for a united city, a united country. Many hundreds of years after the Roman made his plea, a sign carried by a little girl in the crowd caught the attention of another man of great influence, a candidate for his nation's highest office. The sign read simply, "Mr. Nixon, Bring Us Together." But this is impossible when there are privileged and underprivileged classes. Aristotle said it, Rome experienced it, and America is living it today. The little girl was honored with a White House invitation, but years later the nation was still divided—polarized, they said—by those with a plus and those with a minus, by those living in comfortable suburbs and those living somewhere else where dreams don't come true, at least not for many. For most of those living somewhere else, whether it was in the slums of the ancient world or in the slums of contemporary America, it's only a dream. However, it is a dream that Americans can still realize. Time hasn't run out yet for America, and perhaps it won't if the promise of liberty and justice for all is made a reality.

Notes

1 Henri Pirenne, *Medieval Cities* (Garden City, N.Y., Doubleday Anchor, 1956), pp. 148–149.
2 Hans Kohn, *The Idea of Nationalism* (New York, Collier-Macmillan, 1944), p. 68.
3 Aristotle, *The Politics,* trans. by T. A. Sinclair (Harmondsworth, England, Penguin, 1962), p. 193.
4 Livy, *The Early History of Rome,* trans. by Aubrey de Selincourt (Harmondsworth, England, Penguin, 1960) pp. 255–256.
5 *Ibid.,* pp. 242–243.

Factors in the Amer. dream:
1) possibility of growing wealthy.
2) Amer. is God's chosen nation
3) personal freedoms + a governmental structure responsive to the electorate.
4) Amer. are a nation
5) Peace + justice among classes in society.

Americans have recognized the need for differences in society, but they have also recognized the need for dignity and a degree of political and economic equality. In the fourth century B.C. Aristotle avowed that these needs, if not met in a democratic society, would be cause for revolution.

The Politics

Aristotle

There are other 'Republics' beside Plato's; their authors are sometimes professional politicians or philosophers, sometimes not professionals at all. These all sketch constitutions that come nearer than either of Plato's to existing constitutions, under which people actually live; for no other person has even introduced such novelties as the sharing of children and wives, or common messing for women. They prefer to start from essentials; for some that means getting the best possible distribution of wealth, for, they say, it is always about these basic necessities that disputes arise. This was the motive behind Phaleas of Chalcedon, who was the first to propose equalizing the property of all the citizens. He held that this was not difficult to do at the very beginning, and that, although it was more difficult in states already set up and working, still all properties could quickly be brought to the same level, simply by arranging that the rich should bestow dowries but receive none, and the poor give no dowries but only receive them. Plato, when writing the *Laws,* thought that there ought up to a certain point to be freedom from property-control, but that, as has been stated earlier, none of the citizens should have the right to own property more than five times as great as the smallest property owned. Those who legislate along these lines must not forget, as indeed they are apt to do, that while fixing the amount of property they ought also to fix the number of children; for if the number of children becomes too great for the size of the property, it becomes impossible to maintain the law as it stands. And if you do maintain it, many who were rich will become poor; this is a most undesirable consequence, since you can hardly prevent such persons from becoming bent on revolution.

That equality of property has considerable effect on the partner-

From *The Politics* by Aristotle, trans. by T. A. Sinclair. Reprinted by permission of Penguin Books, Ltd.

ship which we call the state has, so we find, been realized by some
long ago; it can be seen in the legislation of Solon; there are cities
where there is a law against unlimited acquisition of land; laws likewise exist which prevent the sale of property, as for example in
Locri, where the law is that property may only be sold where it can
be shown that a misfortune has occurred to make the sale imperative.
Other laws require the ancient lots of land to be maintained intact. It
was the abrogation of such a law that rendered the constitution of
Leucas over-democratic; it ceased to be possible to appoint to office
only those possessed of the proper qualification. Equality of property
may exist and yet the level be fixed either too high, with resultant excess of luxury, or too low, with inevitable discomfort. It is clear,
therefore, that it is not enough for a legislator to equalize property-
holdings; he must aim at fixing an amount mid-way between ex-
tremes. But even if one were to fix a moderate amount for all, that
would still not answer the purpose; for it is more necessary to equalize appetites than property, and that can only be done by adequate
education under the laws. Perhaps, however, Phaleas would say that
this is exactly what he himself meant; for he holds that in states there
ought to be equality of education as well as equality of property. But
one must state what exactly the education is to be; it is no use simply
saying that it is to be one and the same. 'One and the same' education might very well be of such a kind that it would produce men
ambitious to secure for themselves wealth, or distinctions, or both.
And dissension is caused by inequality in privilege no less than by
inequality in wealth, though for opposite reasons on either side; that
is to say, the many are incensed by the sight of inequality in wealth,
the upper classes are incensed if honours are equally shared, for
then, as the Homeric tag has it, 'good and bad are held in equal
esteem'. . . .

The first, and most truly so called, variety of democracy is that
which is based on the principle of equality. In such the law lays down
that the poor shall not enjoy any advantage over the rich, that neither class shall dominate the other but both shall be exactly similar.
For if, as is generally held, freedom is especially to be found in democracy, and also equality, this condition is best realized when all
share in equal measure the whole *politeia*. But since the people are
the more numerous class and the decision of the majority prevails,
such apparent inequality does not prevent its being a democracy. . . .

When we are considering whence arise revolutions and changes
affecting the constitution, we must begin with the fundamental
causes. These fall into three groups, and we must classify them ac-

cordingly: first, the conditions that lead to revolution, second, the objects aimed at, and thirdly all the various origins of political unrest and of violent cleavages among the citizens.

That which causes conditions leading to change is chiefly and generally what we have just been speaking of—inequality. For those who are bent on equality start a revolution if they believe that they, having less, are yet the equals of those who have more. And so too do those who aim at inequality and superiority, if they think that they, being unequal, are not getting more, but equal or less. [The aims are sometimes justifiable, sometimes not.] The lesser rebel in order to be equal, the equal in order to be greater. These then are conditions predisposing to revolution. Now as to motives: we find these to be profit and dignity, also their opposites; for in striving to avoid loss of money and loss of status, whether for their friends' sake or for their own, men often bring about revolutions in their states. Thirdly, the origins and causes of the disorders which make men act in the way described and strive for the objects mentioned—there are perhaps seven of these but the number might well be larger. Two of these are the same as already stated—profit and dignity, but in a different way. They play a part now, not as stimulating men to fight against each other in order to acquire them, as in the former statement, but because men see others getting a larger share of these, some rightly, some wrongly. The five other causes in this group are cruelty, fear, excessive power, contemptuous attitudes, disproportionate aggrandizement. To these we may add, in rather a different way, lobbying and intrigue, sheer inattention, imperceptible changes, dissimilarity.

Cicero, great Roman orator, lawyer, senator, and liberal moderate, wrote extensively on the duties of man. In this selection he gives some clues as to why the dream of liberty and justice failed in the ancient world— clues that might equally apply to the ultimate success or failure of the American Dream.

The Unnaturalness of Doing Wrong

Cicero

Well, then, to take something away from someone else—to profit by another's loss—is more unnatural than death, or destitution, or pain, or any other physical or external blow. To begin with, this strikes at the roots of human society and fellowship. For if we each of us propose to rob or injure one another for our personal gain, then we are clearly going to demolish what is more emphatically nature's creation than anything else in the whole world: namely, the link that unites every human being with every other. Just imagine if each of our limbs had its own consciousness and saw advantage for itself in appropriating the nearest limb's strength! Of course the whole body would inevitably collapse and die. In precisely the same way, a general seizure and appropriation of other people's property would cause the collapse of the human community, the brotherhood of man. Granted that there is nothing unnatural in a man preferring to earn a living for himself rather than for someone else, what nature forbids is that we should increase our own means, property, and resources by plundering others.

Indeed this idea—that one must not injure anybody else for one's own profit—is not only natural law, an international valid principle: the same idea is also incorporated in the statutes which individual communities have framed for their national purposes. The whole point and intention of these statutes is that one citizen shall live safely with another; anyone who attempts to undermine that association is punished with fines, imprisonment, exile, or death.

The same conclusion follows even more forcibly from nature's *rational principle,* the law that governs gods and men alike. Whoever obeys this principle—and everyone who wants to live according to

From *Selected Works* by Cicero, trans. by Michael Grant. Reprinted by permission of Penguin Books, Ltd.

nature's laws must obey it—will never be guilty of coveting another man's goods or taking things from someone else and appropriating them for himself. For great-heartedness and heroism, and courtesy, and justice, and generosity, are far more in conformity with nature than self-indulgence, or wealth, or even life itself. But to despise this latter category of things, to attach no importance to them in comparison with the common good, really does need a heroic and lofty heart.

In the same way, it is more truly natural to model oneself on Hercules and undergo the most terrible labours and troubles in order to help and save all the nations of the earth than (however superior you are in looks or strength) to live a secluded, untroubled life with plenty of money and pleasures. And mankind was grateful to Hercules for his services; popular belief gave him a place among the gods. That is to say, the finest and noblest characters prefer a life of dedication to a life of self-indulgence: and one may conclude that such men conform with nature and are therefore incapable of doing harm to their fellow-men.

A man who wrongs another for his own benefit can be explained in two different ways. Either he does not see that what he is doing is unnatural, or he refuses to agree that death, destitution, pain, the loss of children, relations, and friends are less deplorable than doing wrong to another person. But if he sees nothing unnatural in wronging a fellow-man, is he not beyond the reach of argument?— he is taking away from human beings all that makes them human. If, however, he concedes that this ought to be avoided, yet still regards death, destitution, and pain as even more undesirable, he is mistaken. He ought not to concede that *any* damage, either to his person or to his property, is worse than a moral failure.

So everyone ought to have the same purpose: to identify the interest of each with the interest of all. Once men grab for themselves, human society will completely collapse. But if nature prescribes (as she does) that every human being must help every other human being, whoever he is, just precisely because they are all human beings, then—by the same authority—all men have identical interests. Having identical interests means that we are all subject to one and the same law of nature: and, that being so, the very least that such a law enjoins is that we must not wrong one another. This conclusion follows inevitably from the truth of the initial assumption.

If people claim (as they sometimes do) that they have no intention of robbing their parents or brothers for their own gain, but that robbing their other compatriots is a different matter, they are not talking sense. For that is the same as denying their common interest with their fellow-countrymen, and all the legal or social obligations that follow therefrom: a denial which shatters the whole fabric of national life. Another objection urges that one ought to take account of compatriots but not of foreigners. But people who put forward these arguments subvert the whole foundation of the human community and its removal means the annihilation of all kindness, generosity, goodness, and justice; which is a sin against the immortal gods, since they were the creators of the society which such men are seeking to undermine. And the tightest of the bonds uniting that society is the belief that robbery from another man for the sake of one's personal gain is more unnatural than the endurance of any loss whatsoever to one's person or property—or even to one's very soul. That is, provided that no violation of justice is involved: seeing that of all the virtues justice is the sovereign and queen.

Difficult Moral Decisions

Let us consider possible objections.

1. Suppose a man of great wisdom were starving to death: would he not be justified in taking food belonging to someone who was completely useless? 2. Suppose an honest man had the chance to steal the clothes of a cruel and inhuman tyrant like Phalaris [tyrant of Acgragas (Agrigentum) in Sicily (c. 570–544 B.C.), believed to have roasted his victims alive in a brazen bull], and needed them to avoid freezing to death, should he not do so?

These questions are very easy to answer. For to rob even a completely useless man for your own advantage is an unnatural, inhuman action. If, however, your qualitics were such that, provided you stayed alive, you could render great services to your country and to mankind, then there would be nothing blameworthy in taking something from another person *for that reason*. But, apart from such cases, every man must bear his own misfortunes rather than remedy them by damaging someone else. The possible exception I have quoted does not mean that stealing and covetousness in general are any less unnatural than illness, want, and the rest. The point is rather that neglect of the common interest is unnatural, because it is unjust; that nature's law promotes and coincides with the common interest; and therefore that this law must surely ordain that the means of subsistence may, if necessary, be transferred from the feeble, useless person to the wise, honest, brave man, whose death would be a grave loss to society. But in that case the wise man must guard against any excessive self-regard and conceit, since that could only lead to a wrongful course of action. If he avoids these pitfalls, he will be doing his duty—working for the interests of his fellow-men, and, I repeat yet again, of the human community.

The rise of medieval towns and cities presaged the modern era of business, industry, and concern with money and banking. Our heritage of business enterprise and property values goes back to these cities of seven and eight hundred years ago. In the following excerpt Henri Pirenne, noted Belgian medievalist, describes the growth of city economics and society under newly formed urban laws in the Middle Ages. Freedom was as necessary in the business world then as it is now.

Urban Institutions and Law

Henri Pirenne

The needs and tendencies of the bourgeoisie were so incompatible with the traditional organisation of Western Europe that they immediately aroused violent opposition. They ran counter to all the interests and ideas of a society dominated materially by the owners of large landed property and spiritually by the Church, whose aversion to trade was unconquerable. It would be unfair to attribute to "feudal tyranny" or "sacerdotal arrogance" an opposition which explains itself, although the attribution has often been made. As always, those who were the beneficiaries of the established order defended it obstinately, not only because it guaranteed their interests, but because it seemed to them indispensable to the preservation of society. Moreover, the bourgeois themselves were far from taking up a revolutionary attitude towards this society. They took for granted the authority of the territorial princes, the privileges of the nobility and, above all, those of the Church. They even professed an ascetic morality, which was plainly contradicted by their mode of life. They merely desired a place in the sun, and their claims were confined to their most indispensable needs.

Of the latter, the most indispensable was personal liberty. Without liberty, that is to say, without the power to come and go, to do business, to sell goods, a power not enjoyed by serfdom, trade would be impossible. Thus they claimed it, simply for the advantages which it conferred, and nothing was further from the mind of the bourgeoisie than any idea of freedom as a natural right; in their eyes it was

From *Economic and Social History of Medieval Europe* by Henri Pirenne. Reprinted by permission of Harcourt Brace Jovanovich, Inc., and Routledge & Kegan Paul, Ltd., London.

merely a useful one. Besides, many of them possessed it *de facto;* they were immigrants, who had come from too far off for their lord to be traced and who, since their serfdom could not be presumed, necessarily passed for free, although born of unfree parents. But the fact had to be transformed into a right. It was essential that the villeins [free common villagers], who came to settle in the towns to seek a new livelihood, should feel safe and should not have to fear being taken back by force to the manors from which they had escaped. They must be delivered from labour services and from all the hated dues by which the servile population was burdened, such as the obligation to marry only a woman of their own class and to leave to the lord part of their inheritance. Willy-nilly, in the course of the twelfth century these claims, backed up as they often were by dangerous revolts, had to be granted. The most obstinate conservatives, such as Guibert de Nogent, in 1115, were reduced to a wordy revenge, speaking of those "detestable communes" which the serfs had set up to escape from their lord's authority and to do away with his most lawful rights.[1] Freedom became the legal status of the bourgeoisie, so much so that it was no longer a personal privilege only, but a territorial one, inherent in urban soil just as serfdom was in manorial soil. In order to obtain it, it was enough to have resided for a year and a day within the walls of the town. "City air makes a man free" *(Stadtluft macht frei),* says the German proverb.

But if liberty was the first need of the burgess, there were many others besides. Traditional law with its narrow, formal procedure, its ordeals, its judicial duels, its judges recruited from among the rural population, and knowing no other custom than that which had been gradually elaborated to regulate the relations of men living by the cultivation or the ownership of the land, was inadequate for a population whose existence was based on commerce and industry. A more expeditious law was necessary, means of proof more rapid and more independent of chance, and judges who were themselves acquainted with the professional occupations of those who came under their jurisdiction, and could cut short their arguments by a knowledge of the case at issue. Very early, and at latest at the beginning of the eleventh century, the pressure of circumstances led to the creation of a *jus mercatorum,* i.e., an embryonic commercial code. It was a collection of usages born of business experience, a sort of international custom, which the merchants used among themselves in their transactions. Devoid of all legal validity, it was impossible to invoke it in the existing law courts, so the merchants agreed to choose among themselves arbitrators who had the necessary competence to understand their disputes and to settle them promptly. It is here undoubtedly that we must seek the origin of those law courts, which in England received the picturesque name of courts of *piepowder (pied poudré),* because the feet of the merchants who resorted to them were still dusty from the roads.[2] Soon this *ad hoc* jurisdiction became permanent and was recognised by public authority. At Ypres, in 1116, the Count of Flanders abolished the judicial duel, and it is certain that about the same date he instituted in most of his towns local courts of *échevins* [aldermen], chosen from among the burgesses and alone competent to judge them. Sooner or later the same thing happened in all countries. In Italy, France, Germany and England the towns obtained judicial autonomy, which made them islands of independent jurisdiction, lying outside the territorial custom.

This jurisdictional autonomy was accompanied by administrative autonomy. The formation of urban agglomerations entailed a number of arrangements for convenience of defence, which they had to provide for themselves in the absence of the traditional authorities, who had neither the means nor the wish to help them. It is a strong testimony to the energy and the initiative of the bourgeoisie that it succeeded by its own efforts in setting on foot the municipal organisation, of which the first outlines appear in the eleventh century, and which was already in possession of all its essential organs in the twelfth. The work thus accomplished is all the more admirable because it was an original creation. There was nothing in the existing order of things to serve it as a model, since the needs it was designed to meet were new.

The most pressing was the need for defence. The merchants and their merchandise were, indeed, such a tempting prey that it was essential to protect them from pillagers by a strong wall. The construction of ramparts was thus the first public work undertaken by the towns and one which, down to the end of the Middle Ages, was their heaviest financial burden. Indeed, it may be truly said to have been the starting-point of their financial organisation, whence, for example, the name of *firmitas,* by which the communal tax was always known at Liége, and the appropriation in a number of cities *ad opus castri* (i.e., for the improvement of the fortifications) of a part of the fines imposed by the borough court. The fact that to-day municipal coats of arms are surrounded by a walled crown shows the importance accorded to the ramparts. There were no unfortified towns in the Middle Ages.

Money had to be raised to provide for the expenses occasioned by the permanent need for fortifications, and it could be raised most easily from the burgesses themselves. All were interested in the common defence and all were obliged to meet the cost. The quota payable by each was calculated on the basis of his fortune. This was a great innovation. For the arbitrary seigneurial tallage, [a tax] collected in the sole interest of the lord, it substituted a payment proportionate to the means of the taxpayer and set apart for an object of general utility. Thus taxation recovered its public character, which had disappeared during the feudal era. To assess and collect this tax, as well as to provide for the ordinary necessities whose numbers grew with the constant increase of the town population, the establishment of quays and markets, the building of bridges and parish churches, the regulation of crafts and the supervision of food supplies, it soon became necessary to elect or allow the setting up of a council of magistrates, consuls in Italy and Provence, *jurés* in France and aldermen in England. In the eleventh century they appeared in the Lombard cities, where the consuls of Lucca are mentioned as early as 1080. In the following century, they became everywhere an institution ratified by public authority and inherent in every municipal constitution. In many towns, as in those of the Low Countries, the *échevins* were at once the judges and administrators of the townsfolk.

The lay princes soon discovered how advantageous the growth of the cities was to themselves. For in proportion as their trade grew on road and river and their increasing business transactions required a corresponding increase of currency, the revenues from every kind of toll and from the mints likewise flowed in increasing quantities into the lord's treasury. Thus it is not surprising that the lords assumed on the whole a benevolent attitude towards the townsfolk. Moreover, living as a rule in their country castles, they did not come in contact with the town population and thus many causes of conflict were avoided. It was quite otherwise with the ecclesiastical princes. Almost to a man they offered a resistance to the municipal movement, which at times developed into an open struggle. The fact that the bishops were obliged to reside in their cities, the centres of diocesan administration, necessarily impelled them to preserve their authority and to oppose the ambitions of the bourgeoisie all the more resolutely because they were roused and directed by the merchants, ever suspect in the eyes of the Church. In the second half of the eleventh century the quarrel of the Empire and the Papacy gave the city populations of Lombardy a chance to rise against their simoniacal prelates [churchmen of high rank who engaged in the buying or selling of church offices]. Thence the movement spread through the Rhine valley to Cologne. In 1077, the town of Cambrai rose in revolt against

Bishop Gerard II and formed the oldest of the "communes" that we meet with north of the Alps. In the diocese of Liége the same thing happened. In 1066 Bishop Théoduin was forced to grant the burgesses of Huy a charter of liberties which is several years earlier than those whose text has been preserved in the rest of the Empire. In France, municipal insurrections are mentioned at Beauvais about 1099, at Noyon in 1108–9, and at Laon in 1115.

Thus, by fair means or foul, the towns gained peaceably or by force, some at the beginning, others in the course of the twelfth century, municipal constitutions suitable to the life of their inhabitants. Originating in the "new burgs," in the *portus,* where the merchants and artisans were grouped, they were soon developed to include the population of the "old burgs" and the "cities," whose ancient walls, surrounded on all sides by the new quarters, were falling into ruin like the old law itself. Henceforth, all who resided within the city wall, with the sole exception of the clergy, shared the privileges of the burgesses.

The essential characteristic of the bourgeoisie was, indeed, the fact that it formed a privileged class in the midst of the rest of the population. From this point of view the medieval town offers a striking contrast both to the ancient town and to the town of to-day, which are differentiated only by the density of their population and their complex administration; apart from this, neither in public nor in private law do their inhabitants occupy a peculiar position in the State. The medieval burgess, on the contrary, was a different kind of person from all who lived outside the town walls. Once outside the gates and the moat we are in another world, or more exactly, in the domain of another law. The acquisition of citizenship brought with it results analogous to those which followed when a man was dubbed knight or a clerk tonsured, in the sense that they conferred a peculiar legal status. Like the clerk or the noble, the burgess escaped from the common law; like them, he belonged to a particular estate *(status),* which was later to be known as the "third estate."

The territory of the town was as privileged as its inhabitants. It was a sanctuary, an "immunity," which protected the man who took refuge there from exterior authority, as if he had sought sanctuary in a church. In short, the bourgeoisie was in every sense an exceptional class. Each town formed, so to speak, a little state to itself, jealous of its prerogatives and hostile to all its neighbours. Very rarely was a common danger or a common end able to impose on its municipal particularism the need for alliances or leagues such, for example, as the German Hanse [a medieval league of merchants from free German cities, organized to secure greater safety and privileges in trading]. In general, urban politics were determined by the same sacred egoism which was later to inspire State politics. For the burgesses the country population existed only to be exploited. Far from allowing it to enjoy their franchises, they always obstinately refused it all share in them. Nothing could be further removed from the spirit of modern democracy than the exclusiveness with which the medieval towns continued to defend their privileges, even, and indeed above all, in those periods when they were governed by the crafts.

Notes

1 Guibert de Nogent, *Histoire de sa vie,* ed. G. Bourgin, p. 156 (Paris, 1907). At the beginning of the thirteenth century again Jacques de Vitry preaches against the "violent and pestiferous *communitates*." A. Giry, *Documents sur les relations de la royauté avec les villes en France,* p. 59 (Paris, 1885). Similarly, in England, Richard de Devizes says, "Communia est tumor plebis, timor regni tepor sacerdotii." W. Stubbs, *Select Charters,* p. 252 (Oxford, 1890).
2 "Extraneus mercator vel aliquis transiens per regnum, non habens certam mansionem infra vicecomitatum sed vagans, qui vocatur piepowdrous" (1124–53). Ch. Gross, *The Court of Piepowder,* in *The Quarterly Journal of Economics,* t. XX (1906), p. 231, n. 4.

Many of our democratic achievements have been realized as a result of protest and violence. The barons of England made "demands" on their King in 1215, and when John hesitated, they confronted him with force. Freedom and its synonym liberty are used frequently in the following selection. Freedom for whom? What is the significance of the Magna Carta in the struggle for freedom?

The Magna Carta

An Account of Magna Carta by Roger of Wendover

A.D. 1214 . . . [King John] held his court at Winchester at Christmas for one day, after which he hurried to London and took up his abode at the new temple. And at that place the above-mentioned nobles came to him in gay military array, and demanded the confirmation of the liberties and laws of King Edward, with other liberties granted to them and to the kingdom and Church of England, as were contained in the charter, and above-mentioned laws of Henry the First. They also asserted that, at the time of his absolution at Winchester, he had promised to restore those laws and ancient liberties and was bound by his own oath to observe them. The King, hearing the bold tones of the barons in making this demand, much feared an attack from them, as he saw that they were prepared for battle; he however made answer that their demands were a matter of importance and difficulty, and he therefore asked a truce till the end of Easter. . . . In Easter week of this same year, the above-mentioned nobles assembled at Stamford with horses and arms, for they now induced almost all the nobility of the whole kingdom to join them and constituted a very large army: for in their army were computed to be two thousand knights, besides horse soldiers, attendants, and foot soldiers, who were variously equipped . . . all of these being united by oath, were supported by the concurrence of Stephen, Archbishop of Canterbury, who was at their head. . . . The barons then delivered to the messengers [of the King] a paper containing in great measure the laws and ancient customs of the kingdom, and declared that, unless the King immediately granted them and confirmed them under

From *Problems in Western Civilization*, pp. 86–89, 97–99, edited by Ludwig F. Schaefer, David H. Fowler, and Jacob E. Cooke. Reprinted by permission of Charles Scribner's Sons.

his own seal, they would, by taking possession of his fortresses, force him to give them sufficient satisfaction as to their before-named demands . . . and at length he angrily declared with an oath, that he would never grant them such liberties as would render him their slave . . . and when the nobles heard what John said, they . . . directed their forces towards Northampton. . . . When the army of the barons arrived at Bedford, there also came to them there messengers from the city of London, and, finding the gates open they, on the 24th of May [1215] . . . entered the city without any tumult whilst the inhabitants were performing divine service, for the rich citizens were favorable to the barons, and the poor ones were afraid to murmur against them. . . . They then took security from the citizens and sent letters throughout England to those earls, barons, and knights, who appeared to be still faithful to the King, though they only pretended to be so . . . the greatest part of these, on receiving the message of the barons, set out to London and joined them, abandoning the King entirely. . . . King John, when he saw that he was deserted by almost all, so that out of his regal superabundance of followers he scarcely retained seven knights, was much alarmed lest the barons would attack his castles and reduce them without difficulty, as they would find no obstacle to their so doing . . . told them for the sake of the peace and for the exaltation and honor of the kingdom, he would willingly grant them the laws and liberties they required. He also sent word to the barons by the same messenger to appoint a fitting day and place to meet and carry all these matters into effect. The King's messengers then came in all haste to London and without deceit reported to the barons. . . . They in great joy appointed the fifteenth of June for the King to meet them, at a field lying between Staines and Windsor. . . . There were present upon behalf of the King, the Archbishops, Stephen of Canterbury and H. of Dublin, the bishops W. of London. . . . Those who were on behalf of the barons it is not necessary to enumerate, since the whole nobility of England were now assembled together in numbers not to be computed. At length, after various points on both sides had been discussed, King John, seeing that he was inferior in strength to the barons, without raising any difficulties, granted the underwritten laws and liberties and confirmed them by his charter. . . .

The Great Charter

John, by the grace of God, king of England, lord of Ireland, duke of Normandy and Aquitaine, count of Anjou, to the archbishops, bishops, abbots, earls, barons, justiciars, foresters, sheriffs, reeves, servants, and all bailiffs and his faithful people greeting. Know that by the inspiration of God and for the good of our soul and those of all our predecessors and of our heirs, to the honor of God and the exaltation of holy church, and the improvement of our kingdom by the advice of our venerable fathers Stephen, archbishop of Canterbury, primate of all England and cardinal of the holy Roman church. . . .

1. In the first place, we have granted to God, and by this our present charter confirmed, for us and for our heirs forever, that the English church shall be free, and shall hold its rights entire and its liberties uninjured; and we will that it be thus observed; which is shown by this, that the freedom of elections, which is considered to be most important and especially necessary to the English church, we, of our pure and spontaneous will, granted, and by our charter confirmed before the contest between us and our barons had arisen; and obtained a confirmation of it by the lord Pope Innocent III.; which we shall observe and which we will, shall be observed in good faith by our heirs forever.

We have granted moreover to all free men of our kingdom for us and our heirs forever all the liberties written below, to be had and holden by themselves and their heirs from us and our heirs.

2. If any of our earls or barons, or others holding from us in chief by military service shall have died, and when he has died his heir shall be of full age and owe relief, he shall have his inheritance by the ancient relief. . . .

8. No widow shall be compelled to marry so long as she prefers to live without a husband, provided she gives security that she will not marry without our consent, if she holds from us, or without the consent of her lord from whom she holds, if she holds from another. . . .

12. No scutage or aid shall be imposed in our kingdom except by the common council of our kingdom, except for the ransoming of our body, for the making of our oldest son a knight, and for once marrying our oldest daughter, and for these purposes it shall be only a reasonable aid; in the same way it shall be done concerning the aids of the city of London.

13. And the city of London shall have all its ancient liberties and free customs, as well by land as by water. Moreover, we will and grant that all other cities and boroughs and villages and ports shall have all their liberties and free customs. . . .

16. No one shall be compelled to perform any greater [military] service for a knight's fee or for any other free tenement than is owed from it. . . .

20. A free man shall not be fined for a small offense, except in proportion to the measure of the offense; and for a great offense, saving his freehold; and a merchant in the same way, saving his merchandise; and the villein shall be fined in the same way, saving his wainage [harvested crops for seed and estate needs], if he shall be at our mercy; and none of the above fines shall be imposed except by the oaths of honest men of the neighborhood.

21. Earls and barons shall be fined only by their peers, and only in proportion to their offence. . . .

23. No manor or man shall be compelled to make bridges over the rivers except those which ought to do it of old and rightfully. . . .

28. No constable or other bailiff of ours shall take anyone's grain or other chattels, without immediately paying for them in money, unless he is able to obtain a postponement at the good will of the seller. . . .

30. No sheriff or bailiff of ours or anyone else shall take horses or wagons of any free man for carrying purposes except on the permission of that free man. . . .

35. There shall be one measure of wine throughout our whole kingdom, and one measure of ale, and one measure of grain. . . .

39. No free man shall be taken or imprisoned or dispossessed, or outlawed, or banished, or in any way destroyed, nor will we go upon him, nor send upon him, except by the legal judgment of his peers or by the law of the land. . . .

41. All merchants shall be safe and secure in going from England and coming into England and in remaining and going through England, as well by land as by water, for buying and selling, free from all evil tolls, by the ancient and rightful customs, except in time of war, and if they are of a land at war with us. . . .

45. We will not make justiciars, constables, sheriffs, or bailiffs, except of such as know the law of the realm and are well inclined to observe it. . . .

60. Moreover, all those customs and franchises mentioned above which we have conceded in our kingdom, and which are to be fulfilled, as far as pertains to us, in respect to our men; all men of our kingdom as well clergy as laymen, shall observe as far as pertains to them, in respect to their men.

61. Since, moreover, for the sake of God, and for the improvement of our kingdom, and for the better quieting of the hostility sprung up lately between us and our barons, we have made all these concessions; wishing them to enjoy these in a complete and firm stability forever, we make and concede to them the security described

below; that is to say, that they shall elect twenty-five barons of the kingdom, whom they will, who ought with all their power to observe, hold, and cause to be observed, the peace and liberties which we have conceded to them, and by this our present charter confirmed to them, in this manner, that if we or our justiciar, or our bailiffs, or any of our servants shall have done wrong in any way towards any one, or shall have transgressed any of the articles of peace or security; and the wrong shall have been shown to four barons of the aforesaid twenty-five barons, let those four barons come to us or to our justiciar, if we are out of the kingdom, laying before us the transgression, and let them ask that we cause that transgression to be corrected without delay. And if we shall not have corrected the transgression or, if we shall be out of the kingdom, if our justiciar shall not have corrected it within a period of forty days, . . . the aforesaid four barons shall refer the matter to the remainder of the twenty-five barons, and let these twenty-five barons with the whole community of the country distress and injure us in every way they can; that is to say by the seizure of our castles, lands, possessions, and in such other ways as they can until it shall have been corrected according to their judgment, saving our person and that of our queen, and those of our children; and when the correction has been made, let them devote themselves to us as they did before. . . .

Given by our hand in the meadow which is called Runnymede, between Windsor and Staines, on the fifteenth day of June, in the seventeenth year of our reign.

The Need for Discipline Within Freedom

Jack Perry

My wife and I came back to Washington after seven years in Europe prepared to hear a lot of talk about crime and law and order. We were not disappointed in the expectation.

We were saddened, nevertheless, by the depth and extent of the preoccupation—reflected most recently in the President's [1970] State of the Union message—and in the genuine restriction in daily life compared to what we left in Washington in 1962. One way or another, the problem seems to be making cowards of us all.

More and more, remembering the order of Western Europe and finding Americans living in such worry about disorder and violence, we have been asking ourselves what freedom is in America, how free we really are.

"You can walk the streets at night without fear," is what all the American tourists seem to say nowadays about Paris and other cities in Europe. As a matter of fact, there are sections of Paris, London or Rome where tourists might think twice about walking at night.

But for the most part, it seems true that West Europeans are largely free of concern about crime and violence. Their lives are, by American standards, remarkably safe and orderly. In many ways, however—some large, some small—the European is more restricted, less "free," than the American.

Must Carry a Passport and Register With Police

He must carry a national passport and show it when asked; he must register with the police when traveling or moving to a new place; he cannot have a gun without submitting to controls; he cannot go abroad and take as much money as he wants, and he has far more of his daily life, from travel to medical care to education to general

From "American Freedom" by Jack Perry. Reprinted by permission from the February 15, 1970, issue of *The Washington Post*.

welfare, tied in closely to the central government. He lives, in sum, under many restrictions that Americans have not accepted.

Yet if the European accepts these limits, within them he has the feeling of freedom—without the constant preoccupation with crime and insecurity that now seems to be the American habit. In his day-to-day living he is more in a position to enjoy his freedom than we Americans are.

Here in the United States, my wife and I have sensed that worry about crime and law and order is depressing the quality of life, so that "freedom" becomes unenjoyable. If a man is free to live any way he pleases, free to make as much money as he can, free to buy a gun any time, free to carry no identification and yet is afraid to go on the street after sundown, then his "freedom" has not liberated him.

The societies we call the Old World have explored the limits of order and disorder and come to terms with those limits. They have reached a working compromise between order and liberty.

The individual becomes early aware of his relative place and the limits to permissible behavior. And if order is shaken, as we saw in France during the "May events" of 1968, the limits of disorder are surprisingly strict, and society goes on functioning the next day with surprising continuity.

In America, still in many ways "young," we have not accepted the limits. We talk about the American "tradition of violence," but to my wife and myself it seemed more accurate to speak of America's "tradition of indiscipline"—the refusal to face maturity and its limitations, the refusal to pay the price of balancing order and liberty.

This is of course the frontier mentality, so-called, still seeing our country as without limits to its potentialities or resources. We still act as if there are enough bears for everyone to shoot: If each man goes his own way, musket in hand, and defends his rights, we will all stay free. But the European is older, his bears are all shot.

Three examples of this contrast between the United States and Europe come to mind. The European thinks nothing of showing his "papers" to anyone in authority. The American can refuse to identify himself and (if he refrains from driving) can carry no "papers" at all. Is the American freer?

In fact, keeping closer track of people helps European police keep order. American police, especially in their decentralized status, often operate largely in ignorance, and the criminal can find it all too easy to flee and remain hidden. We pay the price for this "freedom from identification" by making it harder to keep order. This constricts our freedom.

A second example, notorious and disputed, is provided by guns. To us, coming back from Europe, the argument that the indiscriminate sale of guns is freedom, while the control of gun ownership is slavery, simply is not realistic.

The European accepts the idea that if he wants a gun he shows his need for it and gets a license. Our experience showed us—and we think the statistics support the impression—that the European lives in less fear of guns than Americans do. A gun in every man's hands nowadays has not been conducive to an atmosphere of order; our true freedom has been constricted.

A third example is provided by the interesting case of the automobile. And this is a reverse example, where Americans appear less free but are in fact freer—the exception to prove the rule.

Since the Automobile Age as a mass phenomenon came to our country at least a generation before it arrived in Europe, Americans are "old" and "mature" when we deal with cars whereas the Europeans are "young" and "undisciplined." Generally, we accept the sharp limitations that numbers of cars, speed limits, rush hours and dangers of accident place on our "freedom to drive."

In Europe, the tradition persists of adventurous high-speed driving, immune from safety precautions, consideration for others or discipline.

And as any visitor to Europe reports, the result on European roads is danger, fear and complete absence of peace of mind. The European appears "freer," for he refuses to grow up behind the wheel; in effect, he is a slave to insecurity and fear. We Americans are, in fact, much freer in enjoying our cars.

This seemed to us, in reverse, the situation of Americans and their enjoyment of freedom today.

Many Americans Making a New Idol of Security

Our homecoming impression has been that many Americans are erecting a new idol, "security," an idealized condition in which a man could do what he wanted without fear that anyone else will harm him. For many, life in America seems to be a process of defending themselves from vast, shadowy forces who want to "take it away." Some of this feeling of defensiveness is specifically antiblack, but it also seems wider, more of a hedgehog defense against today's world.

This seems to us close to the spirit that engendered fascism in Europe in the '30s. Followed to its end, this logic would dictate closing up America after sunset, or shutting off the threatening elements from our daily life. It could mean erecting walls and closing ourselves into little fortresses of fear.

But "security" is not the aim of life and the truly "secure" man is not wholly alive. The quality of life is what counts, and security is merely one contributor to that. The goal is the freedom to live fully, not to live securely.

Compared to Europe, American society remains immature, "freer" in the sense of irresponsibility, but less and less free in the ability to enjoy freedom.

Sad as it may be for all of us to admit it, when you reach 200 million, you reach limits to any man's freedom, you reach limits to the land and the resources and to democracy itself. You reach the point where discipline and sacrifice are necessary.

Unless all of us agree to sacrifice something to solve the problem, accepting new disciplines, new burdens, we do not think the problem will be solved. This seems to us an essential lesson the Old World still has to teach the new.

In the eternal pendulum between liberty and order, it is time to swing toward greater order, hedging some particular freedoms in order to safeguard the general freedom.

Norman Thomas, the respected and revered successor to Eugene Debs
and other socialists of the turn of the century, lived to see much of the
socialist program enacted into law. The socialist idea of spreading
wealth more equally to impede discontent parallels Aristotle's thinking as
stated in the first reading of this chapter. Writing after the end of
World War II, Thomas abandons (temporarily) his socialist-oriented
criticisms and points out some admirable qualities of the United States—
qualities which suggest the ideals of the American Dream are still alive.

What's Right With America

Norman Thomas

Most of my yesterdays have been spent telling what's wrong with
America—always, I hope, with suggestions for constructive change.
Most of my tomorrows will be similarly employed. Today I am writ-
ing about some of the things that are right with America.

I do not retract my criticisms of American foreign policy or lack of
policy since Pearl Harbor when I say that I know no remote historical parallel to the fact that a nation has emerged victorious in two
world wars, unequaled in economic and military might, with so little
desire for aggressive, imperial power as America has yet shown.

Consider the record. We not only raised and equipped enormous
forces as they never were equipped before, while at the same time we
fed our civilians on an average better than in peacetime; we also gave
to our Allies in lend-lease, according to the latest figures, fifty and a
half billion in reverse lend-lease. Now—and here is the point—our
government has not demanded in return either from its former enemies or its debtor associates any territory or special trade and economic concessions. (Even the Pacific island bases now in controversy
are only partially an exception to this statement since they were held
by Japan only on mandate or by occupation, and the United States
has proposed some recognition of the trusteeship of the United Nations. The problem would disappear under the universal national dis-
armament with international supervision which I have advocated.)

So far from demanding material rewards for victory we made a

From "What's Right With America" by Norman Thomas. Reprinted from the
March, 1947, issue of *Harper's* Magazine. Used by permission of Mr.
Thomas' executors.

further three-billion-dollar loan to Great Britain and extended generous credits to France. Not too graciously or adequately we have carried the main burden of allaying famine. The record is not all that the highest wisdom or the most enlightened humanity would have dictated, but when in history has it been remotely paralleled by any tribe, state, or nation in ancient, medieval, or modern times?

It was not thus that mighty powers from ancient Rome to modern Britain and France gathered and held their empires. It is not thus that the Soviet dictatorship has utilized victory. On the contrary, Stalin has annexed some 270,000 square miles of territory, mostly at the expense of nations with which he had treaties of nonaggression; established his rule through puppet states from the Baltic to the boundaries of Greece and the Adriatic Sea; quartered his armies on starving peoples; stripped them of machinery; extorted more than the Czar's imperial "rights" in Manchuria and taken from this territory more than two billion dollars' worth of machinery necessary to any recovery of Chinese economy.

Nor is this all. We carried through our promise of independence to the Philippines and seem likely to correct the just grievances of Filipinos at the conduct of American troops still quartered in unnecessary numbers in the islands. In Japan MacArthur enjoys a respect and popularity heretofore unheard of in the temporary rule of a conqueror over a defeated foe.

After the First World War America showed a similar disinclination to aggressive imperialism, but also in disappointment over the results of the war it refused to accept the responsibility of membership in the League of Nations. After World War II there was no such attempt at isolation. America fostered and joined the United Nations and all its subsidiaries. Our Senate ratified the Bretton Woods agreement. Most remarkable of all, our government voluntarily proposed to turn over to a properly constituted international authority its temporary monopoly of atomic energy, the greatest physical force in the world. Say, if you will, and as I do, that we ought also to have suspended the making of bombs, and that our action is only what wisdom dictates. So rare is such wisdom in politics that it should count as unprecedented virtue. There was never, of course, a situation remotely like our monopoly of atomic energy, but I could safely offer a reward far beyond my ability to pay for a citation of any action by any other nation since the dim dawn of history which might have suggested such a sharing of power.

It is true that despite these things we and the world drift toward war rather than peace. Our good has not been good enough. But it is a fantastic distortion of truth when a Labour M.P. [member of parliament] in England charges that "ignorant and well-off Americans are talking quite gaily of another war." Most Americans dread a war, which cannot be avoided simply by frantic appeasement of either Russian or any other imperialism. A few Americans—scarcely gaily —think and even talk about preventive war. But nothing is more certain than that the American people will tolerate no such war. Indeed, a recent poll taken by the National Opinion Research Center of Denver University shows that, taking the country as a whole, slightly less than fifty per cent would be willing to attack first with atomic bombs even if they should "ever suspect that a certain country is planning to make a surprise attack on our country within a few days." How would our English critics vote on a similar question?

I had got so far in writing this article when the coal strike and its consequences temporarily dampened my ardor for discussing American virtue and intelligence. Yet even this crisis helped to prove the force of public opinion, and the miners went back to work without any such interlude of violence or drastic repression as have stained some pages of our own history.

By and large, civil liberties in America have survived a Second World War better than almost any prophet feared. The reason, I suspect, is less our virtue than the fact that in the recent war, unlike any of its predecessors, there was no organized political opposition. After Pearl Harbor such opposition seemed impossible. Hence there was little provocation to drastic repression. There were individual conscientious objectors, and they were not as well treated as the public supposes. The alternative service in the camps was really unpaid slave labor. The objectors had to support themselves or get help from friends and pacifist groups. There has as yet been no amnesty for imprisoned objectors.

Nevertheless, the record stands that we and we alone of the major powers got through the Second World War without conscription of labor or any major infringement on the rights of free speech, free press, and assemblage. Our worst blunder—I should rather call it a crime—was our evacuation of the Japanese and Japanese-Americans on the West Coast on terms wholly inconsistent with the finest traditions of Anglo-American justice. Nothing in the First World War equaled this departure from well-established principles of civil liberty in the number of people that it affected or in its danger as a precedent. Unfortunately, the Supreme Court went far to validate it.

But here again it must be recorded that most of the evacuees have been allowed to return to their homes; that at the last session of

Congress the Senate voted partial monetary compensation for their losses; and that in the November election California voters in a referendum rejected proposals for stiffening the land laws to the hurt of the Japanese-American community.

In race discrimination the American record is bad—perhaps the worst made by any nation, always excepting South Africa. Yet as I look back over thirty years of fairly intimate contact with the American scene I take courage because of the genuine progress that has been made in plain human decency and regard for human rights, even in the South. In the light of our history the outstanding fact is not Bilbo and all that he typifies but the growing opposition to him and our sense of shame when we contemplate his version of a master race. We have not lived up to the Four Freedoms nor even to the Bill of Rights of our own Constitution, but our failures would be virtues over large areas of the globe. It is perhaps less a commentary on our own virtue than on the degradation of the world that by comparison Americans walk in such great freedom from the restrictions of a police state upon their conscience and their liberties. We need fear no spies wherever two or three are gathered together. And no police state can compel us to work under conditions at which Simon Legree might have shuddered.

American history has its shameful passages of ruthlessness. Let the Indians, the slaves imported from Africa and bred in America, the Mexicans, victims of a brief imperialist war, bear witness. Yet, in spite of this, the United States has proved on an immense scale the capacity of men of quarreling nationalities to live and work together. We have gone through two world wars during which men and women, the children of warring nations, lived together in American cities without untoward incident while their sons fought side by side in American armies.

From its early beginnings down to the passage of restrictive immigration laws in the second decade of this century, this country was a land of asylum. After 1789, a young nation predominantly, although not exclusively, Protestant and British in its antecedents, imposed no restrictions on religion and opened its doors to all comers from Europe and even for a time from Asia. Its hospitality was less than perfect, but exclusiveness and anti-foreign riots were very definitely the occasional exception and not the rule in our history. The descendants of Puritans acquired a tolerance which was not proof of decadence. In very many parts of America even today it is true that the only groups which can be attacked with complete impunity are Americans with this Puritan or Protestant background. And in saying this I do not forget the Ku Klux Klan, which, by the way, does not trace its lineage to the Pilgrims or Puritan fathers, much less to the men who wrote our Declaration of Independence and our federal Constitution.

There is, moreover, even today, less caste feeling, less snobbery in human relations in America than in any other great nation, not excluding some of those with more radical economic creeds. I came away from Moscow with a feeling that there was far more good fellowship between all kinds and conditions of men, far more social democracy, in New York. And New York is not my ideal.

Nor is ours a democracy with no higher standards than run-of-the-mill Hollywood films. All over our country there is a saving quality of family life, of good-humored and good-neighborly responsibility, that someday a modern novelist may discover. For myself, I have even a good word for church suppers and grange fairs.

For all this relative freedom and fellowship in America there are various explanations in terms of the hospitality of a new, uncrowded land, its climate, its geographic position, its fertility, and its economic conditions. We are of the same blood as less fortunate Europeans. Modesty becomes us, and thankfulness for the extraordinary opportunity that has been ours. But it is not self-righteous for us to be genuinely proud of the great American tradition of liberty, which in the stormy crisis of our time still has strength and validity.

Tomorrow I shall go back to pointing out some of the things wrong in America and to suggesting how they may be made right. I shall do it with more confidence because we have a heritage and a history which justify faith in man's capacity for freedom and fair play.

Questions

1 How are the several parts (economic, religious, democratic, national, social) of the American Dream interrelated?

2 Are some elements of the Dream incompatible? For instance, is it possible to have equality and freedom at the same time?

3 What degrees of inequality are permissible in a free or democratic society?

4 Can you compare Athens and Sparta of the fifth century B.C. with the U.S. and the U.S.S.R. of today? What

about their economics, politics, and attitudes toward freedom and learning?

5   Why does Aristotle place great emphasis on equality?

6   The Magna Carta was instituted only for the benefit of the nobles in England. It had no application to the common people, then or even now. Discuss.

7   Is it necessary for minorities to demonstrate in order to achieve reform?

8   Is Aristotle arguing against "elites" in the operation of a democracy? If he is, discuss whether or not elites are necessary to all societies and whether or not their responsibilities warrant extra compensation.

2

Puritan Truths
and the American Dream

Essay

True Believers in the Promised Land
Frederick Gentles

Readings

The Way to Wealth
Benjamin Franklin

On Puritans
Charles A. Beard

Errand Into the Wilderness
Perry Miller

BYU—A Campus of Peace and Patriotism
John Dart

Rituals—The Revolt Against the Fixed Smile
Melvin Maddocks

The True Believer
Eric Hoffer

Everyone has his own world view according to his time and place on earth, and the ideas he formulates are quickly translated into the "true view" of people and things. The more uncomplicated the mind, the greater the certainty of truth. The Puritans were a simple people who believed in what they considered simple truths. Their truths of God, democracy, and work became fundamental parts of the great American Dream. Even though dreams have a way of being ill-defined, of changing, of fading, and even of vanishing, the American Dream has continued to hold on to Puritan truths. But have these truths been modified to such an extent that they form a new "true view"?

True Believers in the Promised Land

Frederick Gentles

The American Dream was conveyed to the New World by a people dedicated to God, individual initiative, and the sanctity of work. American success in enterprise and technology for the last three hundred and fifty years has been due in good part to these fundamental principles. The Dream from the first took on the certainty that at least some Americans possessed the truth, but from the first there seemed to be inconsistencies between the Dream and its realization in everyday life.

The Puritans stepping onto American shores in the seventeenth century were more a serious God-fearing, militant people of Old Testament character than a Christ-oriented people with boundless love for all mankind. They looked upon themselves as a new Chosen People who had received the Word directly from God, not Jesus, though they were Christians. They were the "new" saints, and they denied the saints of Anglicans, Catholics, Lutherans, and others. They looked to Abraham, Moses, Joshua, Isaiah, Amos, and Ezekiel of the Old Testament rather than to Peter, Paul, and Mary. They went to work immediately to build a world pleasing to God. They were believers.

In *The Puritan Heritage,* Joseph Gaer and Ben Siegel describe the dream of the Chosen People:

In searching Scripture for relevant texts to support their views and needs, the Puritans easily discovered numerous similarities between themselves and the Israelites. They (again like the Pilgrims) viewed England as their Egypt, James I as their Pharaoh, the Atlantic as their Red Sea. They also were an embattled people obviously chosen to carry out divine plans for the world's redemption. They too had been driven from their homes, not as punishment, but to build a promised land. The only significant difference they could see between ancient Israel and themselves was that they were expected to convert the very wilderness to a promised land.

And in such figures as Winthrop, Cotton, and Norton, the Puritans felt they had leaders comparable to Moses and Joshua.[1]

From the ideological seeds of the Puritans sprouted a vigorous new nation. New Joshuas and Moseses appeared from time to time to lead a confident people from one triumph to another over nature and the obstacles set up by fellow men. Washington, Lincoln, Edison, Ford, the Roosevelts, and John F. Kennedy are among those charismatic figures who played leading roles in creating history's wealthiest and most powerful nation. How much of America's success story stems from the Puritan experience? How did the Puritan truths of God, individualism, and work help to fashion the American Dream?

Certainly, Puritans brought with them a strong belief in God, and many were locked into their absolute truths about the deity. Although Puritans were often intolerant of other faiths, the efforts of those opposed to rigid dogmatism helped nudge them out of their narrow and intolerant views. In the colony of Rhode Island, founded by Roger Williams, Ann Hutchinson, and others, religious freedom was guaranteed to everyone who settled there, and a strict separation of church and state was maintained. The concept of toleration was further broadened by the Maryland Act of Toleration in 1649 which granted religious freedom to Trinitarians, and later, the Northwest Ordinance of 1787 provided, among other things, for the freedom of worship. Laws helped create a new morality for many—the morality of tolerance of other beliefs. Evolving out of the experiences of the early settlers, the separation of church and state and religious tolerance have become fundamental traditions and inseparable parts of the American Dream. But our history has continually shown that there have always been some people as intolerant as the most bigoted of the Puritans.

The Puritans were also staunch believers in individualism. They objected to being governed by pope, king, or any other strong centralized power. The wide open spaces of America encouraged individualism, and this concept became part of the Constitution with its explicit provisions for states' rights. But the freedom to be an individual was often denied, and discrimination unfortunately has been a continuing phenomenon of American history. Certainly Puritans and their heirs have been faithful to the Dream of freedom, but at the same time they have been unfaithful, too. Unfaithful to the legal and moral right to be an individual with long hair or different skin color, to be rich or poor, to have a different background or unconventional ideas.

God and individualism were tied into the Puritan-Protestant work ethic which elevated hard work to the status of a religious virtue. God is pleased with those who work, and he is not pleased with those who remain idle. Following the values of the Puritans in regard to industriousness, Americans have always been faithful to the ideas of work, thrift, and the careful investment of time and money. For many, industriousness has come to be a necessary factor in the realization of the American Dream. But though Puritans and their progeny were devoted to the concept of work, the ethic has been modified over the years, and some are now objecting to it.

Work was next to godliness in the Puritan value system, and idleness was associated with Satan. Waste of time was the deadliest of sins—idle talk, luxury, and all that. If the poor refuse to work they must not eat, said Cotton Mather, outspoken Puritan leader and writer. Although workshops and poor relief were established in the English colonies, there was little sympathy for the poor who generally were considered victims of their own idle and wicked ways. The myth of the self-made man developed early in American history, and it may be represented today by a bumper sticker seen recently on an ornate Cadillac in a posh neighborhood: "I'm Fighting Poverty. I Work." The milk of human kindness, if any, is for those who work, not for those spongers on welfare, the sign seems to say.

Work produced wealth, and wealth gave Puritans and other Protestants cause to link capitalism to God and the work ethic. The package of God, individualism, work, wealth, and capitalism merged into a complex that resulted in a huge industrial America, a country far removed from its beginnings on the desolate shores of New England. Max Weber in *The Protestant Ethic and the Spirit of Capitalism* stated that man is dominated by the making of money as the ultimate purpose in life. Benjamin Franklin's moral attitudes, he said, are colored with utilitarianism. Franklin's well-known aphorisms encouraging industriousness have been known to generations of Americans: "Early to bed, early to rise, makes a man healthy, wealthy, and wise. . . . A penny saved is a penny earned. . . . Remember that time is money. . . . The early bird catches the worm. . . . Money can beget money, and its offspring can beget more. . . . Honesty is the best policy." Not necessarily because honesty is moral, of course, but because it pays; crime does not pay.

John Wesley, a contemporary of Franklin and founder of Methodism, questioned the paradoxical relationship between religion and the wealth accumulating from work. Fortunes accumulated by Protestants seemed to divert them from their God. "I fear, wherever riches have increased, the essence of religion has decreased in the same proportion. Therefore I do not see how it is possible, in the nature of things, for any revival of true religion to continue for long."[2] Puritans, Presbyterians, Methodists, Baptists, and soon Catholics and Quakers were caught up in the ethic of work and its most attractive by-product—wealth. Wealth had been an important factor in corrupting ancient Athens, Rome, the Medieval Church, and the Renaissance states. Was Wesley suggesting that wealth was also a corrupting influence in America and England?

But even Wesley capitulated to the work ethic when he urged Christians to gain all they can and save all they can so that they may be able to give all they can to the Church.[3] It would be immoral not to encourage people to be diligent and frugal. Without hard work, how could America have succeeded? However, some people today detect hypocrisy between the crass materialism that work has created and the simple ideals of the Christian faith of brotherly love. They opt for the New Testament gospel of love over the Old Testament emphasis on militancy and rugged individualism as interpreted by the Puritans.

Dr. Evelyn Latowsky, professor of social science at York University in Toronto, said in a recent report to the American Anthropological Association:

> We find more and more young people, and now more older people as well, to be in opposition to what they view as the hypocrisy and superficiality of the modern industrial state. They object to being an appendage of the machine, and they dislike being treated as things. . . . They are looking beyond plenty. They are looking for essential humanity, an alternate purpose in what seems to them an absurd world.[4]

Dr. Latowsky believes the movement is here to stay and sees it as a healthy revitalization of Western society.

A *Time* magazine essay on "America the Inefficient" quoted a Harvard Business School professor, Abraham Zaleznik, as saying that people are no longer turned on by the Protestant Ethic. "To some the Protestant Ethic—hard work is a virtue for its own sake—appears to have been replaced by an almost Mediterranean spirit, a spreading belief that men should work no more than they must to enjoy the good life and worldly pleasures."[5] Many people would rather have their leisure than add to their income. Indeed, leisure is no longer the evil Puritans made it out to be. To some, to be forever affluent and efficient is nauseating and even dangerous, as illustrated by the efficient dictatorships of *Brave New World* and *1984*.

Is the trend toward increasing one's leisure rather than one's wealth a reaction against Puritan values, or against the materialism that has come to be identified with the work ethic? Have we so corrupted the Puritan truths that they are no longer valid ideals of the American Dream? Perhaps the answer lies in returning to the simplistic Puritan "view" of the world—a view that emphasizes the absolute truths of God, individualism, and the sanctity of work. Or perhaps we must reevaluate all of the ideals that constitute the American Dream, in order to make that Dream applicable to the tumultuous times in which we live.

Notes

1 Joseph Gaer and Ben Siegel, *The Puritan Heritage, America's Roots in the Bible* (New York, Mentor, 1964), p. 26.
2 Max Weber, *The Protestant Ethic and the Spirit of Capitalism* (New York, Scribner's, 1958), p. 175.
3 *Ibid.*, pp. 175, 176.
4 *Los Angeles Times,* November 21, 1970.
5 "Inefficiency in America," *Time,* Vol. 95, No. 12, March 23, 1970, p. 77.

For the Puritans in the New World, work was closely associated with their
religious faith. The Puritan (also known as the Protestant) work ethic is a
descriptive term that has since come to characterize, in a secular as well
as in a religious way, a whole attitude toward life: hard work is virtuous.
Benjamin Franklin, an immigrant from Boston to the industrial
Philadelphia, succinctly expressed the maxims Americans have lived by in
the pursuit of the American Dream of rags to riches.

The Way to Wealth

Benjamin Franklin

Preface to Poor Richard Improved: 1758

Courteous Reader:

I have heard that nothing gives an Author so great Pleasure, as to
find his Works respectfully quoted by other learned Authors. This
Pleasure I have seldom enjoyed; for tho' I have been, if I may say it
without Vanity, an *eminent Author* of Almanacks annually now a
full Quarter of a Century, my Brother Authors in the same Way, for
what Reason I know not, have ever been very sparing in their Ap-
plauses, and no other Author has taken the least Notice of me, so
that did not my Writings produce me some solid *Pudding,* the great
Deficiency of *Praise* would have quite discouraged me.

I concluded at length, that the People were the best Judges of my
Merit; for they buy my Works; and besides, in my Rambles, where I
am not personally known, I have frequently heard one or other of my
Adages repeated, with, *as Poor Richard says,* at the End on 't; this
gave me some Satisfaction, as it showed not only that my Instructions
were regarded, but discovered likewise some Respect for my Authority; and I own, that to encourage the Practice of remembering
and repeating those wise Sentences, I have sometimes *quoted myself*
with great Gravity.

Judge, then how much I must have been gratified by an Incident I
am going to relate to you. I stopt my Horse lately where a great
Number of People were collected at a Vendue of Merchant Goods.
The Hour of Sale not being come, they were conversing on the Bad-
ness of the Times and one of the Company call'd to a plain clean old

From *The Autobiography of Benjamin Franklin and Selections From His
Other Writings.* Modern Library Edition, Random House, Inc., 1950.

Man, with white Locks, "Pray, Father Abraham, what think you of the Times? Won't these heavy Taxes quite ruin the Country? How shall we be ever able to pay them? What would you advise us to?" Father *Abraham* stood up, and reply'd, "If you'd have my Advice, I'll give it you in short, for *A Word to the Wise is enough,* and *many Words won't fill a Bushel,* as *Poor Richard* says." They join'd in desiring him to speak his Mind, and gathering round him, he proceeded as follows;

"Friends," says he, and Neighbours, "the Taxes are indeed very heavy, and if those laid on by the Government were the only Ones we had to pay, we might more easily discharge them; but we have many others, and much more grievous to some of us. We are taxed twice as much by our *Idleness,* three times as much by our *Pride,* and four times as much by our *Folly;* and from these Taxes the Commissioners cannot ease or deliver us by allowing an Abatement. However let us hearken to good Advice, and something may be done for us; *God helps them that help themselves,* as *Poor Richard* says, in his Almanack of 1733.

It would be thought a hard Government that should tax its People one-tenth Part of their *Time,* to be employed in its Service. But *Idleness* taxes many of us much more, if we reckon all that is spent in absolute *Sloth,* or doing of nothing, with that which is spent in idle Employments or Amusements, that amount to nothing. *Sloth,* by bringing on Diseases, absolutely shortens life. *Sloth, like Rust, consumes faster than Labour wears; while the used Key is always bright,* as *Poor Richard* says. *But dost thou love Life, then do not squander Time, for that's the stuff Life is made of,* as *Poor Richard* says. How much more than is necessary do we spend in sleep, forgetting that *The sleeping Fox catches no Poultry,* and that *There will be sleeping enough in the Grave,* as *Poor Richard* says.

If Time be of all Things the most precious, wasting Time must be, as *Poor Richard* says, *the greatest Prodigality;* since, as he elsewhere tells us, *Lost Time is never found again; and what we call Time enough, always proves little enough:* Let us then up and be doing, and doing to the Purpose; so by Diligence shall we do more with less Perplexity. *Sloth makes all Things difficult, but Industry all easy,* as *Poor Richard* says; and *He that riseth late must trot all Day, and shall scarce overtake his Business at Night;* while *Laziness travels so slowly, that Poverty soon overtakes him,* as we read in *Poor Richard,* who adds, *Drive thy Business, let not that drive thee;* and *Early to Bed, and early to rise, makes a Man healthy, wealthy, and wise.*

So what signifies *wishing* and *hoping* for better Times. We may make these Times better, if we bestir ourselves. *Industry need not wish,* as *Poor Richard* says, *and he that lives upon Hope will die fasting. There are no Gains without Pains; then Help Hands, for I have no Lands,* or if I have, they are smartly taxed. And, as *Poor Richard* likewise observes, *He that hath a Trade hath an Estate; and he that hath a Calling, hath an Office of Profit and Honour;* but then the *Trade* must be worked at, and the *Calling* well followed, or neither the *Estate* nor the *Office* will enable us to pay our Taxes. If we are industrious, we shall never starve; for, as *Poor Richard* says, *At the working Man's House Hunger looks in, but dares not enter.* Nor will the Bailiff or the Constable enter, for *Industry pays Debts, while Despair encreaseth them,* says *Poor Richard.* What though you have found no Treasure, nor has any rich Relation left you a Legacy, *Diligence is the Mother of Good-luck* as *Poor Richard* says *and God gives all Things to Industry. Then plough deep, while Sluggards sleep, and you shall have Corn to sell and to keep,* says *Poor Dick.* Work while it is called To-day, for you know not how much you may be hindered To-morrow, which makes *Poor Richard* say, *One to-day is worth two To-morrows,* and farther, *Have you somewhat to do To-morrow, do it To-day.* If you were a Servant, would you not be ashamed that a good Master should catch you idle? Are you then your own Master, *be ashamed to catch yourself idle,* as *Poor Dick* says. When there is so much to be done for yourself, your Family, your Country, and your gracious King, be up by Peep of Day; *Let not the Sun look down and say, Inglorious here he lies.* Handle your Tools without Mittens; remember that *The Cat in Gloves catches no Mice,* as *Poor Richard* says. 'Tis true there is much to be done, and perhaps you are weak-handed, but stick to it steadily; and you will see great Effects, for *Constant Dropping wears away Stones,* and by *Diligence and Patience the Mouse ate in two the Cable;* and *Little Strokes fell great Oaks,* as *Poor Richard* says in his Almanack, the Year I cannot just now remember.

Methinks I hear some of you say, *Must a Man afford himself no Leisure?* I will tell thee, my friend, what *Poor Richard* says, *Employ thy Time well, if thou meanest to gain Leisure; and, since thou art not sure of a Minute, throw not away an Hour.* Leisure, is Time for doing something useful; this Leisure the diligent Man will obtain, but the lazy Man never; so that, as *Poor Richard* says, *A Life of Leisure and a Life of Laziness are two Things.* Do you imagine that Sloth will afford you more Comfort than Labour? No, for as *Poor Richard* says, *Trouble springs from Idleness, and grievous Toil from needless Ease. Many without Labour, would live by their Wits only, but they break for want of Stock.* Whereas Industry gives Comfort, and Plenty, and Respect: *Fly Peasures, and they'll follow you. The diligent Spinner has a large Shift; and now I have a Sheep and a Cow, everyBody bids me good Morrow;* all which is well said by *Poor Richard.*

But with our Industry, we must likewise be *steady, settled,* and *careful,* and oversee our own Affairs *with our own Eyes,* and not trust too much to others; for, as *Poor Richard* says

> *I never saw an oft-removed Tree,*
> *Nor yet an oft-removed Family,*
> *That throve so well as those that settled be.*

And again, *Three Removes is as bad as a Fire;* and again, *Keep thy Shop, and they Shop will keep thee;* and again, *If you would have your Business done, go; if not, send.* And again,

> *He that by the Plough would thrive,*
> *Himself must either hold or drive.*

And again, *The Eye of a Master will do more Work than both his Hands;* and again, *Want of Care does us more Damage than Want of Knowledge;* and again, *Not to oversee Workmen, is to leave them your Purse open.* Trusting too much to others' Care is the Ruin of many; for, as the Almanack says, *In the Affairs of this World, Men are saved, not by Faith, but by the Want of it;* but a Man's own Care is profitable; for, saith *Poor Dick, Learning is to the Studious,* and *Riches to the Careful,* as well as *Power to the Bold,* and *Heaven to the Virtuous,* And farther, *If you would have a faithful Servant, and one that you like, serve yourself.* And again, he adviseth to Circumspection and Care, even in the smallest Matters, because sometimes *A little Neglect may breed great Mischief;* adding, *for want of a Nail the Shoe was lost; for want of a Shoe the Horse was lost; and for want of a Horse the Rider was lost, being overtaken and slain by the Enemy; all for want of Care about a Horse-shoe Nail.*

So much for Industry, my Friends, and Attention to one's own Business; but to these we must add *Frugality,* if we would make our *Industry* more certainly successful. A Man may, if he knows not how to save as he gets, *keep his Nose all his Life to the Grindstone,* and die not worth a *Groat* at last. *A fat Kitchen makes a lean Will,* as *Poor Richard* says; and

> *Many Estates are spent in the Getting,*
> *Since Women for Tea forsook Spinning and Knitting,*
> *And Men for Punch forsook Hewing and Splitting.*

If you would be wealthy, says he, in another Almanack, *think of Saving as well as of Getting: The Indies have not made Spain rich, because her Outgoes are greater than her Incomes.*

Away then with your expensive Follies, and you will not then have so much Cause to complain of hard Times, heavy Taxes, and chargeable Families; for, as *Poor Dick* says,

Women and Wine, Game and Deceit,
Make the Wealth small and the Wants great.

And farther, *What maintains one Vice, would bring up two Children.* You may think perhaps, that a *little* Tea, or a *little* Punch now and then, Diet a *little* more costly, Clothes a *little* finer, and a *little* Entertainment now and then, can be no *great* Matter; but remember what *Poor Richard* says, *Many a Little makes a Mickle;* and farther, *Beware of little Expences; A small Leak will sink a great Ship;* and again, *Who Dainties love, shall Beggars prove;* and moreover, *Fools make Feasts, and wise Men eat them.*

Here you are all got together at this Vendue of *Fineries* and *Knicknacks.* You call them *Goods;* but if you do not take Care, they will prove *Evils* to some of you. You expect they will be sold *cheap,* and perhaps they may for less than they cost; but if you have no Occasion for them, they must be *dear* to you. Remember what *Poor Richard* says; *Buy what thou hast no Need of, and ere long thou shalt sell thy Necessaries.* And again, *At a great Pennyworth pause a while:* He means, that perhaps the Cheapness is *apparent* only, and not *Real;* or the bargain, by straitening thee in thy Business, may do thee more Harm than Good. For in another Place he says, *Many have been ruined by buying good Pennyworths.* Again, *Poor Richard* says, 'tis *foolish to lay out Money in a Purchase of Repentance;* and yet this Folly is practised every Day at Vendues, for want of minding the Almanack. *Wise Men,* as *Poor Dick* says, *learn by others Harms, Fools scarcely by their own; but felix quem faciunt aliena pericula cautum.* Many a one, for the Sake of Finery on the Back, have gone with a hungry Belly, and half-starved their Families. *Silks and Sattins, Scarlet and Velvets,* as *Poor Richard* says, *put out the Kitchen Fire.*

These are not the *Necessaries* of Life; they can scarcely be called the *Conveniences;* and yet only because they look pretty, how many *want* to *have* them! The *artificial* Wants of Mankind thus become more numerous than the *Natural;* and, as *Poor Dick* says, *for one poor Person, there are an hundred indigent.* By these, and other Extravagancies, the Genteel are reduced to poverty, and forced to borrow of those whom they formerly despised, but who through Industry and Frugality have maintained their Standing; in which Case it appears plainly, that *A Ploughman on his Legs is higher than a Gentleman on his Knees,* as *Poor Richard* says. Perhaps they have had a small Estate left them, which they knew not the Getting of; they think, *'tis Day, and will never be Night;* that a little to be spent out of *so much,* is not worth minding; *A Child and a Fool,* as *Poor Richard* says, *imagine Twenty shillings and Twenty Years can never be spent* but, *always taking out of the Meal-tub, and never putting in, soon comes to the Bottom;* as *Poor Dick* says, *When the Well's dry, they know the Worth of Water.* But this they might have known before, if they had taken his Advice; *If you would know the Value of Money, go and try to borrow some; for, he that goes a borrowing goes a sorrowing;* and indeed so does he that lends to such People, when he goes *to get it in again. Poor Dick* farther advises, and says,

> *Fond Pride of Dress is sure a very Curse;*
> *E'er Fancy you consult, consult your Purse.*

And again, *Pride is as loud a Beggar as Want, and a great deal more saucy.* When you have bought one fine Thing, you must buy ten more, that your Appearance may be all of a Piece; but *Poor Dick* says, *'Tis easier to suppress the first Desire, than to satisfy all that follow it.* And 'tis as truly Folly for the Poor to ape the Rich, as for the Frog to swell, in order to equal the ox.

> *Great Estates may venture more,*
> *But little Boats should keep near Shore.*

'Tis, however, a Folly soon punished; for *Pride that dines on Vanity, sups on Contempt,* as *Poor Richard* says. And in another Place, *Pride breakfasted with Plenty, dined with Poverty, and supped with Infamy.* And after all, of what Use is this *Pride of Appearance,* for which so much is risked, so much is suffered? It cannot promote Health, or ease Pain; it makes no Increase of Merit in the Person, it creates Envy, it hastens Misfortune.

> *What is a Butterfly? At best*
> *He's but a Caterpillar drest*
> *The gaudy Fop's his Picture just,*

as *Poor Richard* says.

But what Madness must it be to *run in Debt* for these Superfluities! We are offered, by the Terms of this Vendue, *Six Months' Credit;* and that perhaps has induced some of us to attend it, because we cannot spare the ready Money, and hope now to be fine without it. But, ah, think what you do when you run in Debt; *you give to another Power over your Liberty.* If you cannot pay at the Time, you will be ashamed to see your Creditor; you will be in Fear when you speak to him; you will make poor pitiful sneaking Excuses, and by Degrees come to lose your Veracity, and sink into base downright lying; for, as *Poor Richard* says, *The second Vice is Lying, the first is running in Debt.* And again, to the same Purpose, *Lying rides upon Debt's Back.* Whereas a free-born *Englishman* ought not to be ashamed or afraid to see or speak to any Man living. But Poverty often deprives a Man of all Spirit and Virtue: *'Tis hard for an empty Bag to stand upright,* as *Poor Richard* truly says.

What would you think of that Prince, or that Government, who should issue an Edict forbidding you to dress like a Gentleman or a Gentlewoman, on Pain of Imprisonment or Servitude? Would you not say, that you were free, have a Right to dress as you please, and that such an Edict would be a Breach of your Privileges, and such a Government tyrannical? And yet you are about to put yourself under that Tyranny, when you run in Debt for such Dress! Your Creditor has Authority, as his Pleasure to deprive you of your Liberty, by confining you in Gaol for Life, or to sell you for a Servant, if you should not be able to pay him! When you have got your Bargain, you may, perhaps, think little of Payment; but *Creditors, Poor Richard* tells us, *have better Memories than Debtors;* and in another Place says, *Creditors are a superstitious Sect, great Observers of set Days and Times.* The Day comes round before you are aware, and the Demand is made before you are prepared to satisfy it, Or if you bear your Debt in Mind, the Term which at first seemed so long, will, as it lessens, appear extreamly short. *Time* will seem to have added Wings to his Heels as well as Shoulders. *Those have a short Lent,* saith *Poor Richard, who owe Money to be paid at Easter.* Then since, as he says, *The Borrower is a Slave to the Lender, and the Debtor to the Creditor,* disdain the Chain, preserve your Freedom; and maintain your Independency: Be *industrious* and *free;* be *frugal* and *free.* At present, perhaps, you may think yourself in thriving Circumstances, and that you can bear a little Extravagance without Injury; but,

> *For Age and Want, save while you may;*
> *No Morning Sun lasts a whole day,*

as *Poor Richard* says. Gain may be temporary and uncertain, but ever while you live, Expence is constant and certain; and *'tis easier to build two Chimnies, than to keep one in Fuel,* as *Poor Richard* says. So, *Rather go to Bed supperless than rise in Debt.*

> *Get what you can, and what you get hold;*
> *'Tis the Stone that will turn all your lead into Gold,*

as *Poor Richard* says. And when you have got the Philosopher's Stone, sure you will no longer complain of bad Times, or the Difficulty of paying Taxes.

This Doctrine, my Friends, is *Reason* and *Wisdom;* but after all, do not depend too much upon your own *Industry,* and *Frugality,* and

Prudence, though excellent Things, for they may all be blasted without the Blessing of Heaven; and therefore, ask that Blessing humbly, and be not uncharitable to those that at present seem to want it, but comfort and help them. Remember, *Job* suffered, and was afterwards prosperous.

And now to conclude, *Experience keeps a dear School, but Fools will learn in no other, and scarce in that;* for it is true, *we may give Advice, but we cannot give Conduct,* as *Poor Richard* says: However, remember this, *They that won't be counselled, can't be helped,* as *Poor Richard* says: and farther, That, *if you will not hear Reason, she'll surely rap your Knuckles."*

Thus the old Gentleman ended his Harangue. The People heard it, and approved the Doctrine, and immediately practised the contrary, just as if it had been a common Sermon; for the Vendue opened, and they began to buy extravagantly, notwithstanding, his Cautions and their own Fear of Taxes. I found the good Man had thoroughly studied my Almanacks, and digested all I had dropt on these Topicks during the Course of Five and twenty Years. The frequent Mention he made of me must have tired any one else, but my Vanity was wonderfully delighted with it, though I was conscious that not a tenth Part of the Wisdom was my own, which he ascribed to me, but rather the *Gleanings* I had made of the Sense of all Ages and Nations. However, I resolved to be the better for the Echo of it; and though I had at first determined to buy Stuff for a new Coat, I went away resolved to wear my old One a little longer. *Reader,* if thou wilt do the same, thy Profit will be as great as mine. I *am, as ever, thine to serve thee,*

RICHARD SAUNDERS
July 7, 1757

Writing three hundred years after the landing of the Mayflower, Beard
challenges the ignorance of all of us who so glibly stereotype the
Puritans. We are all vulnerable to the easy generalization and to
accepting such generalizations as absolute truths.

On Puritans

Charles A. Beard

The solemn hour approaches. It will soon be just three hundred
years since the Pilgrims let go their anchor off the coast of Cape Cod.
A flood of oratory will surely descend upon us. The New England
societies, the Pilgrim societies, the Forebears societies, the Colonial
Dames, and the French and Indian War societies, and all those who
need an excuse for a night out will attend banquets given under the
benign auspices of astute hotel managers. College presidents, serene,
secure, solemn, and starched will rise and tell again to restless youths
the story of Miles Standish and Cotton Mather. Evangelical clergymen will set aside special days for sermons and thanksgivings. The
Archbishop of Canterbury (shades of Laud!) will send a cablegram
to the Back Bay Brotherhood! We shall be shown again, as Henry
Jones Ford (Scotch-Irish) once remarked, "how civilization entered
the United States by way of New England." We shall hear again how
it was the Puritans who created on these shores representative and
democratic republics, wrested the sword of power from George III,
won the Revolutionary war, and freed the slaves. It has ever been
thus. Egomania must be satisfied and after dinner speakers must have
their fees.

The flood of half truth, honest ignorance, and splendid conceit will
produce an equal reaction—a cry of rage and pain from the improv-
ers of America. Mr. H. L. Mencken will burst upon our affrighted
gaze in full war paint, knife in teeth, a tomahawk dripping with ink in
one hand, a stein of Pilsner in the other, and the scalps of Professors
Phelps, Sherman, and Matthews hanging to his belt. He will spout a
huge geyser of pishposh and set innumerable smaller geysers in motion near Greenwich Village.

In view of the clouds on the horizon and the impending deluge, it
would be well to take our latitude now and find our course lest we

From "On Puritans" by Charles A. Beard. Reprinted from the December 13,
1920, issue of *The New Republic*.

should be blown ashore and wrecked upon the rocks of Plain Asininity. Nothing would be more sensible than to renew our acquaintance with Green, Gardiner, Prothero, Hallam, Lingard, Clarendon, Ludlow, Bradford, Usher, Bancroft, and the other serried volumes that flank the wall. The record seems to stand fairly clear: an autocratic Stuart monarchy and an intolerant ear-clipping Church, the protests of the purifiers, qui . . . receptam Ecclesiae Anglicanae disciplinam, liturgiam, episcoporum vocationem in quaestionem palam vocarunt, immo damnarunt, the propositions of Cartwright, the godliness of the independents, the Mayflower Compact, Cotton Mather's Magnalia, and all the rest.

But neither the orators nor the contemners are content with the plain record. They must show how the Puritans had all the virtues or all the vices. Once the term Puritanism had fairly definite connotations. Now it has lost them all. By the critics it is used as a term of opprobrium applicable to anything that interferes with the new freedom, free verse, psychoanalysis, or even the double entendre.

Evidently in the midst of much confusion, some definition is necessary, and for that purpose I have run through a dozen eulogiums on the Puritans (not omitting G. W. Curtis's orations) and an equal number of attacks on the Puritans (not omitting Mencken's Prefaces). From these authentic documents I have culled the following descriptive terms applied to Puritans. I append a table for the benefit of the reader. Puritanism means:

Godliness	Philistinism
Thrift	Harsh restraint
Liberty	Beauty-hating
Democracy	Sour-faced fanaticism
Culture	Supreme hypocrisy
Industry	Canting
Frugality	Demonology
Temperance	Enmity to true art
Resistance to tyranny	Intellectual tyranny
Pluck	Brutal intolerance
Principle	Grape juice
A free church	Grisly sermons
A free state	Religious persecution
Equal rights	Sullenness
A holy Sabbath	Ill-temper
Liberty under law	Stinginess
Individual freedom	Bigotry
Self-government	Conceit
The gracious spirit of Christianity	Bombast

I look upon this catalogue and am puzzled to find "the whole truth." When I think of Puritan "temperance" I am reminded of cherry bounce and also the good old Jamaica rum which New England used to make in such quantities that it would float her mercantile marine. When I think of "demonology," I remember that son of Boston, Benjamin Franklin, whose liberality of spirit even Mencken celebrates, when he falsely attributes it to French influence, having never in his omniscience read the Autobiography. When I think of "liberty and individual freedom," I shudder to recall stories of the New England slavers and the terrible middle passage which only Ruskin's superb imagination could picture. When I think of "pluck and industry," I recollect the dogged labors of French peasants, Catholic in faith and Celtic in race. When I see the staring words "brutal intolerance" I recall the sweet spirit of Roger Williams, aye, the sweeter spirit of John Milton whose Areopagitica was written before the school of the new freedom was established. When I read "hypocrisy" and "canting" I cannot refrain from associating with them the antics of the late Wilhelm II who, I believe, was not born in Boston. So I take leave of the subject. Let the honest reader, standing under the stars, pick out those characteristics that distinctly and consistently mark the Puritans through their long history.

If we leave generalities for particulars we are equally baffled. Some things of course are clear. The art of reading and writing was doubtless more widely spread in New England than in the other colonies, but that has little or no relation to education or wisdom. Until about 1890 New England did most of the Northern writing for "serious thinkers." It is not necessary to name authors or magazines. New England early had a considerable leisure class free for excursions into the realm of the spirit, but whether that was the product of Puritanism or catches of cod is an open question. Most of our histories have been written in New England, but the monopoly has long passed. New England contributed heavily to western settlement, to the Union army, and to the annual output of textiles. Puritanism did not build our railways, construct our blast furnaces or tunnel our hills.

But when one goes beyond so many pages of poetry, so many volumes of history and sermons, and the Puritan Sabbath one is in a quaking bog. Critics attribute the raucous and provincial note in our literature to the Puritans. No student of the history of civilization would make that mistake. What have the millions of French who have lived and died in Canada produced to compare with the magnificent literature of France? How many Greek colonies scattered along the shores of the Mediterranean could rival the metropolis in sculpture or tragedy? The rusticity of the province was not monopolized by Puritans.

Take then the matter of government. The Mayflower Compact, the Fundamental Orders of Connecticut, and the Fundamental Articles of New Haven set forth a form of religious brotherhood as old as the Church at Jerusalem described in the Acts. The Pilgrims were not Puritans anyway, but even if they were they did not invent the term or the idea of a compact. The so-called democracy of the Massachusetts Bay Corporation was nothing but the democracy of an English company of merchant adventurers brought to America. What was not religious was English. Nothing was new. Nothing in the realm of ideas was contributed by the Puritans.

Consider also the spirit of our government. If we speak of American democracy, must we not think of Jefferson rather than John Adams or Fisher Ames? And Jefferson was born in Virginia, the original home of slavery, indentured servitude, an aristocracy, and an Established Church. Moreover his doctrines, especially his political views, were not as Mencken implies "importations" from France. Any schoolboy who ever heard of John Locke knows better. Was John Locke a Puritan?

Did Jefferson create American democracy? I resort to a Puritan of the Puritans, who according to authentic documents knew and loved good whiskey, Daniel Webster. He delivered an oration at Plymouth on the two hundredth anniversary of the landing of the Pilgrims, and he told more solid truth than will be found in all the oratorical eruptions that will break forth in this harassed land next December. And what did he say? "Our New England ancestors . . . came to a new country. There were as yet no land yielding rent, and no tenants rendering service. . . . They were themselves either from their original condition or from the necessity of their common interest, nearly on a general level in respect to property. Their situation demanded a parcelling out and division of the lands and it may be fairly said that this necessary act fixed the future frame and form of their government. The character of their political institutions was determined by the fundamental laws respecting property."

For more than two hundred years the freeholder and his wife who labored with their own hands shaped the course of American development. This fact has more to do with American democracy, American art, American literature, as Mencken himself knows and says, than all the Puritanism ever imported into New England. The yeoman and his wife were too busy with honest work to give long hours

to problem plays, sex stories, or the other diversions of "the emancipated age." Imagine Bernard Shaw, Gilbert Chesterton, or Baude-
laire doing a turn at log rolling or at spring plowing in the stormy
fields of New Hampshire! Sufficient unto the day is what comes out
of it. Whoever will not try to see things as they really are need not set
himself up as a critic or teacher. And let it be remembered that the
Irish, Germans, Poles, Hungarians, and Jews are not the only people
who can be objective, high, diaphanous, Olympian and understand
"poor, crude America, with its dull, puritanical, Philistine history."

It was not the Puritans that inflicted professors and doctors of philosophy upon us and doctors' dissertations, seminars, research, and
"thoroughness." It was not a Puritan nor even an Englishman who
first spent five years on the gerundive in Caesar. It was not a Puritan
who devised the lecture system, or professorships in English literature. The Puritan may not measure up to Mencken's ideal of art, but
he did build houses that are pleasing to the eye and comfortable to
live in, and he never put his kitchen midden before his front door.
Let us remember also that it was not the Puritans who expelled Shel-
ley from Oxford, and that Lincoln, of New England origin, loved a
ripping story, wrote a good hand, had irregular notions about Providence, was not a Sabbatarian, and did not advocate the eighteenth
amendment.

In learning how the Puritans dealt with their absolute truths, and how impure citizens in the society resisted those truths, we learn something of ourselves. Professor Perry Miller of Harvard relates problems of the Puritan past to problems of the perturbed present as he describes how early Americans contended with godlessness, profanity, dissension, sex, alcohol, mixed dancing, wearing of false locks, nakedness, and telling of lies, "especially when selling anything."

Errand Into the Wilderness

Perry Miller

Because the errand was so definable in advance, certain conclusions about the method of conducting it were equally evident: one, obviously, was that those sworn to the covenant should not be allowed to turn aside in a lust for mere physical rewards; but another was, in Winthrop's simple but splendid words. "we must be knit togeher in this worke as one man, wee must entertaine each other in brotherly affection." We must actually delight in each other, "always having before our eyes our Commission and community in the worke, our community as members of the same body." This was to say, were the great purpose kept steadily in mind, if all gazed only at it and strove only for it, then social solidarity (within a scheme of fixed and unalterable class distinctions) would be an automatic consequence. A society despatched upon an errand that is its own reward would want no other rewards: it could go forth to possess a land without ever becoming possessed by it; social gradations would remain eternally what God had originally appointed; there would be no internal contention among groups or interests, and though there would be hard work for everybody, prosperity would be bestowed not as a consequence of labor but as a sign of approval upon the mission itself. For once in the history of humanity (with all its sins), there would be a society so dedicated to a holy cause that success would prove innocent and triumph not raise up sinful pride or arrogant dissension.

Or, at least, this would come about if the people did not deal falsely with God, if they would live up to the articles of their bond. If we do not perform these terms, Winthrop warned, we may expect immediate manifestations of divine wrath; we shall perish out of the land we are crossing the sea to possess. And here in the 1660s and 1670s, all the jeremiads (of which Danforth's is one of the most poignant) are castigations of the people for having defaulted on precisely these articles. They recite the long list of afflictions an angry God had rained upon them, surely enough to prove how abysmally they had deserted the covenant: crop failures, epidemics, grasshoppers, caterpillars, torrid summers, arctic winters, Indian wars, hurricanes, shipwrecks, accidents, and (most grievous of all) unsatisfactory children. The solemn work of the election day, said Stoughton in 1668, is "Foundation-work"—not, that is, to lay a new one, "but to continue, and strengthen, and beautifie, and build upon that which has been laid." It had been laid in the covenant before even a foot was set ashore, and thereon New England should rest. Hence the terms of survival, let alone of prosperity, remained what had first been propounded:

If we should so frustrate and deceive the Lords Expectations, that his Covenant-interest in us, and the Workings of his Salvation be made to cease, then All were lost indeed; Ruine upon Ruine, Destruction upon Destruction would come, until one stone were not left upon another.

Since so much of the literature after 1660—in fact, just about all of it—dwells on this theme of declension and apostasy, would not the story of New England seem to be simply that of the failure of a mission? Winthrop's dread was realized: posterity had not found their salvation amid pure ordinances but had, despite the ordinances, yielded to the seductions of the good land. Hence distresses were being piled upon them, the slaughter of King Philip's War and now the attack of a profligate king upon the sacred charter. By about 1680, it did in truth seem that shortly no stone would be left upon another, that history would record of New England that the founders had been great men, but that their children and grandchildren progressively deteriorated.

This would certainly seem to be the impression conveyed by the assembled clergy and lay elders who, in 1679, met at Boston in a formal synod, under the leadership of Increase Mather, and there prepared a report on why the land suffered. The result of their deliberation, published under the title *The Necessity of Reformation,* was the first in what has proved to be a distressingly long succession of investigations into the civic health of Americans, and it is probably the most pessimistic. The land was afflicted, it said, because corruption had proceeded apace; assuredly, if the people did not quickly reform, the last blow would fall and nothing but desolation be left. Into what a moral quagmire this dedicated community had sunk, the synod did not leave to imagination; it published a long and detailed inventory of sins, crimes, misdemeanors, and nasty habits, which makes, to say the least, interesting reading.

We hear much talk nowadays about corruption, most of it couched in generalized terms. If we ask our current Jeremiahs to descend to particulars, they tell us that the republic is going on the rocks, or to the dogs, because the wives of politicians aspire to wear mink coats and their husbands take a moderate five per cent cut on certain deals to pay for the garments. The Puritans were devotees of logic, and the verb "methodize" ruled their thinking. When the synod went to work, it had before it a succession of sermons, such as that of Danforth and the other election-day or fast-day orators, as well as such works as Increase Mather's *A Brief History of the Warr With the Indians,* wherein the decimating conflict with Philip was presented as a revenge upon the people for their transgressions. When the synod felt obliged to enumerate the enormities of the land so that the people could recognize just how far short of their errand they had fallen, it did not, in the modern manner, assume that regeneration would be accomplished at the next election by turning the rascals out, but it digested this body of literature; it reduced the contents to method. The result is a staggering compendium of iniquity, organized into twelve headings.

First, there was a great and visible decay of godliness. Second, there were several manifestations of pride—contention in the churches, insubordination of inferiors toward superiors, particularly of those inferiors who had, unaccountably, acquired more wealth than their betters, and, astonishingly, a shocking extravagance in attire, especially on the part of these of the meaner sort, who persisted in dressing beyond their means. Third, there were heretics, especially Quakers and Anabaptists. Fourth, a notable increase in swearing and a spreading disposition to sleep at sermons (these two phenomena seemed basically connected). Fifth, the Sabbath was wantonly violated. Sixth, family government had decayed, and fathers no longer kept their sons and daughters from prowling at night. Seventh, instead of people being knit together as one man in mutual love, they were full of contention, so that lawsuits were on the increase and lawyers were thriving. Under the eighth head, the synod described the sins of sex and alcohol, thus producing some of the juiciest prose of the period:

militia days had become orgies, taverns were crowded; women threw temptation in the way of befuddled men by wearing false locks and displaying naked necks and arms "or, which is more abominable, naked Breasts"; there were "mixed Dancings," along with light behavior and "Company-keeping" with vain persons, wherefore the bastardy rate was rising. In 1672, there was actually an attempt to supply Boston with a brothel (it was suppressed, but the synod was bearish about the future). Ninth, New Englanders were betraying a marked disposition to tell lies, especially when selling anything. In the tenth place, the business morality of even the most righteous left everything to be desired: the wealthy speculated in land and raised prices excessively; "Day-Labourers and Mechanicks are unreasonable in their demands." In the eleventh place, the people showed no disposition to reform, and in the twelfth, they seemed utterly destitute of civic spirit.

There is still much of the strict Puritan spirit in America. In the West
one finds it especially among the Mormons, who created a garden out of
the desert in Utah and who carefully observe the teachings of their
faith. Brigham Young University, the intellectual center of the Church of
Latter-Day Saints, emphasizes moral, spiritual, and intellectual
development in the old American tradition, according to this article by the
"Los Angeles Times" religious editor.

BYU—A Campus of Peace and Patriotism

John Dart

Brigham Young University, in the eyes of its energetic and outspoken president, is destined to excel the likes of Harvard, Yale and
Stanford.

BYU, operated by the Mormon Church, is already the nation's
largest private university in fulltime day enrollment with more than
22,000 students.

When Ernest L. Wilkinson, now 70, took over as president of the
5,000-student school in 1951, the buildings and facilities on the
mountain-backdrop campus were only 20 percent of what they are
today.

BYU has yet to acquire an academic reputation comparable to the
nation's major universities. Reputations of this kind are made in a
university's graduate schools, and BYU began the first of its doctoral
programs only in 1959.

Church Influence Still Felt

However, unlike other universities founded by churches and reli-
gious-minded persons such as John Harvard and Elihu Yale, noted
Wilkinson in a speech to students recently, BYU has not thrown off
the yoke of church influence in its 95-year existence.

"In altogether too many instances Harvard has become a mecca
for those who are crassly materialistic—or rootlessly idealistic," said
Wilkinson, who also pointed to Yale's and Stanford's secularization.

Himself a 1927 Harvard law school graduate, Wilkinson predicted:

"BYU is destined to be as peculiarly different from and to excel

From "BYU—A Campus of Peace and Patriotism" by John Dart. Reprinted
by permission from the March 23, 1970, issue of *Los Angeles Times*.

other universities to the same degree that the church differs from other churches and is destined to excel them.

"This premise is not a mere hypothesis; it is a fact. The Lord said that this church is 'the only true and living church upon the face of the whole earth with which I, the Lord, am well pleased' and this university is a part of the church."

Such doctrinal-based convictions are rarely presented to non-Mormon audiences, and not every Mormon would necessarily agree with that logic of inevitability.

Liked by Conservatives

But many non-Mormon conservatives in the country feel BYU already has a fine reputation in areas they feel really matter, and President Wilkinson could not be more pleased.

A recognition from the political right of BYU's adherence to "enduring values," said Wilkinson in an interview, "is a great opportunity for us and enhances our responsibility."

The campus' lack of protest demonstrations, beards, miniskirts, cigarettes or stimulants of any kind plus evidence of patriotism and reverence have brought glowing praise from persons who view most other large campuses as havens for the immoral and politically radical.

Conservative columnists James J. Kilpatrick and Max Rafferty, California's superintendent of public instruction, in similar style came to BYU's defense in December, 1969, after Stanford University said it would schedule no further intercollegiate competition with Mormon-sponsored schools.

Stanford said it took the action because many of its black and white students found it offensive to have institutional links with a university whose sponsoring church denies the priesthood and some other church privileges to Negroes.

Wilkinson fired off a blistering reply to Stanford President Kenneth Pitzer and Mormons in general cried religious discrimination, explaining as they have on numerous occasions in recent years that the church doctrine is God-given and can be changed only by God through revelation.

BYU athletic teams traveling to other Western campuses frequently encounter demonstrations against discrimination by the church. Mormons and BYU protest that they are open to Negroes and are believers in the brotherhood of man.

Although Stanford's actions and much of the protest elsewhere referred to church doctrine, BYU students, faculty and administrators have debated whether there is discrimination on campus.

Opinions were about evenly divided among 12 students in a recent random poll taken by the student newspaper.

Two Student Opinions

Karen McDonnel of Long Beach said she thinks BYU students "tend to be a little racially prejudiced because of the Mormon doctrine," but Vandra Paullin of Palos Verdes said, "The prejudice here at BYU is built in because we're white, not because we're Mormon."

Twenty percent of the students are from California and 33 percent from Utah. More than 95 percent are members of the Mormon Church, or more formally the Church of Jesus Christ of Latter-Day Saints. The Mormon students apply to the university through their local church officials.

Since relatively few Negroes belong to the Mormon Church there are only a handful of blacks at BYU. Thus, when students talk about discrimination they refer more to attitudes than actions.

Brigham Young University has attempted to change its image a bit lately. Last fall, BYU announced it would actively recruit Negro players for its football team and last month, defensive back Ron Knight, a transfer from Northeastern Oklahoma A&M, enrolled at the university. Knight would be the first Negro varsity football player at BYU.

Wilkinson, in an interview, said BYU will have a black faculty member this semester, Oscar Udo, a Nigerian graduate student in sociology who will be a teaching assistant.

"We have a course at this college which is not new," Wilkinson said. "We teach African history and the contributions to American history of blacks such as Booker T. Washington and those people."

Asked about black studies programs begun at other colleges, Wilkinson replied, "I feel it's probably a violation of the Civil Rights Act to have black teachers teaching black history to black students."

The university president, unsuccessful Republican candidate for U.S. senator from Utah in 1964, said that geography has shaped BYU's relationship to minority groups. "I don't think you'd find a lot of American Indians at a college in Brooklyn," he said.

300 Indians at BYU

There are about 300 Indians at BYU, most of them students who have lived with white Mormon families for a while and gone to white schools in the church's expanding Indian placement program. Although church officials now want to put a ceiling on BYU enrollment at about the present level, Wilkinson said he hopes the Indian enrollment can be brought up to 1,000 students.

Wilkinson's law firm, based in Washington, D.C., handles many Indian claims against the government. One case in which he was involved for the Ute Indians resulted in four judgments totaling $31.5 million.

BYU officials point out that about 1,000 students are from foreign lands—as an indication that the university is open to students of all races and religions.

The Mormon Church has special religious interest in converting and educating American Indians, Latin Americans and Polynesians. They, according to the Book of Mormon, are "the blood of Israel," descendants of Jacob, the father of the 12 tribes of Israel. The Book of Mormon says that Lehi, a grandson of Jacob, and his party came to South America from Palestine about 600 B.C. The church believes that natives of North and South America and—for additional reasons —inhabitants of Polynesia are all related to Lehi.

Hereditary Members

"We have a special concern for the Israelites for in the 'last days' there will be a gathering of all tribes of Israel, including Jews," said Dr. Roy W. Doxey, assistant dean of religion at BYU. The predominant European-heritage membership of the Mormon Church can gain Israelite status after joining the church, but the native Indian, Polynesian and Latin American already has this distinction by heredity, according to church doctrine.

A topic of debate more widely discussed than race is the dress code at BYU.

Although the namesake of BYU—Mormon pioneer Brigham Young—and many succeeding Mormon Church presidents wore beards, chin whiskers are grounds for suspension or expulsion if a student refuses to shave them off.

So is the wearing of miniskirts, or tight clothing, or slacks (except on a few occasions) by girls. Young men are warned not to wear tight-fitting pants or let their hair grow down to the collar.

"One reason for this policy, apart from the virtue of modesty itself," said Wilkinson in a letter to parents, "is that our students have gained a great reputation for being clean, modestly dressed, good-looking young men and women."

He added: "Almost every week we get favorable newspaper and radio comments about our students . . . As a consequence, the appearance of even one person on our campus who deviates from our standards in dress or appearance impairs our reputation."

In registration for the spring semester "spotters" from the dean of students office talked with 80 to 90 students about their dress length or hair length. About 50 girls were stopped, compared with 250 last fall.

"I noticed a lot of girls that wore longer dresses on registration day, then were back to shorter ones the next day," said Ken Kartchner, the student body president.

Kartchner, an engineering student, has urged students to stop fighting the code and get their minds on more important things. At the same time, he has told Wilkinson privately that he opposes enforcement of dress standards—which drew a desk-pounding response from the university president, he said.

"For the minority of students who are fashion-conscious it's a problem," said Kartchner, "but for the majority of administrators it's a preoccupation." One administrator said beards were opposed because they are considered a symbol of the radical movement.

Cases of thievery and drug-taking do occur, administrators readily admit.

The social-political tensions that exist find their vent in groups like Young Democrats and Young Americans for Freedom (permission for a Students for a Democratic Society chapter was refused), a weekly open forum at the student center and the 92 church wards (200–250 students each) on campus where Sunday discussions often range widely.

Another outlet are boy-girl relationships. "Each year thousands of our students find marriage partners on the campus," Wilkinson said. Early marriages are officially discouraged, but church officials obviously view BYU as one of the best places for young Mormons to meet one another.

However, many BYU men wear sideburns and hair as long as the rules will allow and many young women wear boots and skirts at various lengths above the knee.

BYU administrators are unhesitant about confirming the concept that the university is supposed to be a reflection of the Mormon Church. The church provides about 70 percent of its funds and tuition is $500 a year for church members and $750 a year for nonmembers.

However, Wilkinson said the various departments are not supposed to function merely as corroborators of Mormon doctrine. "We tell them they ought to teach any concept," said the president. "Undoubtedly, the anthropology department teaches the concepts of the Book of Mormon, but that's not the only one. You can't arrive at the truth by teaching only one phase of it."

Two of the touchiest subjects at BYU are evolution and birth control, said Dr. Joseph R. Murphy, zoology department chairman.

To church members who complain from time to time that the theory of organic evolution is given credibility in BYU classrooms, Dr. Murphy said he replies with letters from church authorities stating that the Mormon Church has never officially said that evolution contradicts the Bible.

The church has gone on record opposing contraceptives while leaving the ultimate responsibility for the decision up to the individual members, said Dr. Murphy.

A book used as supplementary reading in some courses is "Population, Evolution and Birth Control: A Collage of Controversial Ideas."

"Makes you feel you ought to have a plain brown wrapper on it here at BYU," quipped Dr. Murphy.

The zoologist said most faculty members feel the responsibility to give a synthesis of modern science to students.

"We give many of them an entirely different perspective on genetics," said Dr. Murphy. "If we tell them there is no such thing as 'Negro blood' that surprises some—forcing them to think to what extent differences are cultural rather than biological."

More than 56 percent of the faculty hold Ph.D.s, most of the degrees obtained from other universities because of the recent beginnings of doctoral programs at BYU.

The chemistry and chemical engineering departments are considered most likely to be rated among the nation's top dozen graduate schools in those fields in the next five to 10 years, said Dr. Chauncey Riddle, dean of the graduate school.

Outstanding faculty members include Dr. Harvey Fletcher, "father of stereophonic sound," Dr. H. Tracy Hall, the first man to produce artificial diamonds in high-pressure, high-temperature experiments, and Dr. Armin Hill, who helped the motion picture industry develop new types of light sources, including the radio frequency lamp.

Federal funds are not accepted by BYU for buildings or equipment, but grants are sought from federal agencies for research.

Even the Reserve Officer Training Corps buildings on campus were built by the university from nongovernment funds.

About 850 students are enrolled in BYU's Air Force and Army ROTC programs, making it second only to Notre Dame's 950 enrollees among private universities where the ROTC program is voluntary. The Army ROTC unit is only two years old at BYU and is expected to increase in numbers.

Neither the ROTC programs nor job recruiters from companies such as Dow Chemical Corp. have encountered any demonstrable opposition from BYU students, school officials have noted.

Wilkinson notes: "Our attitude of insisting on moral and spiritual as well as intellectual standards is admittedly contrary to the prevailing trend in a great many universities and colleges which have abandoned any attempt to supervise the moral life of their students. We feel, however, that to indulge irresponsible student conduct is to abdicate our role as educators."

"America began as a ritual of rebirth—the world's best publicized new beginning. Now the original American Dream is dying by bits and pieces, and that is our panic. Do the new rituals represent fumbling attempts to initiate a second beginning? . . . Are we witnessing, at last, the erratic rites of America's coming of age? . . . most Americans find themselves in a kind of no man's land, between Plymouth and Merry Mount, between Middletown and Woodstock." —Melvin Maddocks

Rituals—The Revolt Against the Fixed Smile

Melvin Maddocks

In the spring of 1627, the Pilgrim settlement at Plymouth was scandalized when a rather different American named Thomas Morton decided to show the New World how to celebrate. At Merry Mount, which may have been America's first counterculture community, Morton erected a Maypole—80 feet of priapic pine—and by his own account "brewed a barrell of excellent beare" to be distributed with "other good cheare, for all commers of that day." Other good cheare included Indian girls, according to "a song fitting to the time and present occasion" written by the host himself:

Lasses in beaver coats, come away,
Ye shall be welcome to us night and day.

Myles Standish, that well-known non-womanizer, accompanied by America's first vice squad, interrupted the revels, which were subsequently described by Plymouth Governor William Bradford as "the beastly practices of the mad Bacchinalians." Morton eventually was busted, placed in the stocks and returned to England in a state of mortifying near-starvation.

It is only simplifying history, not distorting it, to suggest that on May Day 1627, the struggle for the American soul was settled once and almost for all. Score: Ants, 1; Grasshoppers, 0. The devil had been unmasked as the imp of play, the demon who made song and dance the pulsebeat of life. And so the men in the gray Puritan suits went their unmerry way: sober, industrious, thrifty, starkly Protestant, with absolutely no use for Maypoles. For Maypoles meant not only untrammeled festivity but something of larger significance: rituals. And rituals meant not only feelings and passions but coded repetitions of the past—things that New Man had come to the New World to escape. On May Day 1627, cool, clear American voices of reason said a firm no to all that.

The no was firm, but it was not, and could not have been, final. As Philosopher George Santayana, looking at the American Puritan through half-Spanish eyes, noted: "For the moment, it is certainly easier to suppress the wild impulses of our nature than to manifest them fitly, at the right times and with the proper fugitive emphasis; yet in the long run, suppression does not solve the problem, and meantime those maimed expressions which are allowed are infected with a secret misery and falseness." Nearly three and a half centuries later, the Merry Mount case no longer seems so open and shut. Not only could contemporary man use a Maypole in his blighted Garden of Eden, but he is just beginning to realize the damage caused by not having one. Consider those maimed excuses for Merry Mount that have come to serve, ever so ineptly, as its substitute. On New Year's Eve (Oh, God! A year older and what have we accomplished?) the children of Myles Standish are condemned to gather with noisemakers, paper hat and lamp shades, and out of sheer embarrassment get smashed. The stocks could not hurt worse than such gross incompetence at ritual gaiety. Every New Year's Eve, Thomas Morton is avenged.

Is this really so small a price to pay, this emptiness of heart? In between un-Mortonlike holidays—the Christmas ringing with carols to shop by, the Easter that means chocolate bunnies and an annual visit to the church of one's unfaith, the Labor Day spent dourly traveling to nowhere along clogged highways—there occur other public rites, as grimly forgettable as scenes in a bad home movie. The lady with a champagne bottle, weighed down by her furs and obligatory Fixed Smile, whacks like an inept murderer at the prow of a receding ship. The politician, equipped with a trowel and the Fixed Smile, gobs mortar on a cornerstone, or noshes his way along the campaign trail.

America's unacknowledged but cheerlessly compulsive rituals make up a montage of trivia that boggles the eye. Brother Masons shake their In-group hands. Boy Scouts extend *rigor mortis* salutes. Shriners vibrate their fezzes. Drum majorettes goose-step. Plastic Miss Americas and Nixon's Graustarkian palace guard seem to pass together in surreal review, followed by that parody of Roman triumph, the Veterans Day parade—all paunch, sourly dispirited bugle blasts, and flat feet hitching to keep step. The banal, hand-held camera pans on, showing no pity. There go the Rose Bowl floats; where does the papier-mâché end, where do the people begin? Here come the shaman-orators and all the Babbitt snake dancers. Dear Lord, another political convention!

The gift for ritual is not exactly prospering in the 20th century; secularity, urbanism, technology—all contrive to separate modern man from the kind of community that encourages, even demands, a sense of ceremony. But is this the best that America can do for a bill of rites? Other people's rituals tend to release them—as they should. Rituals are society's unwritten permission for civilized man to express primitive emotions: fear, sexuality, grief. Other people's rituals invite them to be more human in public—more themselves—than they dare to be in private. Greek Zorbas whirl like fertility gods, Irishmen keen at their friends' funerals or even the funerals of strangers. Americans smile their Fixed Smile: the smile as anti-smile—no pleasure, no love, no silliness. The smile that tries to hide the face of American Gothic and only betrays it. The smile that says, "I cannot be myself in public."

Lately a ghastly doubt has begun to mock us, and it refuses to go away. We aren't sure, but we wonder: Is a sense of ritual—a sense of formal, sanctified public ceremonial—the preliminary state to a special kind of wisdom, a higher seriousness of the heart than Puritan hearts can ever know? Through some hideous gaffe did the anti-Maypolers reject not the devil but one face of God? By being so busy conquering nature that they could not celebrate it, by insisting with prim spiritual pride on reason, did the first Americans cut us all off from the more chaotic but deeper rhythms of life?

When his first child is born, an American father finds how criminally inadequate it is to pass out cigars. When his father dies, an American son discovers that the national habits of grief and commemoration are even worse. A son honors his father by buying a cosmetic job from an undertaker who was a stranger to the living face. Mass-produced casket, mass-produced headstone, all-purpose prayers. Amen.

At the life-and-death occasions, the common-sense, I-can-do-it-myself American bumps up against the humbling truth: rituals teach men how to behave at the best and the worst moments of their lives. If one has learned no way to behave—or only a superficial way—the meaning of those moments, the meaning of life itself, hangs in jeopardy. The greatest of the American watchers, Alexis de Tocqueville, put his finger on the risk. No-frills rugged individualism, he warned over a hundred years ago, not only makes "every man forget his ancestors, but it hides his descendants and separates his contemporaries from him; it throws him back forever upon himself alone and threatens in the end to confine him entirely within the solitude of his own heart."

But now a new tribal generation has arrived. It knows nothing of Merry Mount because it knows nothing of history. But in its blood runs Morton's cursed inspiration. It is determined to raise a Maypole. With beads and real Indian headdress and peace symbols, Woodstock Nation wanders the countryside looking for its own Merry Mount: the perfect rock festival.

No one can begin to understand the young people—including the young people—until one astonishing fact is grasped: they are not kicking against the System because they think it has too many values, but because they think it has too few—and those too thin. In its preoccupation with doing, the System has let the big moments, the festive moments, the very bright and the very dark moments—the ritual moments—get away. The System has just hustled on past with its Fixed Smile in place. And for this, the young are not about to forgive it.

Woodstock Nation is staging a kind of reverse revolution, it may be the first young generation to demand more rather than less ritual. And despite its ignorance, despite its boorishness, the revolution of the children is becoming the education of us all. For though they have not made the fathers trust their values, they have made them distrust their own. Young and old, we are all developing a new respect for ritual. We are learning that knowledge without the ritual element of wonder is barren and self-mocking. We are beginning to understand that the need for ritual is a human constant, not just a craving of primitive Indians and decadent Englishmen, and that if good rituals are not invented, bad rituals happen.

Almost 20 years ago, Dr. Rollo May (*Love and Will*) speculated whether modern man, suffering "in our commercial and industrial society from a suppression of fantasy life and imagination," would seize upon "new forms of magic." His prophecy has come true with a vengeance. At the profoundest levels, as well as at the most trivial, we hunger to ritualize our everyday lives. Like a humorless orgy, the Living Theater spills its rites of the stage into the audience and finally into the street. The young read as holy writ Allen Ginsberg's *How to Make a March/Spectacle*. Protests against war, or even air pollution, find men in saffron robes with shaven heads carrying joss sticks and chanting the *Hare Krishna*. For other instructions, people consult the *I Ching*—including how to stage a new-life-style marriage. The mood reaches even the middle-aged, who tentatively toy with beards and hair styles—the least radical forms of period costuming—and adopt sensitivity training as a kind of labor-relations device. With a fever to be relevant, priests and ministers are bringing religious services into the coffeehouse, the factory, the supermarket. More often than not, the music that enhances these mod liturgies comes from an electric guitar pulsating to a rock beat. Once again, "Make a joyful noise unto the Lord" is our collective text.

What all this suggests is that a touch of madness is in the air and Americans have, as usual, gone from one extreme to the other. In *The Making of a Counter Culture,* Historian Theodore Roszak protests: "We begin to resemble nothing so much as the cultic hothouse of the Hellenistic period, where every manner of mystery and fakery, ritual and rite, intermingled with marvelous indiscrimination." Rituals threaten to be the next epidemic. Consider the games of ritual that people play: group-encounter institutes, hippie communes, mate-swapping clubs—all with varied seriousness are peddling salvation to the Fixed Smilers. The medicine men are setting up their booths. You want to be yourself in public? Have they got a ritual for you! Mysticism has become a carnival sell. Right on, scientology.

The '70s are seeing the American launched on a curiously un-American quest. He has order—the order of the machine and the punch card, the order he once thought he wanted—and he is sick to death of all the well-oiled predestination. He is off and hunting for a richer order than technology can provide, a more organic sense of meaning. Confusedly, belatedly, he is searching for something very like his soul. No one has a right to feel very optimistic about the prospects. If young people associate the Fixed-Smile syndrome with Viet Nam, older Americans see behind all the Dionysian huggermugger the face of Charles Manson. And they sense that what the children are saying to the fathers is this: We will put the Maypole back up, even if it kills us—and you.

By the most insufferable of history's practical jokes, "letting it all hang out" could produce the same results as holding it all in. Instead of Salem witches, the California breed; instead of the Ku Klux Klan, the Weathermen. If Plymouth without Merry Mount was a mistake, Merry Mount without Plymouth could be a disaster. The country that began with theocracy could end with demonology. But such an end would be cheap parody. Rituals are not quick cures for civilization and its discontents. Nor are they self-indulgence for psychic escape artists. Rituals are ultimately the SOS of terrorized hearts trapped between knowledge of their own mortality and ignorance of the dark and quite possibly hostile universe about them. What they are desperately signaling for is a deal. They are the new compact that man tries to make with reality after the death of his illusion that he is God.

America began as a ritual of rebirth—the world's best publicized new beginning. Now the original American Dream is dying by bits and pieces, and that is our panic. Do the new rituals represent fumbling attempts to initiate a second beginning? Is all the writhing and the agony, all the violent self-division, the schizophrenia of an old self dying, a new self being born? Are we witnessing, at last, the erratic rites of America's coming of age? Of its coming to a self-awareness chastened by defeats into being more human? It is too soon to speculate—even to dream a second dream. One's hope is so guarded that it dares express itself only as these tentative questions. All that can be said now is that most Americans find themselves in a kind of no man's land, between Plymouth and Merry Mount, between Middletown and Woodstock. Between too much reason and too much passion. Between the impulse to act and the impulse to be.

According to Hawthorne's short story *The Maypole of Merry Mount,* the peal of a psalm from Plymouth would occasionally collide with "the chorus of a jolly catch" from Merry Mount and echo in a splendid confusion of styles. Suppose a little band of displaced Americans had lived exactly in the middle, in that no man's land between culture and counterculture. Suppose they had listened to that collision of psalm and catch tune for weeks, for months. Would the double echo have ceased to be two competing sounds? Would one new sound have fallen in the ear, with a new rhythm and harmony of its own, neither hymn nor May dance: a third way?

We will be the first to know, for 343 years after May Day 1627, we have become those displaced Americans. We are the people that both sides warned against.

Eric Hoffer, San Francisco longshoreman and philosopher, asserts in
"The True Believer" that there are obvious differences between fanatical
Christians, fanatical Mohammedans, fanatical nationalists, and fanatical
Communists and Nazis, but that there are also certain uniformities in all
types of dedication. "However different the holy causes people die for,
they perhaps die basically for the same thing."

The True Believer

Eric Hoffer

The fanatic is perpetually incomplete and insecure. He cannot gen-
erate self-assurance out of his individual resources—out of his rejected self—but finds it only by clinging passionately to whatever support
he happens to embrace. This passionate attachment is the essence of
his blind devotion and religiosity, and he sees in it the source of all
virtue and strength. Though his single-minded dedication is a holding
on for dear life, he easily sees himself as the supporter and defender
of the holy cause to which he clings. And he is ready to sacrifice his
life to demonstrate to himself and others that such indeed is his role.
He sacrifices his life to prove his worth.

It goes without saying that the fanatic is convinced that the cause
he holds on to is monolithic and eternal—a rock of ages. Still, his
sense of security is derived from his passionate attachment and not
from the excellence of his cause. The fanatic is not really a stickler to
principle. He embraces a cause not primarily because of its justness
and holiness but because of his desperate need for something to hold
on to. Often, indeed, it is his need for passionate attachment which
turns every cause he embraces into a holy cause.

The fanatic cannot be weaned away from his cause by an appeal to
his reason or moral sense. He fears compromise and cannot be persuaded to qualify the certitude and righteousness of his holy cause.
But he finds no difficulty in swinging suddenly and wildly from one
holy cause to another. He cannot be convinced but only converted.
His passionate attachment is more vital than the quality of the cause
to which he is attached.

Though they seem at opposite poles, fanatics of all kinds are actu-

From *The True Believer* by Eric Hoffer, pp. 80–82. Copyright 1951 by Eric
Hoffer. Reprinted by permission of Harper & Row, Publishers, Inc.

ally crowded together at one end. It is the fanatic and the moderate who are poles apart and never meet. The fanatics of various hues eye each other with suspicion and are ready to fly at each other's throat. But they are neighbors and almost of one family. They hate each other with the hatred of brothers. They are as far apart and close together as Saul and Paul. And it is easier for a fanatic Communist to be converted to fascism, chauvinism or Catholicism than to become a sober liberal.

The opposite of the religious fanatic is not the fanatical atheist but the gentle cynic who cares not whether there is a God or not. The atheist is a religious person. He believes in atheism as though it were a new religion.[1] He is an atheist with devoutness and unction. According to Renan, "The day after that on which the world should no longer believe in God, atheists would be the wretchedest of all men."[2] So, too, the opposite of the chauvinist is not the traitor but the reasonable citizen who is in love with the present and has no taste for martyrdom and the heroic gesture. The traitor is usually a fanatic—radical or reactionary—who goes over to the enemy in order to hasten the downfall of a world he loathes. Most of the traitors in the Second World War came from the extreme right. "There seems to be a thin line between violent, extreme nationalism and treason."[3]

The kinship between the reactionary and the radical has been dealt with in . . . [a previous section]. All of us who lived through the Hitler decade know that the reactionary and the radical have more in common than either has with the liberal or the conservative.

Notes

1 Fëdor Dostoyevsky, *The Idiot,* Part IV, Chap. 7.
2 Ernest Renan, *History of the People of Israel* (Boston, Little, Brown & Company, 1888–1896), Vol. V., p. 159.
3 Harold Ettlinger, *The Axis on the Air* (Indianapolis, Bobbs-Merrill Company, 1943), p. 39.

Questions

1 Puritan truths have been called Puritan myths. But do not all cultures have to build their customs and laws on myths—that is, on ideas that man has created and accepts as true?

2 Is indoctrination necessary to every culture's educational system? How much and what kind of indoctrination?

3   Both the Christian church and its work ethic have come under attack in recent times. Why?

4   What will the further development of cybernation and automation do to the work ethic?

5   What has been the influence of Benjamin Franklin on the American Dream?

6   In what ways are the Puritan "truths" with us in America today?

7   What is the importance of ritual in life? How does ritual evolve, and why is it difficult to change?

8   What has been the role of ritual in American industrial history?

9   Is there some fanaticism in all of us? Why?

3

The Declaration of Independence as Dream and Reality

Essay

Dissecting the Declaration of Independence
Melvin Steinfield

Readings

Hedging on Slavery
Thomas Jefferson

The Myth of the Savage Indian
Ashley Montagu

The Literary Qualities of the Declaration
Carl Becker

The Promise of Equality
William Lloyd Garrison

Is Freedom Dying in America?
Henry Steele Commager

Equality of Educational Opportunity
Andrew Billingsley, Douglas Davidson, Theresa Loya

Every student of history is familiar with the following words of Thomas Jefferson: "We hold these truths to be self-evident: that all men are created equal, that they are endowed by their creator with certain unalienable rights, that among these are life, liberty, and the pursuit of happiness." Those words in the Declaration of Independence seem to express the quintessence of the American Dream of equal opportunity. Perhaps that is why they have been repeated so often. Though they have been repeated, they have not often been dissected, and the Declaration of Independence remains for most Americans a document that is essentially unread. Many people are unaware that Jefferson's ideas had been expressed by others long before they found their way into the Declaration of Independence. Or that Jefferson distorted some facts when he listed grievances of the colonists against England. Or that Negro slaves were never intended by the Founding Fathers to be included among those who were endowed with natural rights. The essay below employs a running commentary approach as a means of dissecting the Declaration of Independence and penetrating the facade of the American Dream. The result may be a less idealistic picture than many Americans will wish to acknowledge.

Dissecting the Declaration of Independence

Melvin Steinfield

When, in the Course of human events,

Jefferson could have said "When." His use of "in the course of human events" broadens the statement to reflect the cosmopolitan orientation of the Enlightenment in which the "whole" of society was held in higher esteem than its individual parts. Jefferson is trying to achieve a universal appeal to all mankind. This approach corresponds to the Newtonian world-view which dominated eighteenth-century thought.

it becomes necessary for one people to dissolve the political bands which have connected them with another,

"When there is a revolution" is what Jefferson means. He avoids the use of blunt terms here because he wants to soften the fact that this revolution is a violent action. Violence is frowned upon in Enlightenment thought. Rational approaches to problem-solving are the only acceptable means of establishing that one's cause is just. "Dissolve the political bands" is a perfectly tailored phrase that makes the

illegal and violent revolution Jefferson is projecting sound like a justifiable and praiseworthy movement.

In his other writings, Jefferson shows no reluctance to speak bluntly when discussing revolution and violence. For instance, he wrote to
James Madison in 1787: "A little rebellion, now and then, is a good
thing." And in that same year he wrote, in a letter to Colonel Smith:
"The tree of liberty must be refreshed from time to time with the
blood of patriots and tyrants." But in the Declaration, he shows
restraint.

*and to assume among the Powers of the earth the separate and equal
station to which the Laws of Nature and of Nature's God entitle them,
a decent respect to the opinions of mankind requires that they should
declare the causes which impel them to the separation.*

The reference to "Laws of Nature and Nature's God" is a typical
Enlightenment statement. By the eighteenth century it was believed
that natural laws could be applied not only to the physical world but
also to the realm of human affairs. In plain Anglo-Saxon, what Jefferson has said in the entire first paragraph is: When there is a revolution, the world should be informed of the reasons.

We hold these truths to be self-evident,

John Locke, in his *Essay Concerning Human Understanding,* mentioned the *tabula rasa,* or blank tablet, which he said represented an
individual's mind at birth. Only by years of experiences which make
firm impressions upon this blank tablet are individual attitudes
formed. Thus, Locke held that through exposure to common experiences, there is a "common sense" which all individuals possess. Indeed, Thomas Paine, in titling his revolutionary pamphlet *Common
Sense,* borrowed on this theory. Jefferson shows the influence of
Locke and of the Enlightenment in general when he employs the concept of truths which are obvious to all men. And, likewise, he appeals
to the sensibilities of Enlightenment-oriented thinkers through the use
of such phrases. Who can quarrel with something that is self-evident
to rational beings?

*that all men are created equal, that they are endowed by their Creator
with certain unalienable Rights, that among these are Life, Liberty
and the pursuit of Happiness.*

Basically, Jefferson is merely saying that men are born with natural
rights. He restates, with much embellishment, an idea that John
Locke presented in his essay *On Civil Government* in 1690. In that

essay Locke developed the concept of a natural rights theory to justify the Glorious Revolution of 1688, which gave Parliament supremacy over the King. Additional support for the natural rights theory came in 1762 with Rousseau's *The Social Contract*. We can be safe in assuming that Jefferson was familiar with the ideas of these theorists. We know that only a few years before writing the Declaration of Independence, he acquired a copy of John Locke's works. Thus, Jefferson was able to draw from the best minds of the Enlightenment period in presenting some of the least controversial ideas of the age. Who could disagree with his stand on natural rights?

Of course, it is important to realize that "all men are created equal" did not apply, nor was it intended to apply, literally. Negro slaves and American Indians were especially understood to be excluded from the conception of "all men." In the Dred Scott decision of 1857, Chief Justice Roger Taney explicitly argued that the Founding Fathers never meant for Negro slaves to be included among those men having equal natural rights. It is interesting to note that Jefferson himself, like Washington and other Founding Fathers, owned slaves.

That to secure these rights, Governments are instituted among Men, deriving their just powers from the consent of the governed,

This part of the Declaration reiterates two ideas familiar to its eighteenth-century audience: popular sovereignty and social contract. People form governments to protect their rights, and while they delegate responsibility to the government, they retain the ultimate power. Hobbes, Locke, and Rousseau employed the concept of social contract (sometimes referred to as "compact"), and Locke developed the concept of popular sovereignty. Again, Jefferson was not presenting revolutionary theories as much as he was restating ideas from the current body of Enlightenment thought.

That whenever any Form of Government becomes destructive of these ends, it is the Right of the People to alter or to abolish it, and to institute new Government, laying its foundation on such principles and organizing its powers in such form, as to them shall seem most likely to effect their Safety and Happiness.

We have already mentioned that Jefferson's Declaration of Independence owed a great deal to theorists of the Enlightenment. In fact, Jefferson paraphrased John Locke's *Essay on Civil Government* (1690) throughout most of the Declaration. A comparison of the above wording with an excerpt from Locke's essay provides considerable insight to the extent of Jefferson's "borrowing":

> Whenever, therefore, the legislative shall transgress this fun-
> damental rule of society, and either by ambition, fear, folly, or
> corruption, endeavour to grasp themselves, or put into the hands
> of any other, an absolute power over the lives, liberties, and
> estates of the people, by this breach of trust forfeit the power the
> people had put into their hands for quite contrary ends, and it
> devolves to the people, who have a right to resume their original
> liberty, and by the establishment of a new legislative (such as
> they shall think fit), provide for their own safety and security,
> which is the end for which they are in society.

"All Power to the people," wrote Locke and Jefferson two centuries
before that idea was reechoed by the Black Panthers.

Note that up to this point Jefferson has not named the antagonists
he hints at. He is trying to present a general argument for revolution
that would be applicable to any people in similar circumstances. In so
doing, he hopes to gain the support of all who can agree with the rational principles he is enunciating. What Enlightenment-oriented man
could quarrel with his claim that a government which violates natural
rights should be replaced by one that protects natural rights?

Prudence, indeed, will dictate that Governments long established
should not be changed for light and transient causes; and accordingly
all experience hath shewn, that mankind are more disposed to suffer,
while evils are sufferable, than to right themselves by abolishing the
forms to which they are accustomed.

Even though Jefferson has completed the basic argument justifying
revolution, he still shrewdly avoids bringing up specifics. We still do
not hear about George III or Parliament or colonial grievances. Jefferson creates the impression that the American revolutionaries are
bending over backwards to avoid revolution, long after a revolution
was justified. In effect, he skillfully forestalls the possibility that the
revolutionaries will be accused of being trigger-happy. We are willing
to live with some tyranny, he implies, if it will avoid bringing on
greater disaster. Sometimes, even when a revolution is more than justified, restraint should be exercised. We do not advocate revolution
the minute a government violates individual rights. What could be
more reasonable than this point of view? The Enlightenment emphasis upon calm, tranquil, tolerant, patient, peaceful, and prudent rational behavior was never more effectively employed than in the fox-like
skill of image-building Jefferson.

But when a long train of abuses and usurpations, pursuing invariably
the same Object evinces a design to reduce them under absolute Des-

potism, it is their right, it is their duty, to throw off such Govern-
ment, and to provide new Guards for their future security.

This line was inevitable. Jefferson points out that even the most rational Enlightenment-type individuals have limits beyond which they
cannot continue to permit injustice. In some extreme cases, Jefferson
intimates that even though we are generally not in favor of revolution, a revolution is the only course open to reasonable men. Note
the reminder that the purpose of government is to protect rights.
Again, compare this to John Locke *(Essay on Civil Government,*
1690; italics added for emphasis):

> The reason why men enter into society is the preservation of
> their property; and the end while they choose and authorise a leg-
> islative is that there may be laws made, and rules set, *as guards*
> *and fences to the properties of all the society,* to limit the power
> and moderate the dominion of every part and member of the
> society.

—Such has been the patient sufferance of these Colonies; and such is
now the necessity which constrains them to alter their former Systems
of Government.

Finally, Jefferson mentions specifics. At last he brings the reader of
the Declaration of Independence to a particular case. Up to this point,
the Declaration could be used by anyone to justify revolution against
any form of tyranny. In fact, many revolutions have borrowed heavily
from Jefferson's justification.

The history of the present King of Great Britain is a history of re-
peated injuries and usurpations, all having in direct object the estab-
lishment of an absolute Tyranny over these States. To prove this, let
Facts be submitted to a candid world.

Jefferson knows that Parliament, not the King, exercised the real
power in England. By selecting George III as the object of his criticism, he cleverly personifies the government, thus making it easier to
project the image of tyranny. Strictly speaking, Jefferson "fudged" a
little to sharpen his point.

He has refused his Assent to Laws, the most wholesome and neces-
sary for the public good.

He has forbidden his Governors to pass Laws of immediate and
pressing importance, unless suspended in their operation till his As-
sent should be obtained; and when so suspended, he has utterly
neglected to attend to them.

He has refused to pass other Laws for the accommodation of large districts of people, unless those people would relinquish the right of Representation in the Legislature, a right inestimable to them and formidable to tyrants only.

He has called together legislative bodies at places unusual, uncomfortable, and distant from the depository of their Public Records, for the sole purpose of fatiguing them into compliance with his measures.

He has dissolved Representative Houses repeatedly, for opposing with manly firmness his invasions on the rights of the people.

He has refused for a long time, after such dissolutions, to cause others to be elected; whereby the Legislative Powers, incapable of Annihilation, have returned to the People at large for their exercise; the State remaining in the meantime exposed to all the dangers of invasion from without and convulsions within.

He has endeavoured to prevent the population of these States; for that purpose obstructing the Laws of Naturalization of Foreigners; refusing to pass others to encourage their migration hither, and raising the conditions of new Appropriations of Lands.

He has obstructed the Administration of Justice, by refusing his Assent to Laws for establishing Judiciary Powers.

He has made Judges dependent on his Will alone, for the tenure of their offices, and the amount and payment of their salaries.

He has erected a multitude of New Offices, and sent hither swarms of Officers to harass our People, and eat out their substance.

He has kept among us, in times of peace, Standing Armies without the Consent of our legislature.

He has affected to render the Military independent of and superior to the Civil Power.

He has combined with others to subject us to a jurisdiction foreign to our constitution, and unacknowledged by our laws; giving his Assent to their acts of pretended legislation:

For quartering large bodies of armed troops among us:

For protecting them, by a mock Trial, from Punishment for any Murders which they should commit on the Inhabitants of these States:

For cutting off our Trade with all parts of the world:

For imposing taxes on us without our Consent:

For depriving us in many cases, of the benefits of Trial by Jury:

For transporting us beyond Seas to be tried for pretended offences:

For abolishing the free System of English Laws in a neighbouring Province, establishing therein an Arbitrary government, and enlarging its Boundaries so as to render it at once an example and fit instrument for introducing the same absolute rule into these Colonies:

For taking away our Charters, abolishing our most valuable Laws, and altering fundamentally the Forms of our Governments:

For suspending our own Legislature, and declaring themselves invested with Power to legislate for us in all cases whatsoever.

He has abdicated Government here, by declaring us out of his Protection and waging War against us.

He has plundered our seas, ravaged our Coasts, burnt our towns, and destroyed the lives of our people.

He is at this time transporting large armies of foreign mercenaries to compleat the works of death, desolation and tyranny, already begun with circumstances of Cruelty & perfidy scarcely paralleled in the most barbarous ages, and totally unworthy the Head of a civilized nation.

He has constrained our fellow Citizens taken Captive on the high Seas to bear Arms against their Country, to become the executioners of their friends and Brethren, or to fall themselves by their Hands.

He has excited domestic insurrections amongst us, and has endeavoured to bring on the inhabitants of our frontiers, the merciless Indian Savages, whose known rule of warfare, is an undistinguished destruction of all ages, sexes and conditions.

The several dozen accusations which Jefferson makes fall into three categories: those which are essentially correct, those which are somewhat exaggerated, and those which are highly exaggerated. Certainly Jefferson is correct when he cites the "quartering [of] large bodies of armed troops among us." This was a major grievance of the colonists which had led to the Boston Massacre six years before the Declaration was signed. There is some exaggeration when he refers to "protecting them, by a mock Trial, from Punishment for any Murders which they should commit on the Inhabitants of these States." Actually, it was the Boston mob that provoked the confrontation which led to the massacre. The small detachment of British troops reacted, after extreme provocation, in self-defense. At the trial a jury of Bostonians, hearing the arguments of defense attorney John Adams, found the soldiers guilty only of manslaughter and they were given token punishments. Jefferson, however, perpetuated the fabrications of Samuel Adams, who had built up the incident as a "Massacre."

As an example of grievances that are highly overstated, one could cite the following exaggeration by Jefferson: "He has plundered our seas, ravaged our Coasts, burnt our towns, and destroyed the lives of our people." Is this really the truth? Jefferson's pen produced an interesting combination of grievances, some true, some mostly true, and some mostly untrue. The next lines of the Declaration give us a clue as to why he did this.

In every stage of these Oppressions We have Petitioned for Redress in the most humble terms; Our repeated Petitions have been answered only by repeated injury. A Prince, whose character is thus marked by every act which may define a Tyrant, is unfit to be the ruler of a free People.

Nor have We been wanting in attention to our British brethren. We have warned them from time to time of attempts by their legislature to extend an unwarrantable jurisdiction over us. We have reminded them of the circumstances of our emigration and settlement here. We have appealed to their native justice and magnanimity, and we have conjured them by the ties of our common kindred to disavow these usurpations, which would inevitably interrupt our connections and correspondence. They too have been deaf to the voice of justice and of consanguinity. We must, therefore, acquiesce in the necessity, which denounces our Separation, and hold them, as we hold the rest of mankind, Enemies of War, in Peace Friends.

Jefferson tries to show how the American revolutionaries are perfect paragons of Enlightenment virtue, and how the King is a perfect example of a tyrant. The Americans have "petitioned, warned, appealed," and tried every conceivable nonviolent rational method of expressing patient dissatisfaction; the British have "plundered, ravaged, burnt, and murdered." What more proof does one need? Look at the sharp contrast between the brutal tyrants of Britain and the peaceful moderates of America! Everything the Americans have done is in line with the Establishment-Enlightenment value-system. Everything the British have done is out of line with that system. (If this was not actually the case, it did not stop Jefferson from presenting the "facts" in that manner.)

We, therefore, the Representatives of the united States of America, in General Congress, Assembled, appealing to the Supreme Judge of the world for the rectitude of our intentions, do, in the Name, and by Authority of the good People of these Colonies, solemnly publish and declare, That these United Colonies are, and of Right ought to be Free and Independent States; that they are Absolved from all Allegiance to the British Crown, and that all political connection between them and the State of Great Britain, is and ought to be totally dissolved; and that as Free and Independent States, they have full Power to levy

War, conclude Peace, contract Alliances, establish Commerce, and to do all other Acts and Things which Independent States may of right do. And for the support of this Declaration, with a firm reliance on the Protection of Divine Providence, we mutually pledge to each other our Lives, our Fortunes, and our sacred Honor.

Thus, we are forced to take this unwanted but necessary step.

In summary, the ideas expressed in the Declaration of Independence were not new. John Locke and other political theorists had developed those ideas long before Jefferson restated them. What was new was that these ideas were being used for the first time to justify a revolution that was about to take place. And the formula which Jefferson, borrowing from the Enlightenment political heritage, set forth was to be employed again and again as other nations made their bid for independence. In the French Revolution, and in revolutions in Latin America in the nineteenth century, and in Africa in the twentieth century, the concepts emphasized in the American Declaration of Independence were to reappear.

As a convenient guide, here is a twentieth-century summary of the American Declaration of Independence:

1. When there is a revolution, the world should be informed of the reasons.
2. All men have natural rights.
3. Governments should protect natural rights.
4. Whenever a government fails to protect natural rights, it should be replaced with one which does protect them.
5. No government should be overthrown merely because it does not do a perfect job of protecting natural rights.
6. But, if it violates rights over a long period of time without making any attempt to correct the injustice, then it must be overthrown.
7. Our rights have been violated for a long time.
8. Here is proof of how bad it has been.
9. We have tried all known rational means of pleading with the government and reasoning with it so that it will stop violating our natural rights.
10. It is obvious that nothing short of a revolution will be effective in restoring the power of government and the protection of our rights to the people.
11. Therefore, we have no choice but to declare our independence and to try to regain our rights which were given by God, whose support we feel we have.

Tho following passage was part of Jefferson's original draft of the
Declaration of Independence. It is a "vehement philippic against negro
slavery," as John Adams described it. Congress, which did not want to go on
record as an opponent of the slave trade, dropped this section from
the final draft. Thus, the primary document of the American Dream
was tainted from the start.

Hedging on Slavery

Thomas Jefferson

He has waged cruel war against human nature itself, violating its
most sacred rights of life and liberty in the persons of a distant people
who never offended him, captivating and carrying them into slavery in
another hemisphere, or to incur miserable death in their transportation
thither. This piratical warfare, the opprobrium of infidel powers, is the
warfare of the Christian king of Great Britain. Determined to keep
open a market where men should be bought and sold, he has prostituted his negative for suppressing every legislative attempt to prohibit
or to restrain this execrable commerce; and that this assemblage of
horrors might want no fact of distinguished die, he is now exciting
these very people to rise in arms among us, and to purchase that
liberty of which he deprived them, by murdering the people upon
whom he also obtruded them; thus paying off former crimes committed against the liberties of one people, with crimes which he
urges them to commit against the lives of another.

In the following essay a distinguished anthropologist argues that the
myth of the savage Indian was enshrined and perpetuated in the
Declaration of Independence. Since the Declaration, America has not let
its Indians pursue happiness; instead it has bombarded them with
assaults from all directions. Is this another legacy of the
Declaration of Independence?

The Myth of the Savage Indian

Ashley Montagu

*A Century of Dishonor: A Sketch of the United States Govern-
ment's Dealings With Some of the Indian Tribes,* by Helen Hunt
Jackson, was published in 1881 and ceased to be in print in the year
of her death, 1885. Her novel *Ramona,* dealing with the same subject,
has been reprinted more than 300 times! Such is the superiority of
imaginative over historic literature. The history elicited nowhere
nearly as much interest as the novel, the novel being read for pleasure, the history being relegated to the archives. And this, indeed, has
been the fate of the American Indian, to be treated as a novelistic figure rather than as a historic living accusing reality. Mrs. Jackson's
Century of Dishonor presented a devastating account of the mistreatment of the American Indian by the government of the United States
during the century preceding the publication of the book. There have
been other books of a similar sort on the subject, but all of them have
suffered the same fate, for they seem to have had very little effect on
whatever it is that serves most Americans for a conscience.

The treatment of the American Indian by American whites is a
story, not only of dishonor, but also of infamy. The treachery,
murder, dispossession, disfranchisement, genocide, destruction, robbery, cruelty, exile, and injustice which the American Indian has suffered at the hands of American whites constitute one of the blackest
records in the history of the relations between peoples. Whole tribes
exterminated, pledges, promises, treaties broken, dispossession and
forced migrations from his native lands, forced to live on reservations
as wards of the United States government under the rule of venal

agents, without voting rights or representation, abandoned, disregarded, and often brutally hunted down and murdered in a spirit of sheer wantonness, the American Indian constitutes the shame of the American people.

In the name of making the world safe for democracy or self-determination, we intrude with armed force or the threat of it or with money or food or matériel in the internal affairs of other nations but neglect to secure the benefits of democracy to the original inhabitants of the United States, the original inhabitants who welcomed the first white men to their land with love, friendship, and admiration.

The discoverer of America, Christopher Columbus, described the American Indians as "a loving, uncovetous people, so docile in all things that there is no better people or better country. . . . They loved their neighbors as themselves and they had the sweetest and gentlest way of speaking in the world, and always with a smile."

In 1584 the Englishman Captain Arthur Barlowe wrote Sir Walter Raleigh about the Indians encountered on the Carolina coast: "We were entertained with all love and kindness, and with as much bounty as they could possibly devise. We found the people most gentle, loving, and faithful, void of all guile and treason, and such as live after the manner of the golden age."

Little, alas, did these innocents know that in return for their friendship, these creatures from another world would steal their lands and property, destroy their way of life, and turn them into refugees and beggars in their own country—and then, for attempting to resist the inhuman incursions on them, be branded as fierce savages, who must be subdued or unmercifully destroyed. With the logic that is the rule in such matters, the American Indian was saddled with the crimes committed against him. For example, history and folklore tell us that the American Indian scalped his victims. What is not told us is that this practice was taught the American Indian by the invading whites, who offered a bounty for every Indian scalp taken.

Those who commit atrocities against others are shocked and outraged when their victims rise up and retaliate in kind and then, of course, proceed to condemn them for being what their teachers have taught them to become . . . [E]ven in the Declaration of Independence, in spite of the fact that American Indians had in innumerable ways greatly assisted the Revolutionary forces in their struggle for freedom, it is stated that the King of Great Britain "has excited domestic insurrections amongst us, and has endeavoured to bring on the inhabitants of our frontiers, the merciless Indian Savages, whose known rule of warfare is an undistinguished destruction of all ages, sexes and conditions." Thus was the myth of the savage American Indian enshrined and perpetuated in the most important and basic of all historic American documents.

The crimes and cruelties committed against the American Indian can no longer be shrugged off by continuing to subscribe to the mythology that was created to justify white infamy, nor can they be evaded by pretending that the American Indian will soon cease to exist. The birthrate of the American Indian is among the highest in the land, but so, owing to the depressed conditions under which these once free people are forced to live, are their sickness and death rates. Let Americans of the "Not So Great Society" shed their hypocrisies for making the world safe for democracy abroad and devote some attention to making it safe at home for all Americans—and who has a greater claim to the title of American than the American Indian? Americans owe an incalculable debt to the American Indian. It is time they began making some attempt to repay that debt.

It is only natural to approach traditional patriotic symbols with
reverence and, in the course of time, to inject them with idealistic
qualities which they perhaps never had. Thus, it is refreshing, if not
shocking, to examine a distinguished scholar's analysis of the rhetorical
style of the Declaration of Independence, and his appraisal of what
Jefferson was attempting to accomplish by this style. It's quite a
comedown for the American Dream.

The Literary Qualities of the Declaration

Carl Becker

The last of Jefferson's charges against the king was what John
Adams called the "vehement philippic against negro slavery."[1]

He has waged cruel war against human nature itself, violating
its most sacred rights of life and liberty in the persons of a distant people who never offended him, captivating and carrying
them into slavery in another hemisphere, or to incur miserable
death in their transportation thither. This piratical warfare, the
opprobrium of *infidel* powers, is the warfare of the *Christian*
king of Great Britain. Determined to keep open a market where
MEN should be bought and sold, he has prostituted his negative
for suppressing every legislative attempt to prohibit or to restrain
this execrable commerce; and that this assemblage of horrors
might want no fact of distinguished die, he is now exciting these
very people to rise in arms among us, and to purchase that liberty of which *he* deprived them, by murdering the people upon
whom *he* also obtruded them; thus paying off former crimes
committed against the *liberties* of one people, with crimes which
he urges them to commit against the *lives* of another.

Congress omitted this passage altogether. I am glad it did. One
does not expect a declaration of independence to represent historical
events with the objectivity and exactitude of a scientific treatise; but
here the discrepancy between the fact and the representation is too
flagrant. Especially, in view of the subsequent history of the slave
trade, and of slavery itself, without which there would have been no
slave trade, these charges against the king lose whatever plausibility,

From *The Declaration of Independence* by Carl Becker. Copyright 1922, 1942
by Carl Becker. Reprinted by permission of Alfred A. Knopf, Inc.

slight enough at best, they may have had at the time. But I have quoted this passage in full . . . not on account of its substance but on account of its form, which is interesting, and peculiarly significant in its bearing upon Jefferson's qualities and limitations as a writer. John Adams thought it one of the best parts of the Declaration. It is possible that Jefferson thought so too. He evidently gave much attention to the wording of it. But to me, even assuming the charges against the king to be true, it is the part of the Declaration in which Jefferson conspicuously failed to achieve literary excellence.

The reason is, I think, that in this passage Jefferson attempted something which he was temperamentally unfitted to achieve. The passage was to have been the climax of the charges against the king; on its own showing of facts it imputes to him the most inhuman acts, the basest motives; its purpose, one supposes, is to stir the reader's emotions, to make him feel a righteous indignation at the king's acts, a profound contempt for the man and his motives. Well, the passage is clear, precise, carefully balanced. It employs the most tremendous words—"murder," "piratical warfare," "prostituted," "miserable death." But in spite of every effort, the passage somehow leaves us cold; it remains, like all of Jefferson's writing, calm and quiescent; it lacks warmth; it fails to lift us out of our equanimity. There is in it even (something rare indeed in Jefferson's writings) a sense of labored effort, of deliberate striving for an effect that does not come.

This curious effect, or lack of effect, is partly due to the fact that the king's base actions are presented to us in abstract terms. We are not permitted to see George III. George III does not repeal a statute of South Carolina in order that Sambo may be sold at the port of Charleston. No, the Christian king wages "cruel war against human nature," he prostitutes "his negative for the suppression of every legislative attempt to prohibit or to restrain this execrable commerce." We have never a glimpse of poor dumb negroes gasping for breath in the foul hold of a transport ship, or driven with whips like cattle to labor in a fetid rice swamp; what we see is human nature, and the "violation of its most sacred rights in the persons of a distant people." The thin vision of things in the abstract rarely reaches the sympathies. Few things are less moving than to gaze upon the concept of miserable death, and it is possible to contemplate "an assemblage of horrors that wants no fact of distinguished die" without much righteous indignation.

Yet the real reason lies deeper. It is of course quite possible to invest a generalized statement with an emotional quality. Consider the famous passage from Lincoln's second Inaugural:

> Fondly do we hope—fervently do we pray—that this mighty scourge of war may speedily pass away. Yet, if God wills that it continue until all the wealth piled by the bondman's two hundred and fifty years of unrequited toil shall be sunk, and until every drop of blood drawn with the lash shall be paid by another drawn by the sword, as was said three thousand years ago, so still it must be said, "the judgments of the Lord are true and righteous altogether."

Compare this with Jefferson's [wording]:

> And that this assemblage of horrors might want no fact of distinguished die, he is not exciting these very people to rise in arms against us, and to purchase that liberty of which *he* deprived them, by murdering the people upon whom *he* also obtruded them; thus paying off former crimes committed against the *liberties* of one people, with crimes which he urges them to commit against the *lives* of another.

Making every allowance for difference in subject and in occasion, these passages differ as light differs from darkness. There is a quality of deep feeling about the first, an indefinable something which is profoundly moving; and this something, which informs and enriches much of Lincoln's writing, is rarely, almost never present in the writing of Jefferson.

This something, which Jefferson lacked but which Lincoln possessed in full measure, may perhaps for want of a better term be called a profoundly emotional apprehension of experience. One might say that Jefferson felt with the mind, as some people think with the heart. He had enthusiasm, but it was enthusiasm engendered by an irrepressible intellectual curiosity. He was ardent, but his ardors were cool, giving forth light without heat. One never feels with Jefferson, as one does with Washington, that his restraint is the effect of a powerful will persistently holding down a profoundly passionate nature. One has every confidence that Jefferson will never lose control of himself, will never give way to purifying rage, relieving his overwrought feelings by an outburst of divine swearing. All his ideas and sentiments seem of easy birth, flowing felicitously from an alert and expeditious brain rather than slowly and painfully welling up from the obscure depths of his nature. "I looked for gravity," says Maclay, giving his first impressions of Jefferson, "but a laxity of manner seemed shed about him. He spoke almost without ceasing; but even his discourse partook of his personal demeanor. It was loose and rambling; and yet he scattered information wherever he went, and some even brilliant sentiments sparkled from him."

Jefferson's writing is much like that—a ceaseless flow, sparkling, often brilliant, a kind of easy improvisation. There are in his writings few of those ominous overtones charged with emotion, and implying more than is expressed. Sometimes, indeed, by virtue of a certain facility, a certain complacent optimism, by virtue of saying disputed things in such a pleasant way, his words imply even less than they mean. When, for example, Jefferson says "the tree of liberty must be refreshed from time to time with the blood of patriots and tyrants," so far from making us shudder, he contrives to throw about this unlovely picture a kind of arcadian charm. You will hardly think of Jefferson, with lifted hand and vibrant voice, in the heat of emotion striking off the tremendous sentence, "Give me liberty or give me death!" I can imagine him saying, "Manly spirit bids us choose to die freemen rather than to live slaves." The words would scarcely lift us out of our seats, however we might applaud the orator for his peculiar felicity of expression.

Felicity of expression—certainly Jefferson had that; but one wonders whether he did not perhaps have too much of it. This sustained felicity gives one at times a certain feeling of insecurity, as of resting one's weight on something fragile. Jefferson's placidity, the complacent optimism of his sentiments and ideas, carry him at times perilously near the fatuous. One would like more evidence that the iron had some time or other entered his soul, more evidence of his having profoundly reflected upon the enigma of existence, of having more deeply felt its tragic import, of having won his convictions and his optimisms and his felicities at the expense of some painful travail of the spirit. What saved Jefferson from futility was of course his clear, alert intelligence, his insatiable curiosity, his rarely failing candor, his loyalty to ideas, his humane sympathies. Yet we feel that his convictions, his sympathies, his ideas are essentially of the intellect, somehow curiously abstracted from reality, a consciously woven drapery laid over the surface of a nature essentially aristocratic, essentially fastidious, instinctively shrinking from close contact with men and things as they are.

Not without reason was Jefferson most at home in Paris. By the qualities of his mind and temperament he really belonged to the philosophical school, to the Encyclopaedists, those generous souls who loved mankind by virtue of not knowing too much about men, who worshipped reason with unreasoning faith, who made a religion of Nature while cultivating a studied aversion for 'enthusiasm,' and strong religious emotion. Like them, Jefferson, in his earlier years especially, impresses one as being a radical by profession. We often feel that he defends certain practices and ideas, that he denounces certain customs or institutions, not so much from independent reflection or deep-seated conviction on the particular matter in hand as because in general these are the things that a philosopher and a man of virtue ought naturally to defend or denounce. It belonged to the eighteenth-century philosopher, as a matter of course, to apostrophize Nature, to defend Liberty, to denounce Tyranny, perchance to shed tears at the thought of a virtuous action. It was always in character for him to feel the degradation of Human Nature when confronted with the idea of Negro Slavery.

This academic accent, as of ideas and sentiments belonging to a system, of ideas uncriticized and sentiments no more than conventionally felt, is what gives a labored and perfunctory effect to Jefferson's famous 'philippic against negro slavery.' Adams described it better than he knew. It is indeed a philippic; it is indeed vehement; but it is not moving. It is such a piece as would be expected of a *'philosopher'* on such an occasion. We remain calm in reading it because Jefferson, one cannot but think, remained calm in writing it. For want of phrases charged with deep feeling, he resorts to italics, vainly endeavoring to stir the reader by capitalizing and underlining the words that need to be stressed—a futile device, which serves only to accentuate the sense of artifice and effort, and, in the case of 'the *Christian* king of Great Britain,' introduces the wholly incongruous note of snarling sarcasm, reminding us for all the world of Shylock's 'these be the *Christian* husbands.' Jefferson apprehended the injustice of slavery; but one is inclined to ask how deeply he felt it.

It may be said that Jefferson touches the emotions as little in other parts of the Declaration as in the philippic on slavery. That is in great measure true; but in the other parts of the Declaration, which have to do for the most part with an exposition of the constitutional rights of the colonies, or with a categorical statement of the king's violations of these rights, the appeal is more properly to the mind than to the heart; and it was in appealing to the reader's mind, of course, that Jefferson was at his best. Taking the Declaration as a whole, this is indeed its conspicuous quality: it states clearly, reasons lucidly, exposes felicitously; its high virtue is in this, that it makes a strong bid for the reader's assent. But it was beyond the power of Jefferson to impregnate the Declaration with qualities that would give to the reader's assent the moving force of profound conviction. With all its precision, its concise rapidity, its clarity, its subtle implications and engaging felicities, one misses a certain unsophisticated directness, a certain sense of impregnable solidity and massive strength, a certain effect of passion restrained and deep convictions held in reserve, which would have given to it that accent of perfect sincerity and that emotional content which belong to the grand manner.

The Declaration has not the grand manner—that passion under control which lifts prose to the level of true poetry. Yet it has, what is the next best thing, a quality which saves it from falling to the prosaic. It has elevation. I have said that Franklin had, equally with Jefferson, clarity, simplicity, precision, felicity. If Franklin had written the Declaration it would have had all of these qualities; but Franklin would have communicated to it something homely and intimate and confidential, some smell of homespun, some air of the tavern or the print shop. Franklin could not, I think, have written this sentence:

> When in the course of human events it becomes necessary for one people to dissolve the political bands which have connected them with another, and to assume among the powers of the earth the separate and equal station to which the laws of nature and of nature's god entitle them, a decent respect to the opinions of mankind requires that they should declare the causes which impel them to the separation.

Or this one:

> Prudence indeed will dictate that governments long established should not be changed for light and transient causes; and accordingly all experience hath shewn that mankind are more disposed to suffer while evils are sufferable, than to right themselves by abolishing the forms to which they are accustomed.

Or this:

> And for the support of this declaration we mutually pledge to each other our lives, our fortunes, and our sacred honor.

These sentences may not be quite in the grand manner; but they have a high seriousness, a kind of lofty pathos which at least lift the Declaration to the level of a great occasion. These qualities Jefferson was able to communicate to his writing by virtue of possessing a nature exquisitely sensitive, and a mind finely tempered; they illustrate, in its subtler forms, what John Adams called his 'peculiar felicity of expression.'

Note

1 *Works of John Adams,* II, 514.

103

The Declaration of Independence promised equality to all men. It has since been invoked by those who did not (or even yet do not) enjoy the full benefits of American life. Today, for example, it is an important pillar of the women's liberation movement, which argues that all men and women were created equal. One of the widest applications of the promise of the Declaration has been in the area of civil rights for black people. The following selection is from William Lloyd Garrison's first issue of "The Liberator," January 1, 1831, in which he rests his position upon the words of the Declaration of Independence.

The Promise of Equality

William Lloyd Garrison

In the month of August, I issued proposals for publishing *"The Liberator"* in Washington City; but the enterprise, though hailed in different sections of the country, was palsied by public indifference. Since that time, the removal of the *Genius of Universal Emancipation* to the Seat of Government has rendered less imperious the establishment of a similar periodical in that quarter.

During my recent tour for the purpose of exciting the minds of the people by a series of discourses on the subject of slavery, every place that I visited gave fresh evidence of the fact, that a greater revolution in public sentiment was to be effected in the free states—*and particularly in New England*—than at the south. I found contempt more bitter, opposition more active, detraction more relentless, prejudice more stubborn, and apathy more frozen, than among slave owners themselves. Of course, there were individual exceptions to the contrary. This state of things afflicted, but did not dishearten me. I determined, at every hazard, to lift up the standard of emancipation in the eyes of the nation, *within sight of Bunker Hill and in the birth place of liberty.* That standard is now unfurled; and long may it float, unhurt by the spoilations of time or the missiles of a desperate foe—yea, till every chain be broken, and every bondman set free! Let Southern oppressors tremble—let their secret abettors tremble—let their Northern apologists tremble—let all the enemies of the persecuted blacks tremble.

I deem the publication of my original Prospectus unnecessary, as it has obtained a wide circulation. The principles therein inculcated will be steadily pursued in this paper, excepting that I shall not array myself as the political partisan of any man. In defending the great cause of human rights, I wish to derive the assistance of all religions and of all parties.

Assenting to the "self evident truth" maintained in the American Declaration of Independence, "that all men are created equal, and endowed by their Creator with certain unalienable rights—among which are life, liberty and the pursuit of happiness," I shall strenuously contend for the immediate enfranchisement of our slave population. In Park-Street Church, on the Fourth of July, 1829, in an address on slavery, I unreflectingly assented to the popular but pernicious doctrine of *gradual* abolition. I seize this opportunity to make a full and unequivocal recantation, and thus publicly to ask pardon of my God, of my country, and of my brethren the poor slaves, for having uttered a sentiment so full of timidity, injustice and absurdity. A similar recantation, from my pen, was published in the *Genius of Universal Emancipation* at Baltimore, in September, 1829. My conscience is now satisfied.

I am aware, that many object to the severity of my language; but is there not cause for severity? I *will be* as harsh as truth, and as uncompromising as justice. On this subject, I do not wish to think, or speak, or write, with moderation. No! No! Tell a man whose house is on fire, to give a moderate alarm; tell him to moderately rescue his wife from the hands of the ravisher; tell the mother to gradually extricate her babe from the fire into which it has fallen;—but urge me not to use moderation in a cause like the present. I am in earnest—I will not equivocate—I will not excuse—I will not retreat a single inch— *AND I WILL BE HEARD.* The apathy of the people is enough to make every statue leap from its pedestal, and to hasten the resurrection of the dead.

It is pretended, that I am retarding the cause of emancipation by the coarseness of my invective, and the precipitancy of my measures. *The charge is not true.* On this question my influence,—humble as it is,—is felt at this moment to a considerable extent, and shall be felt in coming years—not perniciously, but beneficially—not as a curse, but as a blessing; and posterity will bear testimony that I was right. I desire to thank God, that he enables me to disregard "the fear of man which bringeth a snare," and to speak his truth in its simplicity and power.

The Declaration of Independence does not carry the force of law because it is not a Constitution—it served merely to express the spirit of the Founding Fathers before a constitution was formulated. Nevertheless, its heavy emphasis on liberty presents a correct image of the kind of government which the Constitution and Bill of Rights ultimately prescribed. In the selection below, a distinguished American historian cites the dangers he saw in 1970 to the Bill of Rights, and to the spirit of the Declaration of Independence.

Is Freedom Dying in America?

Henry Steele Commager

There are certain words,
Our own and others', we're used to—words we've used,
Heard, had to recite, forgotten,
Rubbed shiny in the pocket, left home for keepsakes,
Inherited, stuck away in the back-drawer,
In the locked trunk, at the back of the quiet mind.

Liberty, equality, fraternity,
To none will we sell, refuse or deny, right or justice.
We hold these truths to be self-evident.

I am merely saying—what if these words pass?
What if they pass and are gone and are no more . . . ?

It took long to buy these words.
It took a long time to buy them and much pain.

—STEPHEN VINCENT BENÉT*

"Those, who would give up essential liberty to purchase a little temporary safety," said Benjamin Franklin, two centuries ago, "deserve neither liberty nor safety."

Today we are busy doing what Franklin warned us against. Animated by impatience, anger and fear, we are giving up essential liber-

From "Is Freedom Dying in America?" by Henry Steele Commager. Reprinted by permission from the July 14, 1970, issue of *Look* Magazine. Henry S. Commager © Look Magazine.

*From *The Selected Works of Stephen Vincent Benét*. Holt, Rinehart and Winston. Copyright 1940 by Stephen Vincent Benét. Reprinted by permission of Brandt & Brandt.

ties, not for safety, but for the appearance of safety. We are corroding due process and the rule of law not for Order, but for the semblance of order. We will find that when we have given up liberty, we will not have safety; and that when we have given up justice, we will not have order.

"We in this nation appear headed for a new period of repression," Mayor John V. Lindsay of New York recently warned us. We are in fact already in it.

Not since the days when Sen. Joseph McCarthy bestrode the political stage, fomenting suspicion and hatred, betraying the Bill of Rights, bringing Congress and the State Department into disrepute, have we experienced anything like the current offensive against the exercise of freedom in America. If repression is not yet as blatant or as flamboyant as it was during the McCarthy years, it is in many respects more pervasive and more formidable. For it comes to us now with official sanction and is imposed upon us by officials sworn to uphold the law: the Attorney General, the FBI, state and local officials, the police, and even judges. In Georgia and California, in Lamar, S.C., and Jackson, Miss., and Kent, Ohio, the attacks are overt and dramatic; on the higher levels of the national administration, it is a process of erosion, the erosion of what Thomas Jefferson called "the sacred soil of liberty." Those in high office do not openly proclaim their disillusionment with the principles of freedom, but they confess it by their conduct, while the people acquiesce in their own disinheritance by abandoning the "eternal vigilance" that is the price of liberty.

There is nothing more ominous than this popular indifference toward the loss of liberty, unless it is the failure to understand what is at stake. Two centuries ago, Edmund Burke said of Americans that they "snuff the approach of tyranny in every tainted breeze." Now, their senses are blunted. The evidence of public-opinion polls is persuasive that a substantial part of the American people no longer know or cherish the Bill of Rights. They are, it appears, quite prepared to silence criticism of governmental policies if such criticism is thought— *by the Government*—damaging to the national interest. They are prepared to censor newspaper and television reporting if such reports are considered—*by the Government*—damaging to the national interest! As those in authority inevitably think whatever policies they pursue, whatever laws they enforce, whatever wars they fight, are in the national interest, this attitude is a formula for the ending of all criticism, which is another way of saying for the ending of democracy.

Corruption of language is often a first sign of a deeper malaise of mind and spirit, and it is ominous that invasions of liberty are carried on, today, in the name of constitutionalism, and the impairment of due process, in the name of Law and Order. Here it takes the form of a challenge to the great principle of the separation of powers, and there to the equally great principle of the superiority of the civil to the military authority. Here it is the intimidation of the press and television by threats both subtle and blatant, there of resort to the odious doctrine of "intent" to punish anti-war demonstrators. Here it is the use of the dangerous weapon of censorship, overt and covert, to silence troublesome criticism, there the abuse of the power of punishment by contempt of court. The thrust is everywhere the same, and so too the animus behind it: to equate dissent with lawlessness and nonconformity with treason. The purpose of those who are prepared to sweep aside our ancient guarantees of freedom is to blot out those great problems that glare upon us from every horizon, and pretend that if we refuse to acknowledge them, they will somehow go away. It is to argue that discontent is not an honest expression of genuine grievances but of willfulness, or perversity, or perhaps of the crime of being young, and that if it can only be stifled, we can restore harmony to our distracted society.

Men like Vice President Spiro T. Agnew simplistically equate opposition to official policies with effete intellectualism, and cater to the sullen suspicion of intellectuals, always latent in any society, to silence that opposition. Frightened people everywhere, alarmed by lawlessness and violence in their communities, and impatient with the notion that we cannot really end violence until we deal with its causes, call loudly for tougher laws, tougher cops and tougher courts or—as in big cities like New York or small towns like Lamar—simply take authority into their own hands and respond with vigilante tactics. Impatient people, persuaded that the law is too slow and too indulgent, and that order is imperiled by judicial insistence on due process, are prepared to sweep aside centuries of progress toward the rule of law in order to punish those they regard as enemies of society. Timid men who have no confidence in the processes of democracy or in the potentialities of education are ready to abandon for a police state the experiment that Lincoln called "the last best hope of earth."

The pattern of repression is, alas, all too familiar. Most ominous is the erosion of due process of law, perhaps the noblest concept in the long history of law and one so important that it can be equated with civilization, for it is the very synonym for justice. It is difficult to remember a period in our own history in which due process has achieved more victories in the courts and suffered more setbacks in the arena of politics and public opinion than in the last decade. While the Warren Court steadily enlarged the scope and strengthened the thrust of this historic concept, to make it an effective instrument for creating a more just society, the political and the law-enforcement agencies have displayed mounting antagonism to the principle itself and resistance to its application. The desegregation decision of 1954 has been sabotaged by both the Federal and local governments—a sabotage dramatized by the recent decision of the Justice Department to support tax exemption for private schools organized to frustrate desegregation.

There are many other examples. Pending legislation, including the Organized Crime Control Act of 1969, provides for "preventive detention" in seeming violation of the constitutional guarantee of presumption of innocence; limits the right of the accused to examine evidence illegally obtained; permits police to batter their way into a private house without notice (the no-knock provision); and provides sentences of up to 30 years for "dangerous special offenders." And the government itself, from local police to the Attorney General, persists in what Justice Holmes called the "dirty business" of wiretapping and bugging to obtain evidence for convictions, though this is a clear violation of the right of protection against self-incrimination.

Equally flagrant is the attack on First Amendment freedoms— freedom of speech, press, petition and assembly—an attack that takes the form of intimidation and harassment rather than of overt repudiation. The President and the Vice President have joined in a crusade designed to force great newspapers like the New York *Times* and the Washington *Post* to moderate their criticism of Administration policies, and to frighten the television networks into scaling down their coverage of events that the Government finds embarrassing; a position that rests on the curious principle that the real crime is not official misconduct but the portrayal of that misconduct. Mr. Agnew, indeed, has gone so far as to call on governors to drive the news purveyed by "bizarre extremists" from newspapers and television sets; it is an admonition that, if taken literally, would deny newspaper and TV coverage to Mr. Agnew himself. All this is coupled with widespread harassment of the young, directed superficially at little more than hairstyle, dress or manners—but directed in fact to their opinions, or perhaps to their youthfulness. And throughout the country, government officials are busy compiling dossiers on almost all citizens prominent enough to come to their attention.

Government itself is engaged increasingly in violating what President Dwight D. Eisenhower chose as the motto for the Columbia University bicentenary: "Man's right to knowledge and the free use thereof." The USIA proscribes books that criticize American foreign policy at the same time that it launches a positive program of celebrating the Nixon Administration and the conduct of the Vietnam war through films and a library of "safe" books selected by well-vetted experts. The Federal Government spends millions of dollars presenting its version of history and politics to the American people. The Pentagon alone spends $47 million a year on public relations and maintains hundreds of lobbyists to deal with Congress, and the Defense Department floods schools and clubs and veterans organizations with films designed to win support for the war.

Meantime, the growing arrogance of the military and its eager intervention in areas long supposed to be exclusively civilian gravely threaten the principle of the superiority of the civil to the military power. Military considerations are advanced to justify the revival of the shabby practices of the McCarthy era—security clearances for civilians working in all establishments that have contracts with Defense —a category that includes laboratories, educational institutions and research organizations. What the standards are that may be expected to dictate security "clearance" is suggested by Vice President Agnew's proposal to "separate the [protest leaders] from our society—with no more regret than we should feel over discarding rotten apples from a barrel." That is, of course, precisely the philosophy that animated the Nazis. Military considerations, too, are permitted to dictate policies of secrecy that extend even to censorship of the *Congressional Record,* thus denying to congressmen, as to the American people, information they need to make decisions on foreign policy. Secrecy embraces, not unnaturally, facts about the conduct of the war; Attorney General Mitchell, it was reported, hoped to keep the Cambodian caper secret from Congress and the people until it was a *fait accompli.* So, too, the CIA, in theory merely an information-gathering agency, covers its far-flung operations in some 60 countries with a cloak of secrecy so thick that even Congress cannot penetrate it. The Army itself, entering the civilian arena, further endangers freedom of assembly and of speech by employing something like a thousand agents to mingle in student and other assemblies and report to the Army what they see and hear. This is, however, merely a tiny part of the some $3 billion that our Government spends every year in various types of espionage —more every year than the total cost of the Federal Government from its foundation in 1789 to the beginning of the Civil War in 1861!

It would be an exaggeration to say that the United States is a garrison state, but none to say that it is in danger of becoming one.

The purpose of this broad attack on American freedoms is to silence criticism of Government and of the war, and to encourage the attitude that the Government knows best and must be allowed a free hand, an attitude Americans have thought odious ever since the days of George III. It is to brand the universities as a fountainhead of subversion and thus weaken them as a force in public life. It is to restore "balance" to the judiciary and thereby reverse some of the great achievements of the 16 years of the Warren Court and to reassure the Bourbons, North and South, who are alarmed at the spectacle of judicial liberalism. It is to return to a "strict" interpretation of the power of states over racial relations and civil liberties—a euphemism for the nullification of those liberties.

The philosophy behind all this, doubtless unconscious, is that government belongs to the President and the Vice President; that they are the masters, and the people, the subjects. A century ago, Walt Whitman warned of "the never-ending audacity of elected persons"; what would he say if he were living today? Do we need to proclaim once more the most elementary principle of our constitutional system: that in the United States, the people are the masters and all officials are servants—officials in the White House, in the Cabinet, in the Congress, in the state executive and legislative chambers; officials, too, in uniform, whether of the national guard or of the police?

Those who are responsible for the campaign to restrict freedom and hamstring the Bill of Rights delude themselves that if they can but have their way, they will return the country to stability and order. They are mistaken. They are mistaken not merely because they are in fact hostile to freedom, but because they don't understand the relation of freedom to the things they prize most—to security, to order, to law.

What is that relationship?

For 2,500 years, civilized men have yearned and struggled for freedom from tyranny—the tyranny of despotic government and superstition and ignorance. What explains this long devotion to the idea and practice of freedom? How does it happen that all Western societies so exalt freedom that they have come to equate it with civilization itself?

Freedom has won its exalted place in philosophy and policy quite simply because, over the centuries, we have come to see that it is a necessity; a necessity for justice, a necessity for progress, a necessity for survival.

How familiar the argument that we must learn to reconcile the rival claims of freedom and order. But they do not really need to be reconciled; they were never at odds. They are not alternatives, they are two sides to the same coin, indissolubly welded together. The community—society or nation—has an interest in the rights of the individual because without the exercise of those rights, the community itself will decay and collapse. The individual has an interest in the stability of the community of which he is a part because without security, his rights are useless. No community can long prosper without nourishing the exercise of individual liberties for, as John Stuart Mill wrote a century ago, "A State which dwarfs its men, in order that they may be more docile instruments in its hands . . . will find that with small men no great thing can really be accomplished." And no individual can fulfill his genius without supporting the just authority of the state, for in a condition of anarchy, neither dignity nor freedom can prosper.

The function of freedom is not merely to protect and exalt the individual, vital as that is to the health of society. Put quite simply, we foster freedom in order to avoid error and discover truth; so far, we have found no other way to achieve this objective. So, too, with dissent. We do not indulge dissent for sentimental reasons; we encourage it because we have learned that we cannot live without it. A nation that silences dissent, whether by force, intimidation, the withholding of information or a foggy intellectual climate, invites disaster. A nation that penalizes criticism is left with passive acquiescence in error. A nation that discourages originality is left with minds that are unimaginative and dull. And with stunted minds, as with stunted men, no great thing can be accomplished.

It is for this reason that history celebrates not the victors who successfully silenced dissent but their victims who fought to speak the truth as they saw it. It is the bust of Socrates that stands in the schoolroom, not the busts of those who condemned him to death for "corrupting the youth." It is Savonarola we honor, not the Pope who had him burned there in the great Piazza in Florence. It is Tom Paine we honor, not the English judge who outlawed him for writing the *Rights of Man*.

Our own history, too, is one of rebellion against authority. We remember Roger Williams, who championed toleration, not John Cotton, who drove him from the Bay Colony; we celebrate Thomas Jefferson, whose motto was "Rebellion to tyrants is obedience to God," not Lord North; we read Henry Thoreau on civil disobedience, rather than those messages of President Polk that earned him the title "Polk the Mendacious"; it is John Brown's soul that goes marching on, not that of the judge who condemned him to death at Charles Town.

Why is this? It is not merely because of the nobility of character of these martyrs. Some were not particularly noble. It is because we can see now that they gave their lives to defend the interests of humanity, and that they, not those who punished them, were the true benefactors of humanity.

But it is not just the past that needed freedom for critics, nonconformists and dissenters. We, too, are assailed by problems that seem insoluble; we, too, need new ideas. Happily, ours is not a closed system—not yet, anyway. We have a long history of experimentation in politics, social relations and science. We experiment in astrophysics because we want to land on the moon; we experiment in biology because we want to find the secret of life; we experiment in medicine because we want to cure cancer; and in all of these areas, and a hundred others, we make progress. If we are to survive and flourish, we must approach politics, law and social institutions in the same spirit that we approach science. We know that we have not found final truth in physics or biology. Why do we suppose that we have found final truth in politics or law? And just as scientists welcome new truth wherever they find it, even in the most disreputable places, so statesmen, jurists and educators must be prepared to welcome new ideas and new truths from whatever sources they come, however alien their appearance, however revolutionary their implications.

"There can *be* no difference anywhere," said the philosopher William James, "that doesn't make a difference elsewhere—no difference in abstract truth that doesn't express itself in a difference in concrete fact. . . ."

Let us turn then to practical and particular issues and ask, in each case, what are and will be the consequences of policies that repress freedom, discourage independence and impair justice in American society, and what are, and will be, the consequences of applying to politics and society those standards and habits of free inquiry that we apply as a matter of course to scientific inquiry?

Consider the erosion of due process of law—that complex of rules and safeguards built up over the centuries to make sure that every man will have a fair trial. Remember that it is designed not only for the protection of desperate characters charged with monstrous crimes; it is designed for every litigant. Nor is due process merely for the benefit of the accused. As Justice Robert H. Jackson said, "It is the best insurance for the Government itself against those blunders which leave lasting stains on a system of justice. . . ."

And why is it necessary to guarantee a fair trial for all—for those accused of treason, for those who champion unpopular causes in a disorderly fashion, for those who assert their social and political rights against community prejudices, as well as for corporations, labor unions and churches? It is, of course, necessary so that justice will be done. Justice is the end, the aim, of government. It is implicitly the end of all governments; it is quite explicitly the end of the United States Government, for it was "in order to . . . establish justice" that the Constitution was ordained.

Trials are held not in order to obtain convictions; they are held to find justice. And over the centuries, we have learned by experience that unless we conduct trials by rule and suffuse them with the spirit of fair play, justice will not be done. The argument that the scrupulous observance of technicalities of due process slows up or frustrates speedy convictions is, of course, correct, if all you want is convictions. But why not go all the way and restore the use of torture? That got confessions and convictions! Every argument in favor of abating due process in order to get convictions applies with equal force to the use of the third degree and the restoration of torture. It is important to remember that nation after nation abandoned torture (the Americans never had it), not merely because it was barbarous, but because, though it wrung confessions from its victims, it did not get justice. It implicated the innocent with the guilty and outraged the moral sense of the community. Due process proved both more humane and infinitely more efficient.

Or consider the problem of wiretapping. That in many cases wiretapping "works" is clear enough, but so do other things prohibited by civilized society, such as torture or the invasion of the home. But "electronic surveillance," said Justice William J. Brennan, Jr., "strikes deeper than at the ancient feeling that a man's home is his castle; it strikes at freedom of communication, a postulate of our kind of society. . . . Freedom of speech is undermined where people fear to speak unconstrainedly in what they suppose to be the privacy of home or office."

Perhaps the most odious violation of justice is the maintenance of a double standard: one justice for blacks and another for whites, one for the rich and another for the poor, one for those who hold "radical" ideas, and another for those who are conservative and respectable. Yet we have daily before our eyes just such a double standard of justice. The "Chicago Seven," who crossed state lines with "intent" to stir up a riot, have received heavy jail sentences, but no convictions have been returned against the Chicago police who participated in that riot. Black Panthers are on trial for their lives for alleged murders, but policemen involved in wantonly attacking a Black Panther headquarters and killing two blacks have been punished by demotion.

Turn to the role and function of freedom in our society—freedom of speech and of the press—and the consequences of laying restrictions upon these freedoms. The consequence is, of course, that society will be deprived of the inestimable advantage of inquiry, criticism, exposure and dissent. If the press is not permitted to perform its traditional function of presenting the whole news, the American people will go uninformed. If television is dissuaded from showing controversial films, the people will be denied the opportunity to know what is going on. If teachers and scholars are discouraged from inquiring into the truth of history or politics or anthropology, future generations may never acquire those habits of intellectual independence essential to the working of democracy. An enlightened citizenry is necessary for self-government. If facts are withheld, or distorted, how can the people be enlightened, how can self-government work?

The real question in all this is what kind of society do we want? Do we want a police society where none are free of surveillance by their government? Or do we want a society where ordinary people can go about their business without the eye of Big Brother upon them?

The Founding Fathers feared secrecy in government not merely because it was a vote of no-confidence in the intelligence and virtue of the people but on the practical ground that all governments conceal their mistakes behind the shield of secrecy; that if they are permitted to get away with this in little things, they will do it in big things—like the Bay of Pigs or the invasion of Cambodia.

And if you interfere with academic freedom in order to silence criticism, or critics, you do not rid the university of subversion. It is not ideas that are subversive, it is the lack of ideas. What you do is to silence or get rid of those men who have ideas, leaving the institution to those who have no ideas, or have not the courage to express those that they have. Are such men as these what we want to direct the education of the young and advance the cause of learning?

The conclusive argument against secrecy in scientific research is that it will in the end give us bad science. First-rate scientists will not so gravely violate their integrity as to confine their findings to one government or one society, for the first loyalty of science is to scientific truth. "The Sciences," said Edward Jenner of smallpox fame, "are never at war." We have only to consider the implications of secrecy in the realm of medicine: What would we think of doctors favoring secrecy in cancer research on the grounds of "national interest"?

The argument against proscribing books, which might normally be in our overseas libraries, because they are critical of Administration policies is not that it will hurt authors or publishers. No. It is quite simply that if the kind of people who believe in proscription are allowed to control our libraries, these will cease to be centers of learning and become the instruments of party. The argument against withholding visas from foreign scholars whose ideas may be considered subversive is not that this will inconvenience them. It is that we deny ourselves the benefit of what they have to say. Suppose President Andrew Jackson had denied entry to Alexis de Tocqueville on the ground that he was an aristocrat and might therefore be a subversive influence on our democracy? We would have lost the greatest book ever written about America.

There is one final consideration. Government, as Justice Louis D. Brandeis observed half a century ago, "is the potent, the omnipresent teacher. For good or for ill, it teaches the whole people by its example." If government tries to solve its problems by resort to large-scale violence, its citizens will assume that violence is the normal way to solve problems. If government itself violates the law, it brings the law into contempt, and breeds anarchy. If government masks its operations, foreign and domestic, in a cloak of secrecy, it encourages the creation of a closed, not an open, society. If government shows itself impatient with due process, it must expect that its people will come to scorn the slow procedures of orderly debate and negotiation and turn to the easy solutions of force. If government embraces the principle that the end justifies the means, it radiates approval of a doctrine so odious that it will in the end destroy the whole of society. If government shows, by its habitual conduct, that it rejects the claims of freedom and of justice, freedom and justice will cease to be the ends of our society.

Eighty years ago, Lord Bryce wrote of the American people that "the masses of the people are wiser, fairer and more temperate in any matter to which they can be induced to bend their minds, than most European philosophers have believed possible for the masses of the people to be."

Is this still true? If the American people can indeed be persuaded to "bend their minds" to the great questions of the preservation of freedom, it may still prove true. If they cannot, we may be witnessing, even now, a dissolution of the fabric of freedom that may portend the dissolution of the Republic.

The Declaration of Independence protested the political tyranny of
George III. But there are also other kinds, for example educational tyranny.
According to the following article, Third World people in America have been
the victims of a cultural tyranny. In discussing the Ethnic Studies Program
at Berkeley, the authors describe the growing movement that Third World
peoples are joining for independent control over their educational destiny.
Do you see any precedents in the Declaration of Independence?

Equality of Educational Opportunity

Andrew Billingsley, Douglas Davidson, Theresa Loya

When W. E. B. Dubois wrote just before the turn of the century
that the problem of the 20th century would be the problem of the
color line, he could not possibly have known how prophetic a statement he was making. Nor could he or anyone else envision how that
problem would come crashing onto the American college campus
scene after festering in the shadows for more than half of this fateful
century. This issue of racial equality in American higher education
seemed to explode with terrible swift anger and agony in the spring of
1968. Paradoxically, no one, not even the students who were its major
instrument, nor the administrators who were its major target, and
certainly not the faculties who were its major obstacles seemed to be
able to understand or control the nature of this explosion. It seemed
to engulf the whole country like a wild fire, or like an idea whose time
has come.

The cry went out: "Let there be blacks in all areas of higher education; in the administration, the faculty, the student body, the textbooks, the janitorial force, and the purchasing office." In the West, a
slightly different cry went out. It called for the inclusion of all Third
World people—blacks, browns, reds, and yellows. It said, "We who
are the colors of the earth have been too long left out in the land of
our birth. And we want in, in the worst way—not later than the fall of
next year." These demands were non-negotiable.

In California, the concept of the Third World took on new signifi-

From "Equality of Educational Opportunity" by Andrew Billingsley, Douglas
Davidson, and Theresa Loya. *California Monthly,* Vol. LXXX, No. 4, June–
July, 1970, pp. 13–20. Reprinted by permission of *California Monthly* and
the authors.

cance on college campuses: first at San Francisco State College, and then at the University of California at Berkeley, and eventually at all major urban campuses.

Many people are under the impression that the Third World movement is indigenous to the California scene. This is definitely not the case. The Third World movement represents the growing awareness of the peoples of color throughout the world—Asia, Middle East, Africa, Latin America—of their common experiences under colonial domination. This movement is characterized by struggles on the part of these heretofore colonized peoples for freedom and self-determination. They are seeking and oftentimes fighting for the right to control and develop their own economic, political, and social institutions. They are demanding that the Western European colonial powers cease their interference in the functioning of their respective nations.

This general movement has a number of implications and challenges for American higher education. First, American higher education is primarily an extension of the Western European educational system. Its structure, function, and philosophical basis are essentially Western European. Its methods of instruction and the subject matter or areas of concentration are heavily weighted towards Western Europe. Thus, it does not adequately reflect the histories, cultures, and contributions of Third World peoples. When these areas are subjects of study, they are studied through the eyes of Western Europeans. Third World people have questioned the ability of Western European scholars to accurately research and write about their people. They argue that it is virtually impossible for the colonial scholar to capture the essence of colonized people.

Third World people in this country are in basic agreement with this charge. They argue that American-trained scholars have distorted and created false myths about the lives of Third World people here. They argue further that not only have American and European scholars distorted and created myths about Third World people, but that the truth about America and Europe has not been revealed because the written materials do not include the perspectives of Third World people concerning the nature of America and Europe. Third World students and teachers are now challenging the American higher education system to make the necessary changes to allow for the inclusion of their perspectives.

Thus, Third World peoples are demanding the right to control their own affairs, solve their own problems, make their own mistakes. What they desire from America and Western Europe is technical assistance and financial aid. Their ultimate goal is a new world order composed of independent nations which respect their differences, appreciate their similarities, and recognize that all peoples of the world are struggling to create a better world. They envision a more peaceful, humanistic world where men can grow and develop their complete human potential free of the yokes of racism, ethnocentricism, and cultural imperialism.

Although Third World peoples constitute approximately one fourth of California's total population, they constitute only about 16 percent of the total student enrollment in the state's institutions of higher education.

In 1968 there were approximately 576,000 undergraduate students in California's higher education system. Of this total, approximately 89,000 were minority or Third World students; 32,314 were black; 31,858 were students with Spanish surnames; 21,936 were Oriental or Asian; and approximately 2,900 were American Indians.

Most Third World students are enrolled in two-year community colleges. In the University of California system less than ten percent of the students are from these Third World groups. At Berkeley, as a result of special efforts during the past few years, nearly 12 percent of the student body now comes from Third World groups.

Overall, Third World peoples are grossly under-represented in the state's institutions of higher education, and we anticipate that this under-representation is increasing rather than decreasing, due to current repressive policies such as the cutting back of special equal opportunity funding, the establishment of tuition, and the elimination of the summer quarter in the University system.

The initiative for the Department of Ethnic Studies began with a proposal from the Afro-American Student Union for the establishment of an Afro-American Studies Department. The proposal called for an initially limited curriculum which would evolve into a degree-granting department. This proposal was presented to the chancellor in the spring of 1968.

Upon receiving this proposal, the chancellor appointed an assistant chancellor for academic affairs. He was charged with the responsibility of exploring the feasibility of such a program. This appointment became effective at the beginning of the fall quarter, 1969.

During the fall quarter of 1969, after engaging in considerable study and exploration, there were several meetings and discussions on this proposal. The assistant chancellor for academic affairs and the dean of the College of Letters and Science recommended the establishment of an Afro-American Studies Department. However, after examining all of these proposals, the Executive Committee of the

College of Letters and Science voted against the establishment of a department and approved instead a more limited program of Afro-American Studies. The Afro-American Student Union and the black faculty found this unacceptable.

While this was occurring, groups of Mexican-American and Asian-American students were developing their own programs of study. After noting what had transpired with the Afro-American proposals, the three groups—later joined by the Native Americans—called for a Third World strike. At this point, a uniform set of demands and a proposal were issued. This proposal called for a broadly-based program of ethnic studies which would culminate in a Third World College. The college would be composed of four departments, one for each ethnic group. The strike lasted for six weeks, continuing through the winter quarter. While it was called and led by Third World student groups and endorsed by a group of Third World faculty, it had considerable support from white students and some white faculty.

During the strike, there were a number of meetings and discussions on the issue of ethnic studies among all segments of the University. Consequently, the Academic Senate passed a resolution on March 4, 1969, supporting the establishment of an interim Department of Ethnic Studies. This interim department would be composed of the four ethnic studies programs. It would be administratively responsible to the Chancellor's Office rather than to one of the existing colleges, and it would eventually evolve into the College of Ethnic Studies.

This proved to be a crucial decision. A moratorium was called on the strike shortly thereafter and four weeks later the chancellor announced the establishment of the interim Department of Ethnic Studies.

The student body demonstrated further support of ethnic studies by passing a referendum on May 20–22 which taxed each student $1.50 per quarter to aid in the support of the Ethnic Studies Department. An overwhelming majority of the students—84 percent—supported this referendum.

In July, 1969, the chancellor announced the appointment of faculty advisory committees and four coordinators to guide the development of each of the programs within the department. The budget for the department was finalized on October 6, 1969—the same day that classes began. The department moved to its present offices in Dwinelle Hall two weeks later.

The founding of the department was a going effort on the part of the four major ethnic minorities on Berkeley's campus. The guidelines for departmental development have been developed in the spirit of the Third World. In coming together to plan for the department, three major principles were established as imperative: a) students must play an active and decisive role in initiating and participating in the academic planning for the department, b) academic programs must be made relevant to the specific needs of the ethnic minority communities, both within and without the University campus, and c) a Third World inter-ethnic focus must be emphasized in developing relevant and well-coordinated programs for students, faculty, and the broader ethnic communities.

This underlying philosophy is basically reformist in character. It reflects Third World peoples' perception of the need to change the nature of higher education in this University in order to make it more relevant not only to their educational needs and those of ethnic minority communities, but also for the education of other students and faculty as well. Some have argued that the University as an institution needed ethnic studies more than minority group students do. Surely some of the major problem areas confronting this society are those centering around the experience of ethnic minorities. And universities have largely ignored them.

The Ethnic Studies Department is an autonomous department in that it is not housed in any of the existing colleges or schools. It is administratively responsible to the Chancellor's Office. The assistant chancellor for academic affairs is serving as the acting coordinator of the department until a chairman is selected.

The department is divided into four divisions—the Asian Studies Division, the La Raza Studies Division, the Native American Studies Division, and the Afro-American Studies Division. Each division has a coordinator and an assistant coordinator and its own secretarial and clerk-typist staff.

The department is related to the Academic Senate through the Committee on Courses which has to approve all departmental courses, and the Budget Committee which approves all departmental faculty appointments. In addition, the College of Letters and Science has approved many of the ethnic studies courses as meeting L & S breadth requirements. And as each of these programs moves toward the establishment of degree-granting programs they will have to be approved by the Council on Special Curriculae. Far from being a free-wheeling isolated unit, the department has the support and protection as well as the limitations of being structured into the regular governing mechanisms of the University.

The Ethnic Studies Department began in the fall quarter of 1969 with a budget of $474,785. These funds were divided among the four divisions. The department was allotted approximately 27 academic full-time teaching equivalents (FTE) which were also divided among the four divisions.

With its portion of the budget the Afro-American Studies Division, the largest division, was able to offer 16 courses to 417 students in the fall quarter. They had 11 faculty members. During the winter quarter, this division offered 18 courses to 564 students and increased its faculty to 14. During the spring quarter of this year 26 courses were offered and 611 students enrolled in Afro-American Studies.

The La Raza Studies Division started with a faculty of seven, offering eight courses to 172 students and built to a faculty of nine teaching over 200 students in 14 courses in the spring.

The Asian Studies Division began with six courses and 257 students. Since then the number of courses has tripled and the enrollment has nearly doubled.

The Native American Studies Division, the smallest group, offered five courses to 144 students with only two faculty members in its first quarter. In the spring, with three faculty members, students enrolled in its six courses numbered over 300.

In addition to the courses offered by each division, there were two courses sponsored by the department as a whole, i.e., all four groups, with faculty members and students from each division participating. They were offered in order to increase the cooperative spirit of the Third World as well as to develop models for more Third World—as opposed to divisional—courses. As these Third World core courses evolve, it will become possible for students to obtain degrees either in a particular division or in Third World Studies in general.

The courses offered by the four divisions fell into roughly five categories. First, there were courses on the history of each ethnic group, such as Afro-American Studies 105B (Black World History) and Native American Studies 140 (A Survey of Southern Plains Indian History). Secondly, there were courses on the contemporary socio-economic conditions of each group, for example, Asian Studies 130B (Asian-American Communities). Thirdly, there were courses in each division on the cultural contributions of each group; examples of these courses are: Afro-American Studies 122 (Afro-American Art and Culture); Asian Studies 180 (Asian Music, Theory and Practice); La Raza Studies 1B (Rhetoric and Communication Skills); and Native American Studies 150B (American Indian Arts and Contemporary Development).

The fourth category of courses included those focusing on means of relating the divisions to their larger ethnic communities. Examples of the fourth group are: Afro-American Studies 100 (Experience in the Black Community) and La Raza Studies 198 (Latino Experience in the Barrio). Comprising the fifth category of courses were language and literature courses, offered as a means of dealing with the language problems of the ethnic students to improve the students' written and verbal skills. Examples of these courses are: Afro-American Studies 3 (Black Studies English) and Asian Studies 1A (Asian Studies Reading and Composition). Some of the divisions gave language courses to improve or to teach their students the language of their communities, such as Native American Studies 160 (Introduction to Sioux Language and Culture), Spanish classes offered by the La Raza division, conversational Cantonese and Japanese given by Asian Studies, and a Swahili course given by Afro-American Studies.

There is a great deal of diversity in the ethnic studies faculty. However, most members are young—between the ages of 25 and 35—and all are committed both to academic excellence and their respective minority communities. A number of them are not established or traditional academic types, but are graduate students or community people. Most of them have master's degrees, and some are continuing their studies while teaching in the department.

These characteristices vary from division to division. The La Raza Studies faculty has more Ph.D.s than any of the other divisions. The Afro-American Studies faculty, however, is composed of a number of community professionals (the principal of a Bay Area elementary school, the former director of Berkeley's poverty program, the president of a local black college, a local minister, etc.). As was noted above, all of these people have graduate degrees or are doing graduate work presently. The Asian Studies faculty is composed almost entirely of graduate students, most of whom are Ph.D. candidates. The two Native American Studies faculty members are young community leaders who are involved with attempting to change the present conditions of their people on the reservations. Both are pursuing their academic careers; one is a Ph.D. candidate and the other is continuing his studies in art.

Student participation is one of the main features of these programs. Consequently, students are involved at all levels in each division. They are actively involved in the initiation of courses and the selection of faculty. In many cases they serve as teaching assistants, readers, and in some cases acting instructors for courses. For example, the Asian Studies Division wanted to offer a course in Tagalog in order to facilitate their work in the community. There were no faculty available who could teach the language. A student who was well versed in the language was able to fill the void.

Thus, the Ethnic Studies Department is demonstrating quite dramatically that students are responsible and capable, contrary to the attitudes and opinions expressed by many administrators, faculty, and others.

Community involvement is another of the basic principles of the department. The students and faculty in each division are active in developing and implementing programs which relate their department to their larger community. For example, the Asian Studies Division has students and instructors working in Chinatown, Manilatown, and Japantown. They have established community centers in these areas. One of their major tasks has been that of teaching English to the residents in these areas, especially the new immigrants. They also tutor elementary and secondary students. The Asian Studies Division offers its course in Cantonese to give the students a mastery of the language of the community so that they can be effective teachers of English to the residents.

The Native American students and faculty are involved in establishing a cultural center in the community. La Raza Studies students and faculty are working with Mexican-American prisoners and delinquents in the local Bay Area detention institutions and are tutoring and counseling young Mexican-Americans on educational opportunities. The Afro-American Studies students and faculty are involved in working with local community organizations and tutoring and counseling elementary and secondary students in the Bay Area.

As shown here, the Ethnic Studies Department is academically oriented. It's attempting to bring to the University the perspectives of Third World peoples. The University's separate Educational Opportunity Program, which predates the Ethnic Studies Department, functions primarily as a recruitment mechanism. It screens high potential, mostly minority students, many of whose high school grade point average and SAT scores are below the University's regular admissions standards. These high potential students are also given financial aid. Other services, such as tutoring, are available if the student desires. The EOP and the department are inextricably related in consequence, but not in structure. That is, if the EOP program's budget is reduced (as it has been by the state legislature), it will have immediate as well as long-range effects on the Ethnic Studies Department. The vast majority of minority students at Berkeley are supported by EOP funds. If alternative means of recruiting and supporting minority students are not developed, the number of minority students on campus will be reduced and the Ethnic Studies Department could be destroyed before it has a chance to become established.

The relationship between the Ethnic Studies Department and the Graduate Minority Program is similar to that between the department and the EOP. The Graduate Minority Program recruits and supports minority graduate students for all departments. However, some schools and departments—among them business administration, social welfare, criminology, and law—have established their own minority recruitment and support programs. Most of the minority graduate students receive their support from their respective departments or professional schools.

The Graduate Minority Program complements the efforts of those schools and departments.

The Graduate Minority Program, like EOP, is in the midst of a financial dilemma. The number of applicants has increased, but the budget has been cut. This affects ethnic studies in that graduate students are in vital positions in the department. Many graduate students are teaching courses; some are serving as teaching assistants, others are serving as administrators, and still others are enrolled in ethnic studies courses, some with a view toward academic careers in this field. And the potential role of graduate students in ethnic studies is not fully developed. A reduction in their numbers would decrease the scope and quality of the department. Again, if the department is to realize its potential, some alternative means of supporting minority graduate students must be developed.

The Third World presence at UC, Berkeley, is not an isolated phenomenon confined to the developing and implementation of the Ethnic Studies Department. The Third World thrust has had ramifications throughout the University. The impact is reflected in the growing number of Third World faculty and administrators. There are presently seven high-level Third World administrators—four blacks and three Chicanos. There are approximately 49 Third World faculty members presently working on the Berkeley campus, 40 of whom are black, eight Chicano-Latino, and one Native American. They include professors, associates and assistant professors, visiting professors, instructors, and acting instructors. The Asian-American faculty members were not included because they were already well represented, while the numbers of other minority faculty are exceedingly small compared to the total faculty. The University has committed itself to increasing the numbers of Third World faculty in order to reflect the ethnic composition of the student population and the state population.

One of the most direct and profound consequences of the struggle for the Ethnic Studies Department has been an increased awareness on the part of other departments of the absence of and the need for ethnic studies content. This has been especially true of the social sciences, the humanities, and the professions. Among other departments, Comparative Literature is offering a course in West African literature. Sociology gives one called "The Black Family from World War I to Present," Psychology 191C covers the psychological aspects of black identity and "Ethnic Tension and Conflict in Relation to Law Enforcement" is studied in Criminology 119.

The Ethnic Studies Department is demonstrably an established feature of higher education at Berkeley. It is not altogether clear how it will progress, be accepted by other elements of the University, or what its impact will be on the total structure of the University and on the education of minority and other students. Nor is it completely clear what form ethnic studies will ultimately take. The issue of whether it will be an autonomous college or part of the Chancellor's Office, or merge with some other existing school or college is yet to be resolved. The most informed judgment to date suggests that ethnic studies can best develop through an autonomous college. The issue is still alive in the administration, and among the faculty and the student body.

Another issue confronting ethnic studies is that of the size and scope of the program. The question is, should the Department of Ethnic Studies be expanded, or should there be more and more ethnic studies offerings in other departments in the University. Clearly the students and faculty involved in ethnic studies give top priority to expanding the scope and viability of the department. This means an expanded budget, employment of senior faculty members, establishment of an organized curriculum, and degree-granting programs. There are still some lingering feelings on the part of some of the faculty and administration that expansion of the department should be limited and high priority given to expansion in other departments. This issue is still to be resolved.

Still another issue focuses on the internal workings of the department. Whether it remains one department or moves toward a larger unit, the problem is to what extent it can (or should) be molded into a unified (if not uniform) working unit. A very small group of students and faculty have been working hard at that task. The appointment of a chairman or dean would help. But for very understandable reasons Third World cultures are no more ready for instant amalgamation with each other than they are with the dominant group.

Ethnic studies is off to a commendable start and is growing rapidly, but the process of establishing a viable Third World presence at Berkeley is far from complete or simple. It is filled with complexity, a touch of agony, a glimmer of promise, mountains of hard work, and a great deal of excitement.

Questions

1 Does it disturb you to penetrate the romantic aura surrounding the Declaration of Independence?

2 Jefferson's passage condemning George III for permitting the slave trade was dropped from the Declaration, yet his reference to the Indians as savages was retained. Does this have any historical significance for America's treatment of minorities?

3 During the years just prior to the Civil War, there was considerable discussion of the intentions of the Declaration of Independence with regard to slavery. Chief Justice Taney in the Dred Scott decision of 1857, and Senator Douglas in the Lincoln-Douglas debates of 1858, claimed that the author of the Declaration never intended to include black people among those who were endowed with equal rights. Were they correct? Even if they were correct, should we be more concerned with what Jefferson **intended** than with the basic **human rights** he said existed?

4 What influence has the Declaration had on revolutionary movements outside the United States? On reform movements within the United States?

5 Do you feel that the Declaration was a hypocritical "public relations release"?

6 To what extent has the Dream of equality of opportunity as expressed in the Declaration been fulfilled in American life?

7 In 1848, at a feminist convention at Seneca Falls, New York, the Declaration of Independence was paraphrased to read "all men **and women** are created equal. . . ." What are the implications for Women's Liberation today?

4

The Dream of
"One Nation, Indivisible"

Essay

Challenges to the Federal System
Melvin Steinfield

Readings

The Articles of Confederation

The Nullification Crisis
John A. Garraty

The Union Above All
Abraham Lincoln

A More Perfect Union
D. W. Brogan

Federalism in 1970
Henry Brandon

The Federal Role in Education
Clark Kerr

The essay below discusses theoretical and historical problems
encountered in defining the precise powers of the Federal government.
One of these problems, according to the author, is the persistence of
sectionalism in America and its relation to the doctrine of states' rights.
Can you detect a bias on the part of the author?

Challenges to the Federal System

Melvin Steinfield

Can the Federal government require a state to integrate its public
schools? "No!" said Florida governor Claude Kirk in 1970 as he
urged his fellow fair-skinned Floridians to oppose compulsory busing
in defiance of Federal orders. Can the United States government send
a citizen of one of its states to fight in an overseas war if Congress has
not officially declared war? "No!" shouted the Massachusetts Legislature collectively in 1970 as it authorized a court challenge to the right
of the Federal government to send citizens of Massachusetts to fight in
Vietnam.

These two challenges, one in the North and one in the South, were
hardly the first challenges to the authority of the Federal government
by individual states. From the pre-Revolutionary days of Benjamin
Franklin and his rejected Albany Plan, proposing to establish a Union
with strong central government in 1754, through the lifetime of the
Confederacy during the Civil War showdown on secession in the
1860s, to the challenges of the 1970s noted above, Americans have
spent countless years trying to resolve the conflicts of a Federal system of government. They are still there. Benjamin Franklin's failure
to forge a stronger national government in 1754 foreshadowed the
necessity of the North using sledgehammer tactics to preserve a semblance of national unity in the 1860s. One hundred years and more
after the Civil War Between the States, there are still weak links in the
chain of national unity, and the Federal system is still undergoing me-
ticulous scrutiny and is still confronting serious challenges.

Why has there been such controversy surrounding the powers of
the central government as opposed to those of state and local governments? Why can't a precise delineation of powers be made and why
can't there be a definition of the Federal system that would eliminate
the need for periodic reexamination and recurrent conflict?

One reason is the persistence of sectionalism in the United States. "One nation, indivisible" and "E pluribus unum" may be the Federal dream, but they are not the reality. The slogans of national unity mean little to many of the descendants of defeated rebels who are still waiting for the time when "The South shall rise again!" Like their nineteenth-century proslavery ancestors, many Southerners find it convenient to fall back on the states'-rights argument as a mask for their opposition to national civil rights legislation for black citizens. This reluctance to abandon the Southern caste system is symbolized in a determined "NEVER" to which the careers of such men as George Wallace and Lester Maddox are dedicated.

"We are not against black people," so the hypocritical argument goes, "we are just opposed to the Federal government forcing us to do things against our will." Those "things" usually have something to do with black people, but not always. There is a sectional feeling in the South that transcends the race issue. The symbols and tokens of this sectional feeling are abundant in popular life today. One only has to attend a football game at the University of Texas or a fair in Alabama. At many public gatherings in the South, "Dixie" preempts the National Anthem and the Stars and Bars may overshadow Old Glory, which is sometimes referred to as "the Yankee flag."

But economics has also played a large part in the development of sectional feelings. The primarily agricultural orientation of the South, as contrasted with the more industrial orientation of the North, has contributed to the conflict between states' rights and the Federal government. From early Revolutionary days, the farmers had been less inclined than the seaboard merchants to establish a strong central government. And later, when the young industries of the North fought for Federal tariffs and import regulations, the agrarian sections dissented—such tariffs might be advantageous to manufacturing concerns but they would also raise the price of manufactured goods for farmers. A strong central government which could regulate commerce, perhaps at the expense of regional economic interests, did not appeal to many Southern states in the tariff question of the 1820s, and it still does not appeal to some states today. The argument of states' rights has often been used—in both North and South—as a convenient cloak for economic self-interests.

Throughout the history of America's struggle to establish and maintain a Federal system, there have been sectional factors which have hindered that effort. Often the obstacles have come from the South. But not always. It has been stated that the North, as well as the South, has used the states'-rights issue to disguise its economic interests. And, the first serious threat of a state seceding from the Union came at the Hartford, Connecticut, Convention in 1814.

In addition to the historic sectional differences, rivalries, and conflicts, there has been another reason for the difficulty experienced in defining exact powers between Federal and state governments: the Constitution itself. On the surface, the Constitution appears to have provided a simple theoretical explanation of the powers of the Federal government:

> The powers not delegated to the United States by the Constitution, nor prohibited by it to the States, are reserved to the States respectively, or to the people. (Amendment 10.)

Textbooks on American government frequently use a diagram, such as the one below, to represent the division of power between Federal and state governments.

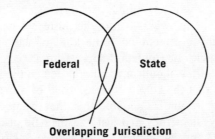

Overlapping Jurisdiction

The implication of allotting equal space in the diagram to both Federal and state governments is that the powers are divided *equally*. Sometimes this concept of equal powers in the Federal system is illustrated by contrasting it with diagrams of confederate and unitary systems.

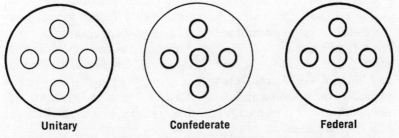

| Unitary | Confederate | Federal |

The *unitary system* exists in England; the central government is the primary power with the local units functioning as administrative arms of the central authority. In a *confederacy,* such as the United Nations, sovereignty is retained by local units that are bound together only in a loose association. But in a *federal* system, such as the United States, both the local (state) and central governments have an approximately equal amount of sovereignty in carefully defined realms, with some overlapping of authority.

Sounds simple enough, but the history of the United States of America is laden with challenges to the Federal system from state and local authorities who did not wish to accept what they perceived as the encroachment of the central or Federal government. One can find this fear of a strong central system and the tendency to lean toward a confederate system in the Revolutionary period. When the American revolutionaries declared their independence as "free and independent states" in 1776 they did not rush into a Federal system. For five years they debated and argued about the best kind of government to establish. The country was governed by the Second Continental Congress until 1781, when our first Constitution, the Articles of Confederation, went into effect.

The need to carry on the military struggle against Britain may help explain why it took five years before the thirteen separate states could manage to reach agreement on some kind of national constitution. But that the Articles of Confederation set up a weak central government with most of the significant authority left to the individual states leaves no doubt that the colonists were afraid of a strong central government. It is quite understandable that they wanted to guard their state sovereignty, since they had just had their fill of a unitary system under George III and Parliament. Also, historic rivalries and sectional differences between the states did not predispose them to unite in any system stronger than a loose confederacy. (The student is referred to the partial text of the Articles of Confederation in the first reading of this chapter.)

Certainly there was much that the colonists of the North and South had in common. One uniting factor was their common opposition to the British unitary system that had dominated them against their protests. It was this mutual dissatisfaction with the rule of the mother country that explains why John Hancock, a New England merchant and shipper, could team up with George Washington, a Virginia plantation-owner and slaveholder. But from the start significant sectional differences presented formidable obstacles to the establishment of a Federal system.

The rural conservatism and race-consciousness of a stable, almost static society primarily agrarian in nature, coupled with the longer growing season, fertile soil, and broad rivers, helped shape the distinctive regional characteristics of the South. The economy was based on such staple crops as tobacco, rice, and cotton. The North developed a more open, dynamic society, with a primarily industrial and commercial economy and a greater ethnic pluralism. Such sectional differences determined the nature of the struggle for political and economic supremacy between North and South. There was rivalry and there was jealousy, and mutual sectional suspicions initially could be resolved only by abandoning efforts to achieve strong national unity; only through a confederate system could the thirteen original states present a united front against Britain and, following the Revolution, against their own problems.

But in reacting against their fears, the American Revolutionary leaders who framed the Articles of Confederation as our first constitution *overreacted*. Under the Articles, the government from 1781 to 1788 was known as the "Critical Period." It was beset with the problems of establishing itself on a firm footing as a new nation, yet its central government was impotent. Though it did reach some notable achievements, as in the Land Ordinance of 1785 and the Northwest Ordinance of 1787, on the whole the government under the Articles was ineffective and it began to totter. This weakness of the government points to the degree of petty rivalries among the states and their inability to cooperate for their mutual benefit. States' rights predominated.

After fighting so hard to win the war against Britain, men like Washington and Hamilton did not want to see their country lose its struggle to succeed. With their support, American leaders met in 1787 at Philadelphia to try to correct the deficiencies of the first American constitution, and they produced what we know simply as The Constitution. The long debates and painstaking compromises of the Constitutional Convention indicated further the reluctance of states to yield power to the central government. One of the major issues was the small states' fears of large-state domination. The small states were opposed from the outset to a Congress based on proportional representation, and a compromise was necessary to allay these fears—there would be a House with the number of representatives from each state determined by population, and a Senate in which each state would be represented equally. At that, only 39 members of the 55 delegates to the Convention put their signature of endorsement on the document.

Then came the struggle to ratify the Constitution. A major issue among several was the power of the central government. Would it be too great? Bitter controversy accompanied the effort to ratify the Constitution, and much of it centered on states' rights. But equally important were the antagonistic economic orientations of the Federalists and Antifederalists. As noted previously, states' rights sometimes has been used as a convenient argument for protecting vested money interests. Supporters of the Constitution were largely commerce-oriented—shippers, manufacturers, merchants—whereas many of those opposed to ratification were agrarian-based.

The vote on ratification in various state conventions was close. For example, the Massachusetts convention ratified the Constitution by only a 53 percent majority, New Hampshire by only 55 percent, Virginia by only 53 percent (against the opposition of Patrick Henry who stayed away from the convention because he "smelt a rat" and because he opposed taking away so much power from the states), and New York by only 55 percent. The first vote taken in North Carolina and Rhode Island was a victory for the opponents of ratification; it was only after the Constitution had already gone into effect that North Carolina (1789) and Rhode Island (1790) ratified it. In the states where the outcome remained so long in question, it was undoubtedly the Federalist papers (mainly written by Alexander Hamilton) and the promise of a Bill of Rights that finally swayed the vote in favor of ratification.

The triumph of the Federal system that was implicit in the ratification of the new Constitution was a triumph that required further battles to protect. An early example of the ambiguous nature of Federal power arose in the controversy concerning the constitutionality of the National Bank in 1790 and 1791. Strictly speaking, the National Bank raised the question of expressed constitutional powers versus implied powers, rather than Federal power versus states' rights. But the implications of the controversy came to have profound consequences for the Federal system. Hamilton, Washington's Secretary of the Treasury, proposed that a National Bank be established to act as fiscal agent for the United States Treasury. Both Edmund Randolph, Washington's Attorney General, and Thomas Jefferson, Washington's Secretary of State, opposed it because they felt that Congress did not have the power to establish such a bank. Note that for the agricultural interests, especially the small farmer, Jefferson had become the prime spokesman; he held that freehold farmers made up the best basis for a *republican* government. Hamilton, on the other hand, appealed particularly to the business interests—such as financiers, manufacturers, and shipowners—and he favored a more *elitist* governmental structure.

Washington listened to both sides and finally requested that Hamilton and Jefferson put their arguments on paper, so that he would not be influenced by verbal rhetoric. In their famous opinions on the constitutionality of the National Bank, both written in February, 1791, Hamilton and Jefferson produced what historian Merrill Jensen calls "two classic and contradictory opinions of the nature of the Constitution." Jensen continues:

> These two basic interpretations may be simply stated. Jefferson held that the central government was sharply limited by the letter of the Constitution; that in effect the states retained their sovereign powers except where they were specifically delegated. Hamilton argued in effect that the central government was a national government which could not be restrained by a strict interpretation of the Constitution or by ideas of state sovereignty. These rival interpretations did not originate with Hamilton and Jefferson, for they had been the very core of constitutional debate ever since the Declaration of Independence, and even before it, for that matter.[1]

Jensen also points out that the issues raised in the debate on the constitutionality of the National Bank had historic implications more than once:

> Jefferson and his followers used the states' rights idea to oppose the plans of the Federalists when they passed the Alien and Sedition Acts in 1798. But when Jefferson became president and purchased Louisiana, he justified his actions by constitutional theories that even Hamilton hardly dared use. Meanwhile Jefferson's opponents seized upon his earlier theories in a vain attempt to block the expansion of the United States. They did so again during the War of 1812 when the Federalists of New England became out-and-out exponents of "states' rights" and threatened secession because they were opposed to the war.
>
> In the decades before the Civil War, Daniel Webster and John C. Calhoun carried on the dispute, each having changed sides since his youthful years in politics. Webster, who had been a states' rights spokesman during the War of 1812, became the high priest of nationalism, while Calhoun, a leading nationalist in 1812, became the high priest of the states' rights idea which he elaborated to defend the slave-owning and aristocracy of the South.[2]

Throughout the years prior to the Civil War Between the States, there were numerous challenges to the Federal system. In addition to the Virginia and Kentucky Resolutions of 1798 that challenged the Alien and Sedition Laws Jensen refers to above, there was the conflict over the tariff and the nullification crisis during Andrew Jackson's administration (see the reading by John Garraty on this topic later in the chapter). The best-known challenge came with the Civil War itself. The victorious North rammed the concept of Federalism down the throats of the defeated anti-Union Southern forces. The coercive settlement resulted in a bitterness that has not yet abated. To this day, it is still felt whenever tensions of a sectional nature flare up.

Whether it be J. Strom Thurmond's Dixiecrats bolting the Democratic Party in 1948 on the issue of civil rights and states' rights, or whether it be that same Senator Thurmond in 1970 decrying President Nixon's policies on the school segregation issue, the same constitutional arguments raised by Hamilton and Jefferson pro and con are paraded out for the inevitable clash once again. There is no shortage of issues to precipitate such a clash. For example, in 1954 the Supreme Court issued its famous Brown decision, declaring segregated schools to be illegal. In 1956, 96 Congressmen issued *The Southern Manifesto: Declaration of Constitutional Principles*. In it they declared:

> We decry the Supreme Court's encroachments on rights reserved to the States and to the people, contrary to established law, and to the Constitution.

> We commend the motives of those States which have declared the intention to resist forced integration by any lawful means.

> We appeal to the States and people who are not directly affected by these decisions to consider the constitutional principles involved against the time when they too, on issues vital to them, may be the victims of judicial encroachment.

Thus the Constitution is the supreme law of the land, but how shall the Constitution be interpreted?

History has decided in Hamilton's favor, and if the present trends continue, *The Southern Manifesto* might function as an epitaph for Thurmond's views. The Federal government has been increasing its exercised powers because of a long-range trend toward bigger, more efficient, and more centralized governments. In effect, each new power that the Federal government has exercised on the basis of *implied power* is a further restriction on the potential powers reserved to the states.

From the early decisions of Supreme Court Chief Justice John Marshall, through the flowering of a nationalistic spirit, to the demands of the late twentieth century, Americans are accepting the inevitable trend toward a stronger central government at the expense of states' rights. When the pioneers were pushing westward, they turned to the Federal government to wage war on Indians, or to help them build a railroad, or to administer the territories; when it was necessary to mobilize the nation for major wars in the twentieth century, Americans did not stress states' rights, they turned to the Federal government. When the Russians launched their 1957 Sputnik, a powerful wound was dealt America's nationalistic pride, and there followed the National Defense Education Act which gave Federal support for science and language education, an area formerly left almost exclusively to states.

With a mounting sense of dependency, Americans turn to the Federal government for assistance in solving their problems: Federal Consumer Bureaus, Food and Drug Acts, interplanetary space exploration, pollution controls—these are areas in which states' rights cannot hope to be effective. And the power of the Federal government thereby increases. Perhaps the clearest signs of the trend are the frantic appeals of mayors of large cities for greater Federal assistance in solving the problems of their metropolises. And the most conservative areas of the country are the first to complain if their Federal Impact Aid is reduced.

There are few areas left in which states can expect to prevail. Perhaps dog, fishing, and marriage licenses will continue to be issued by individual states. But already there is a movement for national auto driving licenses, national teacher and doctor certification, and national banning of tobacco smoking.

What corner of their privacy will Americans be able to control eventually? Will there be a Federal Commissioner of Eugenics Programs? Or will there be some variations permitted on a state-by-state basis? Will the Federal income tax preempt the ability of states and municipalities to acquire significant new tax bases?

"That government is best which governs least," wrote Thomas Jefferson two centuries ago. His wish is coming true. For the state governments, that is. But on the Federal level, each new invention, whether it be radio or television (FCC), airplane or space rocket (FAA), New Deal or Fair Deal (SEC, CCC, WPA, FEPC, etc.), brings forth a new Federal agency. Yet the challenges to the Federal system continue—and that includes more than just whistlin' Dixie!

Will it ever stop?

Notes

1 Merrill Jensen, "The Confederation Period: Perspectives and Significance," *The American Past,* Vol. I, 3rd edition, ed. by Sidney Fine and Gerald S. Brown (New York, Macmillan, 1970), p. 168. Copyright © 1970 by The Macmillan Company.

2 *Ibid.,* pp. 168–169.

Since they had just revolted against a unitary system that had misused its power, the Revolutionary leaders were especially leery of establishing a government that might repeat the earlier tyranny. The Articles of Confederation, the first constitution of the United States, represents an overreaction on the part of the Founding Fathers, whose fears of concentrating too much power in the central government led to the creation of a hopelessly impotent system. The Articles of Confederation provide for states' rights and little else. The central government had no power to levy taxes, regulate trade, or to compel the states to obey the will of the majority of the states; there was no central executive or judicial power. One state alone could veto any proposed legislation. Although the Ordinances of 1785 and 1787 have been hailed as enlightened legislation under the Articles, the text of the document reveals the fundamental weaknesses that doomed the government of 1781–1788.

The Articles of Confederation

To all to whom these Presents shall come, we the under signed Delegates of the States affixed to our Names, send greeting.

ARTICLE I.   The Stile of this confederacy shall be "The United States of America."

ARTICLE II.   Each state retains its sovereignty, freedom, and independence, and every Power, Jurisdiction and right, which is not by this confederation expressly delegated to the United States, in Congress assembled.

ARTICLE III.   The said states hereby severally enter into a firm league of friendship with each other, for their common defence, the security of their Liberties, and their mutual and general welfare, binding themselves to assist each other, against all force offered to, or attacks made upon them, or any of them, on account of religion, sovereignty, trade, or any other pretence whatever.

ARTICLE IV.   . . . If any Person guilty of, or charged with treason, felony, or other high misdemeanor in any state, shall flee from Justice, and be found in any of the united states, he shall, upon demand of the Governor or executive power, of the state from which he fled, be delivered up and removed to the state having jurisdiction of his offence.

Full faith and credit shall be given in each of these states to the records, acts and judicial proceedings of the courts and magistrates of every other state. . . .

ARTICLE VIII.   All charges of war, and all other expences that shall be incurred for the common defence or general welfare, and allowed by the united states in congress assembled, shall be defrayed out of a common treasury, which shall be supplied by the several states in proportion to the value of all land within each state, granted to or surveyed for any Person, as such land and the buildings and improvements thereon shall be estimated according to such mode as the united states in congress assembled, shall from time to time direct and appoint.

The taxes for paying that proportion shall be laid and levied by the authority and direction of the legislatures of the several states within the time agreed upon by the united states in congress assembled.

ARTICLE IX.   . . . The united states in congress assembled shall also have the sole and exclusive right and power of regulating the alloy and value of coin struck by their own authority, or by that of the respective states—fixing the standard of weights and measures throughout the united states—regulating the trade and managing all affairs with the Indians, not members of any of the states, provided that the legislative right of any state within its own limits be not infringed or violated—establishing or regulating post-offices from one state to another, throughout all the united states, and exacting such postage on the papers passing thro' the same as may be requisite to defray the expenses of the said office—appointing all officers of the land forces, in the service of the united states, excepting regimental officers—appointing all the officers of the naval forces, and commissioning all officers whatever in the service of the united states—making rules for the government and regulation of the said land and naval forces, and directing their operations.

The united states in congress assembled shall have authority to appoint a committee, to sit in the recess of congress, to be denominated "A Committee of the States," and to consist of one delegate from each state; and to appoint such other committees and civil officers as may be necessary for managing the general affairs of the united states under their direction—to appoint one of their number to preside, provided that no person be allowed to serve in the office of president more than one year in any term of three years; to ascertain the necessary sums of money to be raised for the service of the united states, and to appropriate and apply the same for defraying the public expences—to borrow money, or emit bills on the credit of the united states, transmitting every half year to the respective states an account of the sums of money so borrowed or emitted,—to build and equip a navy—to agree upon the number of land forces, and to make requisitions from each state for its quota, in proportion to the number of white inhabitants in such state; which requisition shall be binding, and thereupon the legislature of each state shall appoint the regimental officers, raise the men and cloath, arm and equip them in a soldier like manner, at the expence of the united states; and the officers and men so cloathed, armed and equipped shall march to the place appointed, and within the time agreed on by the united states in congress assembled: But if the united states in congress assembled shall, on consideration of circumstances judge proper that any state should not raise men, or should raise a smaller number than its quota, and that any other state should raise a greater number of men than the quota thereof, such extra number shall be raised, officered, cloathed, armed and equipped in the same manner as the quota of such state, unless the legislature of such state shall judge that such extra number cannot be safely spared out of the same, in which case they shall raise officers, cloath, arm and equip as many of such extra number as they judge can be safely spared. And the officers and men so cloathed, armed and equipped, shall march to the place appointed, and within the time agreed on by the united states in congress assembled.

The united states in congress assembled shall never engage in a war, nor grant letters of marque and reprisal in time of peace, nor enter into any treaties or alliances, nor coin money, nor regulate the value thereof, nor ascertain the sums and expences necessary for the defence and welfare of the united states, or any of them, nor emit bills, nor borrow money on the credit of the united states, nor appropriate money, nor agree upon the number of vessels of war, to be built or purchased, or the number of land or sea forces to be raised, nor appoint a commander in chief of the army or navy, unless nine states assent to the same: nor shall a question on any other point, except for adjourning from day to day be determined, unless by the votes of a majority of the united states in congress assembled. . . .

Article X. The committee on the states, or any nine of them, shall be authorized to execute, in the recess of congress, such of the powers of congress as the united states in congress assembled, by the consent of nine states, shall from time to time think expedient to vest them with; provided that no power be delegated to the said committee for the exercise of which, by the articles of confederation, the voice of nine states in the congress of the united states assembled is requisite. . . .

Article XII. All bills of credit emitted, monies borrowed and debts contracted by, or under the authority of congress, before the assembling of the united states, in pursuance of the present confederation, shall be deemed and considered as a charge against the united states for payment, and satisfaction whereof the said united states, and the public faith are hereby solemnly pledged. . . .

More than 30 years before the Civil War Between the States broke out,
sectional tensions ran high, particularly over the tariff issue. The crisis,
which was precipitated by the challenge to Federal authority in
Jackson's administration, is outlined below.

The Nullification Crisis

John A. Garraty

Sectional Tensions Continue

Although Jackson drew support from widely scattered parts of the
country, his election did not quiet the sectional conflicts of the period.
In office he had to say something about western lands, the tariff, and
other issues. He tried to steer a moderate course, urging a slight reduction of the tariff, "constitutional" internal improvements, and suggesting that once the rapidly disappearing federal debt had been paid
off the surplus revenues of the government might be "distributed"
among the states. Even these cautious proposals caused conflict, so
complex were the interrelations of sectional disputes. If the federal
government turned the expected surplus over to the states, it could
not afford to reduce the price of public land without going into the
red. This disturbed some westerners, most notably Senator Thomas
Hart Benton of Missouri. Western anxiety in turn suggested to southern opponents of the protective tariff an alliance of South and West.
These southerners argued that a low tariff, levied for purposes of revenue only, would increase foreign imports, bring more money into the
Treasury, and thus make it possible to lower the price of public land.

The land question came up in the Senate in December 1829, when
an obscure Connecticut senator, Samuel A. Foot, suggested that the
sale of government land should be sharply restricted. Benton promptly attacked this proposal as a plot concocted by eastern manufacturers to check the westward migration of their workers. On January
19, 1830, Senator Robert Y. Hayne of South Carolina, a spokesman
for Vice-President Calhoun, supported Benton vigorously, suggesting
an alliance of South and West for cheap land and low tariffs as out-

From *The American Nation* by John A. Garraty, pp. 264–268. Copyright ©
1966 by John A. Garraty. Reprinted by permission of Harper & Row, Publishers, Inc.

lined above. Daniel Webster then rose to the defense of the northeastern interests, cleverly goading Hayne by accusing South Carolina of
advocating disunionist policies. The South Carolinian, responding to
this attack, launched into an impassioned exposition of the states'-
rights doctrine while Calhoun, observing the debate from his post as
President of the Senate, indicated his approval by occasional nods and
smiles.

Webster then took the floor again and for two days, before galleries
packed with the elite of Washington society, treated the Senate to a
magnificent display of grandiloquence, patriotism, and common sense.
The Constitution was a compact of the American people, not merely
of the states, he insisted, the Union perpetual and indissoluble. Nullification could lead only to civil war. Webster's defense of nationalism
made the states'-rights position appear close to treason and effectively prevented the formation of a West-South alliance. Nominally
directed at Hayne, his attack was actually aimed at Calhoun and the
doctrine of nullification. Generations of school children have mem-
orized his concluding paean in praise of the Union, a remarkable
example of extemporaneous volubility, in which the flag becomes "the
gorgeous ensign of the republic" bearing, in Webster's vivid imagination, the motto: "Liberty *and* Union, now and forever, one and
inseparable!"

Jackson and Calhoun

Of course, the attention focused on the Webster-Hayne debate revived discussion of the idea of nullification. Although southern-born,
a cotton planter, and a personal friend of Senator Hayne, Jackson had
devoted too much of his life to fighting for the entire United States to
countenance disunion on any terms. Therefore, when the states'-
rights faction invited him to a dinner to celebrate the anniversary of
Jefferson's birth, he came prepared. The evening reverberated with
speeches and toasts of a states'-rights tenor, but when the President
was called upon to volunteer a toast he raised his glass, fixed his eyes
grimly on John C. Calhoun, and said: "Our *Federal* Union: It must
be preserved!" Calhoun took up the challenge at once. "The Union,"
he retorted, "next to our liberty, most dear!"

It is difficult to measure the importance of the animosity between
Jackson and Calhoun in the grave crisis to which this clash was a
prelude. Calhoun wanted very much to be President. He had failed to
inherit the office from John Quincy Adams and had accepted the Vice-
Presidency again under Jackson in hopes of succeeding him at the end

of one term, if not sooner, for his health was known to be frail. Yet Old Hickory showed no sign of passing on, or of retiring. He also seemed to place special confidence in the shrewd Van Buren, who, as secretary of state, also had claim to the succession. A silly social fracas in which Calhoun's wife appeared to take the lead in the systematic snubbing by all the ladies of the administration of Peggy Eaton, wife of the secretary of war, had also estranged the two. (Peggy was supposed to have had an affair with Eaton while she was still married to another man, but Jackson, undoubtedly sympathetic because of the slanders he and Rachel had endured, stoutly defended her good name.) Then, shortly after the Jefferson Day dinner, Jackson discovered that back in 1818, when he had invaded Florida and executed the two Englishmen who had been inciting the Indians, Calhoun, secretary of war at the time, had recommended to President Monroe that he be summoned before a court of inquiry and charged with disobeying orders. Since Calhoun had repeatedly led Jackson to believe that he had supported him at the time, this revelation convinced the President that Calhoun was not a man of honor.

These personal difficulties are worth stressing because ideologically Jackson and Calhoun were not very far apart, except on the ultimate issue of the right of a state to resist federal authority. Jackson was a strong President, but he did not believe that the area of national power was large or that it should be expanded. His interests in economy, the distribution of federal surpluses to the states, and in interpreting the powers of Congress narrowly were all similar to Calhoun's. Like most westerners, he favored internal improvements. While President he approved a greatly enlarged program of federal aid to road and canal companies. But he preferred that local projects be left to the states. In 1830 he vetoed a bill providing aid for the construction of the Maysville Road because it was wholly within Kentucky. There were political reasons for this veto, which was a slap at Kentucky's hero, Henry Clay, but it could not fail to please Calhoun.

Indian Problems

Jackson also took a states'-rights position in the controversy between the Cherokee Indians and Georgia. Convinced that progress required the destruction of all Indians, the President decided to "remove" all the tribes to the wilderness beyond the Mississippi. Many of them accepted their fate with resignation; a few, such as Black Hawk's Sac and Fox in Illinois and Osceola's Seminoles in Florida, resisted and had to be subdued by troops. One Indian nation, however, the Cherokees, made a courageous and intelligent effort to hold on to their lands by adjusting to white ways. They took up farming and cattle raising and cultivated the household arts. They even developed a written language, drafted a constitution, and tried to establish a state within a state in northwestern Georgia. Several treaties with the United States seemed to establish the legality of their government. However, Georgia would not recognize the Cherokee Nation. It passed a law in 1828 declaring all Cherokee laws void and the region part of Georgia. Another law of 1830 required all white men in the Cherokee country to procure licenses and take an oath of allegiance to the state.

The Indians challenged both these laws in the Supreme Court. In *Cherokee Nation v. Georgia* (1831) Chief Justice John Marshall refused to rule on Georgia's nullification of the Cherokee laws. In *Worcester v. Georgia* (1832), however, he decided in the Indians' favor. Later, when a Cherokee named Corn Tassel, convicted in a Georgia court of the murder of another Indian, appealed on the ground that the crime had taken place in Cherokee territory, Marshall also declared this Georgia action unconstitutional. But Jackson backed Georgia's position. "John Marshall has made his decision," he said. "Now let him enforce it." Georgia hanged poor Corn Tassel and destroyed the Cherokee Nation, and Jackson did nothing.

Perhaps Jackson's willingness to allow Georgia to "nullify" decisions of the Supreme Court persuaded the extreme southern states'-righters that he would not oppose the doctrine of nullification should it be formally applied to a law of Congress. If so, they deceived themselves egregiously. Jackson did not challenge Georgia because he was prejudiced, like most westerners, against the Indians. He spoke of "the poor deluded . . . Cherokees," and called William Wirt, the lawyer who defended their cause, a "truly wicked" man. He was not one to be bound by principle in such matters or to worry overmuch about being inconsistent. In any case, when South Carolina revived the talk of nullification in 1832, he acted in quite a different manner.

The Nullification Crisis

The proposed alliance of South and West to reduce both the tariff and the price of land had not materialized, partly because Webster had discredited the South in the eyes of western patriots, and partly because the planters of South Carolina and Georgia, fearing the competition of fertile new cotton lands in Alabama and Mississippi, opposed the rapid exploitation of the West almost as vociferously as did northern manufacturers. When a new tariff law was passed in 1832, it lowered duties much less than the southerners desired. At once, talk of nullifying the acts of both 1828 and 1832 began to be heard in South Carolina.

President Jackson considered the new tariff, which had reduced some duties substantially, a reasonable compromise. Nullification was therefore irrational as well as treasonable, in his opinion. "Tell . . . the Nullifiers from me that they can talk and write resolutions and print threats to their hearts' content," he warned a South Carolina representative when Congress adjourned in July 1832. "But if one drop of blood be shed there in defiance of the laws of the United States I will hang the first man of them I can get my hands on to the first tree I can find."

This warning was not taken seriously in South Carolina. In October the state legislature provided for the election of a special convention, which, when it met, proved to contain a solid majority of nullifiers. On November 24, 1832, this convention passed an Ordinance of Nullification, prohibiting the collection of tariff duties in the state after February 1, 1833. The legislature then authorized the raising of an army and appropriated money to supply it with weapons.

Jackson quickly began military preparations of his own, telling friends that he would have 50,000 men ready to move in a little over a month. But he also made a statesmanlike effort to end the crisis peaceably. First he suggested to Congress that it lower the tariff further. Then, on December 10, he addressed a thoughtful but determined "Proclamation to the People of South Carolina." Nullification could only lead to the destruction of the Union, he said. "The laws of the United States must be executed. I have no discretionary power on the subject. . . . Those who told you that you might peaceably prevent their execution deceived you." Old Hickory then added sternly: "Disunion by armed force is *treason*. Are you really ready to incur its guilt?"

Attention now shifted to Congress where administration leaders introduced both a new tariff bill and a Force Bill granting the President additional authority to execute the revenue laws. Calhoun, having resigned as Vice-President to accept appointment as senator from South Carolina, led the fight against the Force Bill. Jackson was eager to see the tariff reduced but absolutely determined to enforce the law. As the February 1 deadline approached, he claimed that he could raise 200,000 men if needed to suppress resistance. Should the governor of Virginia try to block the movement of troops toward South

Carolina, "I would arrest him at the head of his troops," Jackson warned. "Union men, fear not," he said. *"The Union will be preserved."*

Jackson's determination sobered the South Carolina radicals. Their appeal for the support of other southern states brought further discouragement. Calhoun, although a brave man, was really alarmed for his own safety, for Jackson had threatened to "hang him as high as Haman" if nullification were actually attempted. He was suddenly eager to avoid a showdown. Ten days before the deadline, South Carolina postponed nullification pending the outcome of the tariff debate. Then Calhoun joined forces with Henry Clay to push a compromise tariff through Congress. Its passage, early in March 1833, marked the willingness of the North and West to make concessions in the interest of national harmony. Senator Silas Wright of New York, closely affiliated with Van Buren, explained the situation: "People will neither cut throats nor dismember the Union for protection. There is more patriotism and love of country than that left yet. The People will never balance this happy government against ten cents a pound upon a pound of wool."

And so the Union weathered the storm. South Carolina professed to be satisfied with the new tariff (actually, it made few immediate reductions, providing for a gradual lowering of rates over a ten-year period), and repealed the Nullification Ordinance, saving face by nullifying the Force Bill, which was now a dead letter. Having approached the brink of civil war, the nation had drawn hastily back. It would take an issue more potent than the tariff to break the bonds of union.

The Civil War had been raging for nearly two years before
Abraham Lincoln issued the Emancipation Proclamation. In August of
1862, he received public criticism in the form of a letter published as an
editorial in the "New York Tribune." The author, Horace Greeley, berated
Lincoln for showing undue deference to the slaveholding powers and for
not getting on with the cause of abolition. Lincoln's famous reply
emphasized that his primary concern was not to free the slaves.
Rather, it was to preserve the Union.

The Union Above All

Abraham Lincoln

Executive Mansion,
Washington, August 22, 1862.

Hon. Horace Greely:

Dear Sir

I have just read yours of the 19th. addressed to myself through the
New-York Tribune. If there be in it any statements, or assumptions
of fact, which I may know to be erroneous, I do not, now and here,
controvert them. If there be in it any inferences which I may believe
to be falsely drawn, I do not now and here, argue against them. If
there be perceptible in it an impatient and dictatorial tone, I waive it
in deference to an old friend, whose heart I have always supposed to
be right.

As to the policy I "seem to be pursuing" as you say, I have not
meant to leave any one in doubt.

I would save the Union. I would save it the shortest way under the
Constitution. The sooner the national authority can be restored; the
nearer the Union will be "the Union as it was." If there be those who
would not save the Union, unless they could at the same time *save*
slavery, I do not agree with them. If there be those who would not
save the Union unless they could at the same time *destroy* slavery, I
do not agree with them. My paramount object in this struggle *is* to
save the Union, and is *not* either to save or to destroy slavery. If I
could save the Union without freeing *any* slave I would do it, and if I
could save it by freeing *all* the slaves I would do it; and if I could save
it by freeing some and leaving others alone I would also do that. What
I do about slavery, and the colored race, I do because I believe it
helps to save the Union; and what I forbear, I forbear because I do

not believe it would help to save the Union. I shall do *less* whenever I shall believe what I am doing hurts the cause, and I shall do *more* whenever I shall believe doing more will help the cause. I shall try to correct errors when shown to be errors; and I shall adopt views so fast as they shall appear to be true views.

I have here stated my purpose according to my view of *official* duty; and I intend no modification of my oft-expressed *personal* wish that all men every where could be free. Yours,

A. LINCOLN

The advantages of the federal system and the wisdom contained in its
functioning are both presented favorably in the excerpt below.
Does the author attribute more wisdom to the Founding Fathers
than is justified?

A More Perfect Union

D. W. Brogan

The framers of the American Constitution put as their first aim the
provision of the political means to "a more perfect union." They did
not aim at perfect union, at the ironing-out of all regional differences,
at the destruction of all regional independence. One of the organizers
of the movement that led to framing the Constitution did, indeed,
want complete union, did want to abolish local autonomy. But the
ideas of Alexander Hamilton were so remote from any possibilities in
the America of 1787 that they were more or less politely ignored by
his colleagues, and Hamilton left the Convention in disgust. When the
Constitution was put before the people, Hamilton was an effective
fighter for it, and as the first Secretary of the Treasury he helped to
get the machine running. But he was not a maker of the Constitution,
because he thought it was not good enough, that what the United
States needed was complete union, the fusion of the thirteen states
into a unitary body politic.

Although Hamilton did not get his way, it was not necessarily a
silly way. For the weak federal government that went into operation
in 1789, like the strong federal government in operation in 1956, was
a clumsy method of carrying on the business of the American people
if all that is to be done is to carry on that business. It is clumsy to
have the machinery of government in forty-nine units: the States, and
the Union. It is clumsy to have the powers of the federal government
loosely defined, so that they are constantly matters of controversy, so
that many things are not done because it is uncertain what organ of
government has the legal power to do them. It is at best inconvenient
that the uncontested powers of the federal government are divided
among a President, a Senate, and a House of Representatives, and

that the question *what* power is *where* is decided by the majority of a Supreme Court of nine members. A government so organized must often be slow and uncertain in its action, indeed sometimes be incapable of action or, at any rate, incapable of action in time to meet the situation. The existence of an irreducible minimum of power in forty-eight states causes grave inconvenience, since it means that law and political practice vary from state to state. And some of those states are small in area, or in population, or in both; some are also the results of historical accidents; some break up the natural unity of geographical areas in a way to horrify a geopolitician or a political realist of the type that abolishes ancient European nations in an editorial. It is absurd that the empty mountain state of Nevada should be able both to make a good thing out of its lax divorce laws and its legalization of gambling and to hold the United States to ransom to buy its other main asset, silver, at an exorbitant price. It is absurd that the three counties that make up Delaware should be empowered to charter corporations to do business all over the Union on terms more profitable to the corporation's controllers than to the boldly politic. It is absurd that the New York harbor area should be under the control of two states *and* the federal government, and that the pride of Arizona should hold up, for years at a time, the development of water-power that southern California badly needs.

But to cure these absurdities it would be necessary to impose on three million varied square miles a central authority strong enough to suppress local objections. But such a government would have a pretty free hand in deciding what local objections it decided to suppress— and such a government would be too strong for local liberties, so the American people decided in 1789 and have kept on deciding since.

The standard of comparison we should apply to the degree of success with which the American people have achieved "a more perfect union" is not that of a comparatively small, unitary country like Great Britain or New Zealand. We must look at countries with something like the same problems of space to deal with. We must look at Russia, at Canada, at Brazil, at Australia. And if we do look at them, we find that the Soviet Union with its central Russian mass and its control by the Communist Party machine, and Brazil with its dictatorships—that both of these are, from the American point of view, buying union at the expense of liberty. On the other hand, Canada and Australia, while free, are not, by American standards, united; neither, for example, dared to exercise in World War II that most difficult power of government, the imposition of general conscription for service all over the world. Australia is repeatedly in the throes of attempted constitutional reforms designed to give the federal government temporary powers adequate for the times. And Canada, despite the formal powers of its federal government, has had to allow Quebec to exercise a power of nullification which, in kind if not in extent, is like that claimed long ago for South Carolina by John C. Calhoun. South Africa, with a formally unitary government, is divided three ways by race conflicts, by bitter historical feuds, and by possibly insoluble economic and racial problems. Should the world demand for gold and diamonds fall off, the Union of South Africa might have to face, all over again, problems that optimists think were "solved" in 1909.

To have created a free government over a continental area without making a sacrifice of adequate efficiency or of liberty is the American achievement. It is a unique achievement in world history.

And because that achievement is tied up in fact and in legend with the Constitution, with the political system which makes the Constitution work, with a long historical experience (long, as modern political history goes), the American people are entitled to more than tolerance: they are entitled to sympathetic understanding in their worship of their own system of political and social institutions. And sympathetic understanding must begin with understanding of the obstacles to unity that faced and still face the People of the United States.

Henry Brandon, an editor-at-large for "Saturday Review," discusses the latest changes in the Federal system. Is the "New Federalism" really a major step in the direction of states' rights?

Federalism in 1970

Henry Brandon

It is becoming more and more obvious that President Nixon has a conservative heart and a reformist head. He is not a crusader, but he is enough of a modern man to know reforms are necessary. He has been heard to say in meetings with his aides: "I don't want just to defend things; I want to do something."

In his first State of the Union Message, President Nixon touched on three major areas of reform: "total reform" of the welfare system; reforms to give people access to property rights; and "reform of all our institutions of government at the federal, state, and local level." This last he called "a new federalism."

It is nothing new to find that at times a conservative government can more easily push through certain basic reforms than a more liberal party can. Historically this has been true in this country as well as in Great Britain. Now both minority leaders, Senator Hugh Scott and Congressman Gerald Ford, are promising to press hard for the President's new welfare program. This should make it difficult for Republicans, as natural opponents to such a program, to oppose it, but even more difficult for liberal Democrats *not* to support it in the clinches, despite what they may consider to be its shortcomings. The same applies to the new federalism ideas, which Walter Heller began to promote during President Kennedy's days. But neither President Kennedy nor President Johnson thought that such a proposal stood much of a chance with Congress.

The authors of the "old" federalism—Hamilton, Madison, and Jay —argued first, that a strong national union was necessary in the interest of internal monetary order; secondly, that a federal compact was needed to enable the budding nation to make its influence felt in the world; thirdly, that such a compact would lessen the ominous "spirit of faction" stirring among the states; and finally, that national authority would not supersede local sovereignty—the rights of the states—in matters of essentially local character.

Recently, a paper outlining the adaptation of the old federalism to President Nixon's own ideas was drafted in the White House and circulated among Cabinet members. It deals primarily with how to limit central power, and it proposes that "a sea change in the approach to the limitation of centralized power is that 'states' rights' have now become rights of first refusal. . . . States' rights are now more accurately described as states' duties; this is a fundamental change in federalism . . . and provides federalists with two of their prime causes: the cause of regaining control, and the cause of fairness."

The new federalism, therefore, is designed to return certain powers to local authority, depending on the ability of a particular level of government to deliver the services. It also places priority on the distribution of money instead of services or food or clothing, and if that money is squandered on television sets and ice cream, the argument goes, it is the responsibility of the government at every level to educate the person how better to use money to stay healthy, rather than to assume control of the welfare recipients' money "for their own good."

The "cause of fairness" is reminiscent of Lincoln's appeal to the national conscience when he shifted the focus of the Civil War from "preserve the Union" to "end slavery," and of Franklin Roosevelt's referring to the Presidency as "primarily a position of moral authority." Today, this voice of national conscience leads some to favor disengaging "with honor" from Vietnam, while leading others to believe the United States should withdraw immediately because "it is an immoral war." How to resolve the *national* conscience in its clashes with the *local* conscience—a clash that is not new but rather reemphasized by the new federalism—will be one of the tests for this new doctrine. The Democrats, beginning with Franklin D. Roosevelt, realized that an individual, especially a poor or a black person, could no longer get fair treatment locally. At that level, for various parochial reasons, the odds were stacked against such persons, and so the New Deal and the Fair Deal were developed in Washington, and they sought to impose decisions on local authorities.

But today a growing majority of Americans assume that, while fairness *in principle* still lies in federal standards and minimums, fairness in administration usually lies closer to home. An example of how the new federalists must come to grips with a shortage of opportunity is the Philadelphia labor story. In that instance, the Department of Labor required unions supplying labor for contractors on federally assisted projects to show good faith in admitting more Negroes to jobs. The major question is whether, having experienced the lessons of abdication long ago, local governments are now ready for the second chance they will be given.

Could the new federalism blur party labels, as the White House paper tries to suggest: "The old liberal-conservative and centralist-localist calibrations will lose meaning when applied to a fusion of certain elements of liberalism and conservatism, of central concern and local consent"? Progressivism of the late nineteenth century, the paper points out, grew with roots in both parties, and, as a footnote to history, the paper cites an early draft of Nixon's "Bridges to Human Dignity" campaign speech containing an exposition of "black entrepreneurship." In its final version, the phrase was changed to the catchier "black capitalism." When Hubert Humphrey soon thereafter espoused the same idea, he could not, of course, unabashedly lift Nixon's slogan. So he wound up using "black entrepreneurship."

The question, therefore, of where Nixon stands politically becomes more complicated, and it is not easy to come up with new criteria, for the Left-Right syndrome is too simplistic. The shades of the "Southern strategy" continue to be an obvious influence in various Presidential moves and decisions, but Mr. Nixon is far too shrewd to let this idea dominate his policies; some very basic reforms are being injected into Republican policies, reforms that are bound to narrow the differences between the two parties. When that happens, it is usually the party holding the initiative that profits politically.

To avoid exposing their frequent contradictions, Mr. Nixon is careful not to trumpet too emphatically either his conservative or his reformist decisions. But as the anonymous author of that White House paper at one point says: "The new federalists replace the melting pot with the salad bowl." Leaving everybody, I presume, to select his own preferred dressing.

The paper concludes by pointing out a further disadvantage: "The new federalists can seldom operate with the flair and panache of a Theodore Roosevelt. The nature of their approach—the amalgam of national purpose and local purposefulness—condemns them in most cases to the soft sell, the underpromise, the counterpunch. . . . The new federalists' general tone cannot be stridently confident, because the new road is as unfamiliar to the leader as to the led."

Kerr, formerly president of the University of California and chancellor of the University of California at Berkeley, discusses the gradual increase of the Federal role in education from the time of Jefferson to the present. This excerpt is from his essay "New Challenges to the College and University."

The Federal Role in Education

Clark Kerr

The federal government, now facing policy decisions for the next decade, has entered upon its role in American higher education by gradual steps.

The Dartmouth College Case

The first step was unintentional. Most early colleges, including Harvard, had been founded with a special relation to the government of their colony or state. The Jeffersonians argued that the public interest was dominant, that the state had a natural right to control. The Supreme Court decided to the contrary in 1819. The state of New Hampshire was prevented from infringing upon the charter of Dartmouth College and changing the nature of the private college into a state university. Dartmouth was assured its independence and the trustees were confirmed in their control.

As a result, the movement for private colleges was accelerated and scores of them were founded in the period before the Civil War. The distinctive American pattern of many private institutions evolved, each able to go its own way, each started by private initiative, each financed wholly or largely with private funds. Public institutions, as a consequence, had a harder struggle for public funds and prestige. This pattern of private and public higher education, in which the private segment at its best has always stood for independence and quality, is unusual among university systems of the world, most of which were started by public initiative and are publicly financed and controlled.

The diversified American system creates special problems for federal policy. There are questions of the propriety and even the legality of public support for private institutions, some of which are under religious control. The selection of institutions to be supported is difficult; they vary greatly in the quality of their academic programs and in their contributions to social purposes. Accreditation systems, except for that of New York State, are private. Public support of private institutions presents problems of the degree of control that is necessary and proper, or even possible, over the expenditure of public funds by institutions not subject to basic public control. The most difficult problem, as will be noted later, is whether the federal government can and should give general institutional support to private, including religious, institutions to be expended at their discretion.

The Land-Grant Universities and Service to Society

The second step by the federal government came at the time of the Civil War. The Morrill Act of 1862 authorized grants of land to the states to provide colleges giving instruction in agriculture and the mechanic arts. Thus the Congress took the initiative in establishing land-grant institutions, but it worked through the states and did not create federal universities. The land-grant college movement built chiefly on the few state institutions which existed at the time. It borrowed from German universities the combination of teaching with advanced research, added direct service to agriculture, industry, and government, and thus evolved a distinctively American pattern, not only for the state institutions but also for the greatest of the private universities, which adopted a similar course. Nearly two hundred universities, public and private, now follow this pattern, and at least twenty of them have international distinction.

The land-grant model created great possibilities for cooperation with the federal government. Distinguished universities accustomed to giving service to the surrounding society were available to work with the government—willingly and competently. Thus, during and after the Second World War, the federal government turned to them for scientific research at the highest level of capability, while other countries relied more on government agencies, academies, or scientific societies largely separate from the universities.

The land-grant model also gives rise to problems for federal policy. The great universities are under state or private governance, not federal, and are less subject to federal control or even to federal coordination than those in other countries. They are independent to a degree hardly matched elsewhere. A national plan for university development is unlikely in the United States, although an actuality elsewhere. Consequently there may be more duplication of effort or absence of adequate effort than there would be if an effective national plan were in operation; but a national plan could, of course, be ineffective.

The public land-grant university is a chosen instrument of its state. The federal government has also, in effect, chosen its own special university instruments, both state and private. This approach has increased the great inequalities among institutions. In most states, the land-grant university has almost always been preferred over the teachers' college, for example. The quality of the chosen instruments has varied greatly with the wealth of the states and the state commitments to research and training at an advanced level. Among private universities, the Massachusetts Institute of Technology and the California Institute of Technology have benefited much more from their relations with the federal government than less preferred institutions which once viewed themselves as competitors. Private corporations have also followed the chosen instrument approach. One consequence is enormous variation in the facilities, quality, and effectiveness of institutions. A second consequence is that those not chosen demand equal treatment, particularly as the differences have become greater and more noticed. A third consequence is that concentration of effort has led to the development of many of the world's leading universities, to the great gain of the nation. A major problem is posed for future federal support: Should it be on the basis of merit or of equality, with present merit being enormously far from equal?

The land-grant model committed the university to a multiplicity of purposes. The earlier colleges had been more nearly single-purpose institutions devoted to the general education of undergraduates and the preparation of students for the professions. To these functions were added research and training in an ever-widening span of fields, and service to many and increasingly to all segments of society. This multiplicity brought confusion and even conflict. The purposes were not fully consistent with each other: for example, the general education of undergraduates conflicted with the specialized demands of research endeavors. The university was intertwined with the surrounding society and particularly with its powerful special interest groups. This reduced its objectivity and impartiality and made it more vulnerable to interference, outside control, and controversy.

All these added functions and relations required the university to become large, almost mammoth, compared with the small college from which it grew. It also became less governable, less unified, less stable, and less happy with itself—and thus more difficult for the federal government to deal with. The land-grant model has led increasingly to turbulence, not tranquillity. And this has posed problems for the federal government which authored it.

War and Science

The third step came with the Second World War and the subsequent cold war. Military might was based increasingly on scientific capability. The United States, under emergency conditions, turned to the universities for the atomic bomb, radar, and much else. The results were phenomenal; and they were obtained from a handful of universities. Six universities at one time shared one-half of all federal funds spent for scientific research through universities. Special federal agencies were established to work with the institutions. By 1960, 75 percent of all university research was funded by the federal government, most of it in scientific fields. Thus was established one of the most productive relations in history—the nation became stronger, the leading universities more distinguished.

This relation also caused trouble for the universities that participated. Research and graduate training overwhelmed undergraduate instruction. Science rose far above the humanities, and some scientists liked this better than did most humanists. As scientists became attached to their Washington agencies, their loyalty to their academic institutions was reduced. Nonfaculty research workers became the fastest-growing element in the university population and grew to substantial numbers, but they were not admitted into the collegial structure. The institutions became more complex, as well as much larger, and thus more difficult to administer. Parts of universities became integral units or affiliates of the military-industrial complex.

Justified little step by little step, the university was greatly changed, at first, almost without realizing it. Flexner had complained in 1930 that the universities had become "service stations for the general public." By 1960, they were far more in the service—the very willing, even eager service—of the federal agencies than they ever had been of the general public. The modern university with all its built-in tensions, with all its imbalances, had been created. The process begun by the land-grant movement reached a new height—service to science had a more profound effect than had the earlier service to agriculture and industry.

Federal policy is now faced with some of the new problems created by the old success: how to encourage improvement in undergraduate

Instruction, how to satisfy the humanists and to a lesser degree the social scientists, how to give the university more sense of control of its own destiny, how to restore its unity and institutional integrity, and how to diminish the more abject instances of submission to secret research and international intrigue.

Sputnik and the "Tidal Wave"

The fourth evolutionary stage began in 1958, following Sputnik and facing the decade of the "tidal wave" of students. Federal aid took multiple forms in response to multiple problems. The National Defense Education Act of 1958 supported science training, but added language instruction and teacher training. Support for construction beyond research facilities began on a large scale in 1963. Assistance to needy students was greatly expanded in 1965. Support was increased to institutions as such, to selected budding "centers of strength" in the sciences, and to "developing institutions" which meant, in fact, largely Negro colleges.

Federal support, still confined to a limited number of institutions, reached $750 million by 1958. By 1968, it was six times greater—$4,700 million—going to 2,100 institutions and thousands of students through forty federal agencies. This was the decade when the federal government went beyond science and beyond the chosen few institutions.

Both quantity and quality of higher education were greatly benefited by this new federal support, but once again new programs brought new problems. Among them were the administrative difficulties created by many agencies handling many programs with little and sometimes no coordination; little sense of an overall policy and system of priorities, and no sense of how to integrate federal with state and private support of higher education; and a legacy of heavy dependence by all higher education on federal support and of great expectations of even more support in the future.

The first stage of federal involvement with higher education assured the integrity of the private colleges; the second initiated service to society; the third expanded scientific research; the fourth provided broadened support in the decade of assistance to growth. Each stage has given rise to problems, as every policy of importance inevitably does. The lesson for the future is to examine not only the purposes but also the problems of each new policy: this should lead not to inaction but rather to wiser action.

Problems of the Next Decade

Federal involvement with higher education—though federal involvement is only one of many forces at work—has resulted in a system which might be described, in part, as follows:

A strong private segment—numbering half of all the institutions of higher education, and including one-third of the students, about half of the universities of greatest prestige, and nearly all of the leading colleges—which sets standards for autonomy and quality and provides much of the innovative effort.

A remarkable series of multipurpose universities, some of them in the front rank around the world; they are more involved in the total life of society than are universities in any other nation.

A system with supreme strength in the sciences; of the Nobel Prize awards in science 5 percent went to Americans before the First World War, 40 percent since the Second. The Boston area and California have become the two science capitals of the world.

A system that doubled quantity and improved quality simultaneously in a single decade—from 1958 to 1968—with mixed financial support, amounting in 1968 to about a one-quarter share each for the federal government and the states and a one-half share for the private sector.

These are accomplishments of considerable note, but they have left in their train a series of questions concerning the policy of the federal government for the decade ahead:

How can the government aid the private institutions, including those under religious control, with public money; select among them in all their diversity; and at the same time preserve their autonomy, enhance their quality where it exists, and encourage their capacity for innovation?

How can it preserve the excellence of the distinguished universities, which are such a great national asset, while increasing their numbers gradually, and still accommodate the equalitarian pressures rampant in American society; and how can it help these leading universities to absorb and accommodate the myriad pressures placed upon them?

How can it preserve the strength in scientific research while offsetting some of the deleterious side effects of less attention to general education at the undergraduate level, of comparative neglect of the humanities and social sciences, of loyalties divided between the institutions and the federal agencies, of loss of integrity while in the hot pursuit of dollars?

How can it administer, in a coordinated fashion, a series of federal programs without establishing undue control in a single national agency; make creative use of the new dependence of nearly all of higher education on federal funds; continue to increase quantity and quality with federal aid?

These questions are legacies of past federal involvement in the development of American higher education.

Questions

1   Is there a necessary connection between sectionalism and states' rights?

2   A major weakness of the Southern Confederacy during the Civil War was its emphasis on states' rights; the resulting lack of unity and cooperation hindered the Confederacy considerably. Despite this historical precedent, the sentiment for states' rights still runs strongest in the South. What factors account for this?

3   Is it practical to attempt to establish a world federal system? Would national differences ruin the chances of its success?

4   What are the major weaknesses of the United Nations?

5   What powers now exercised by individual states would you recommend be transferred to the Federal government? What powers exercised by the Federal government would you recommend be reserved for the states?

6   Would you be in favor of a national education system controlled by the Federal government? What would be the main advantages and disadvantages of such a system?

7   Is the Federal government too powerful today?

5

Ethnic Minorities
and the American Dream

Essay

The Myth of the Melting Pot
Melvin Steinfield

Readings

Anti-Chinese Riots
Betty Lee Sung

Ethnic Groups and the Melting Pot
Nathan Glazer and Daniel P. Moynihan

The American Irish
William Shannon

Recent Trends in Anti-Semitism
Howard M. Sachar

Today's Ghettos
Paul Jacobs and Saul Landau

Is America the land of equal opportunity for all, regardless of "race, creed, or color"? Are you proud of the American image of many races and ethnic backgrounds working together, living together, going to school together? Do you believe that the beauty of the American Dream is accurately represented in the concept of the Melting Pot?
It's a beautiful dream, shared by many. It's one of the world's most beautiful dreams. The question is, how much of a reality is it?
The following essay, and the reading selections which follow it, investigate the Melting Pot concept as dream—and as reality.

The Myth of the Melting Pot

Melvin Steinfield

> But while more than twenty million blacks continue to live in ghettos, while Orientals, Mexicans, and Filipinos remain in their racial enclaves, while millions of white European descendants also cling to their old languages, Americans cling precariously to the idea that their country is truly a great melting pot, even though, from its very beginnings, what has been indissoluble is America's prejudice.
>
> —PAUL JACOBS AND SAUL LANDAU[1]

By 1970 many Americans were beginning to realize that the Melting Pot had just as often been a boiling cauldron of conflict in which the vehement fury of racism and discrimination has never stopped bubbling. Yet, for most of America's history, her theoreticians have painted the concept of the Melting Pot in glorious terms. According to this myth, America is the land of freedom, democracy, and golden opportunity in which people of all races, creeds, and colors are accepted on equal terms. Pride in the assimilation of huge numbers of immigrants is a vital companion to the myth of the Melting Pot.

Thus we find J. Hector St. John de Crèvecoeur, in his *Letters from an American Farmer* (1782), boasting about America as the great asylum for refugees from all over the world:

I could point out to you a family whose grandfather was an Englishman, whose wife was Dutch, whose son married a French woman, and whose present four sons have now four wives of different nations. HE is an American, who, leaving behind him all his ancient prejudices and manners, receives new ones from the new mode of life he has embraced, the new government he obeys, and the new rank he holds. He becomes an American by being received in the broad lap of our great ALMA MATER. Here individuals of all nations are melted into a new race of men, whose labors and posterity will one day cause great changes in the world.

Throughout our history, foreigners as well as natives romanticized the vision of harmony that is part of the Melting Pot. President Theodore Roosevelt said: "We Americans are children of the crucible." In 1908 there was even a play by Israel Zangwill, entitled *The Melting Pot*, which shared the attitude of the other prophets of peaceful fusion.

As recently as 1959 the distinguished historian Arthur M. Schlesinger described the Melting Pot as a great American achievement. Writing in the March, 1959, issue of *The Atlantic Monthly,* in an article entitled "Our Ten Contributions to Civilization," he listed the Melting Pot concept as contribution number five: "America has been in the best sense of the term, a Melting Pot, every ingredient adding its particular element of strength."

Schlesinger continued, "Many other peoples, it is true, are also of mixed origin; but the American achievement stands alone in the scale, thoroughness, and rapidity of process and, above all, in the fact that it has been the outcome not of forcible incorporation but of peaceful absorption."

Schlesinger did acknowledge one crack in the Melting Pot: "Our most tragic failure has involved our Negro citizens, now a tenth of our number." That acknowledgement, which was the sole qualification of an otherwise unrestrained enthusiasm, seems to characterize most of the Melting Pot theorists of the twentieth century: America is truly the great Melting Pot, with the possible exception of the Negro, who is on the verge of total acceptance because America's conscience is about to be touched.

In a sense, the monumental study by Gunnar Myrdal in 1942 (*An American Dilemma*) shared the Melting Pot faith implicitly. It is precisely because we do harbor so dearly the goals of assimilation and equality that we found ourselves in a dilemma. In Australia or South Africa, there can be no dilemma, for there is no Melting Pot. But in America the disparities between the "American Creed," as Myrdal labeled it, on the one hand, and the bitter realities of race relations on the other hand, require some sort of reconciliation.

The concept of the American Dream reinforced the American Dilemma and also shared the vision of the Melting Pot. The nature of the American Dream was articulated in memorable phrases by Dr. Martin Luther King in the speech which climaxed the March on Washington on August 28, 1963. That speech was perhaps the last noble expression of hope that the sons of former slaves and the sons of former slave owners would be able to live together in harmony and in a spirit of brotherly love; the historical climate was changing and the fulfillment of the Dream soon appeared less attainable than ever before.

The Supreme Court decision in 1954 ordering the desegregation of schools marked the beginning of a new era in the history of the Melting Pot. The American Dilemma was at last being confronted head-on. No longer could the gap between the Dream and the reality be ignored.

For a short time there were hopes that the increasing militancy of the civil rights movement, combined with the awakening of American conscience, would result in eventual victory for the cause of "Freedom Now!" It is true that some barriers based on race did topple in the decade after the Brown decision. Bus boycotts, sit-ins, picket lines, demonstrations, freedom rides and freedom schools, and voter registration drives began to make some dents in the walls of apartheid.

By the late 1960s, however, it became increasingly apparent that racism persisted; that resistance to change was just about as high as ever; and that blacks and browns and others were not going to be welcomed into the great crucible. They were going to have to fight their way in. Earlier optimism at token victories now shifted to a mood of despair, distrust, bitterness, and rage. The climate was ripe for separation and nationalism among ethnic minorities. Although there were very early antecedents of black power, the belief that white America had failed its last chance was now so widespread that an unprecedented movement toward black consciousness, black pride, and black self-determination spread rapidly. This new radical consciousness was observed in other minorities as well, notably among Mexican-Americans. Blacks were beginning to reject the Anglo-chosen term "Negro" in favor of "Black." Browns also registered their protest against Anglo-imposed labels as they proudly replaced "Mexican-American" with "Chicano."

In retrospect, we can view 1954 as the start of a ten-year effort to make the Melting Pot succeed, to reconcile the Dilemma, and to fulfill the Dream. Failure led to frustration and then to more vociferous

cries for black power. The Watts riot in 1965 was an important turning point. So was the firing upon James Meredith on his march in
Mississippi in 1966. The assassination of Martin Luther King in 1968
put the finishing touches on the integration movement.

America in the closing years of the decade was a nation in which
deep and broad cracks were widening even though many people were
reluctant to admit it.

This reluctance was shared by President Lyndon Johnson, for,
while his 1965 Howard University address spoke of our failure to establish justice for Negroes as the "one huge wrong of the American
nation," he continued to express faith that we were on the verge of
solving this problem. At the end of the Johnson administration, in
1968, the President's Advisory (Kerner) Commission on Civil Disorders warned of the imminent danger of America's moving toward
two separate societies. Early in 1969, an independent report issued by
the Urban Coalition and Urban America, Inc., entitled *One Year
Later*, found virtually no progress toward ending the white racism
which the Kerner report indicted. By the end of the 1960s it was clear
that the myth of the Melting Pot was shattered because the last-ditch
effort to keep it together had failed resoundingly. America was coming apart at the seams.

In the 1960s the Melting Pot was under fire because it had come to
symbolize an entire set of values that were themselves being subjected
to skeptical scrutiny. As Nathan Glazer and Daniel P. Moynihan
pointed out in *Beyond the Melting Pot* (1963), "The point about the
Melting Pot . . . is that it did not happen."

The promise of the Statue of Liberty notwithstanding, there are
varying degrees of assimilation into American life. While Anglos and
other immigrants from northern and western Europe were "melting,"
blacks were enslaved, sold, denied voting rights, and lynched; Indians
were shoved off the paths of westward expansion and massacred;
Chinese and Japanese were excluded or interred; Mexicans were conquered and oppressed; and other ethnic minorities were victimized to
the point that Oscar Handlin could write, in *Race and Nationality in
American Life*: "Discrimination was the permanent manifestation of
the hostilities bred by racism."

Thus, while the Melting Pot was the outspoken goal of much official policy, there have been opponents to assimilation from the start,
and American history is replete with instances in which those who
have wanted to assimilate have not been permitted to do so.

Without question, black people in America have met the greatest
resistance to their effort to "melt" into the mainstream of American
life.

Discrimination against black people has received considerable authorization from federal, state, and local legislative and constitutional provisions. For example, the United States Constitution contained three clauses which revealed that from the days of the Declaration of Independence and the Constitution, black people were never intended to be included in the Melting Pot. First among the constitutional provisions respecting slavery and an inferior position for Negroes is the manner of tabulating black people for apportionment purposes. Only three out of every five would be counted. That is to say, a slave was three-fifths of a person, according to the United States Constitution. Secondly, Congress was prohibited from interfering with the slave trade for twenty years. Thirdly, fugitive slaves were to be returned to their masters in their home states. State and local laws reinforced this legal inequality.

Not until the 1860s was the Constitution amended to grant black people equal rights to freedom, due process, and voting. Yet the passage of the Thirteenth, Fourteenth, and Fifteenth Amendments did not mark the end of legal discrimination. In fact, many forms of legal discrimination arose in the postwar period. Thirty years after the Civil War, in *Plessy* v. *Ferguson*, the Supreme Court of the United States ruled that "separate but equal" school facilities were permissible. In 1896 school segregation on the basis of race was upheld as constitutional. There are many instances which support the statement that for most of his history in this country, the black man has been living under a system which is saturated with legal requirements that he be segregated.

Gradually, many discriminatory laws have been overthrown. But the process was so gradual that it was 1954 before the Brown decision by the Supreme Court reversed the ruling in *Plessy* v. *Ferguson*. One hundred years after the Fourteenth Amendment, segregation remains the American way of life. The series of civil rights laws passed in the 1960s was calculated to make more explicit the fundamental guarantees of the Fourteenth Amendment. The fact that they were needed speaks for itself.

Failure to enforce earlier laws guaranteeing equal treatment created the need for additional laws which emphasized enforcement. Housing, employment, and education are three areas in which antidiscrimination laws at various governmental levels have been passed with little practical effect.

Changing the laws has taken several centuries, and the problem of enforcement of the new laws remains. Meanwhile a balanced overview must mention antimiscegenation laws which discriminate equally against black and white since they interfere with the free choice of a marriage partner on account of "race." In the early 1940s there were thirty states with antimiscegenation laws that banned black-white marriages.

A list of legal racism ought to mention, if only briefly, the covert laws which were just as effective in "keeping the Negro in his Place" as the more blatant denials of the Melting Pot. Poll taxes and grandfather clauses were effective devices in preventing Negro citizens from voting, especially when punctuated by acts of terror. Voter registration drives in the 1960s were necessary in places such as Mississippi because of the heritage of legal racism. Even well-organized registration drives did not completely succeed in helping all black Mississippians to overcome their fears that attempts to vote would jeopardize the security of their jobs, homes, and lives. It was easy to conclude that:

> America has always been a separatist society. Whether by slave code, the lash, the lynch mob, Jim Crow laws or subtle, covert discrimination, white separatism has held the black man apart from full and equal participation in this society. The traditional wisdom has been that Americans, when challenged with their democratic credo, would ultimately resolve their "dilemma" in favor of fairness. The Movement provided just such a challenge—it dared white America to be what it said it already was. In the wake of the disillusionment and despair that followed the fragmentation of the Movement, America has been forced to acknowledge the truth about itself—it is racist.[2]

Not every group has wanted integration, however. For example, most American Indians were hoping for peaceful coexistence, without sacrificing their unique cultural distinctiveness. This was not to be, however, for from their earliest contacts with white men four hundred years ago to the present day, American Indians have been the victims of a persistent greed for land and an implicit racism which were revealed in a variety of ways. Indians have been lied to, cheated, herded away from their lands like so many cattle, manipulated, brutalized, and decimated. If some managed to survive physical annihilation, they still had to beat back attempts to rob them of their dignity as a people.

Under the pretense of equipping them for assimilation, Indians have been uprooted from their ancient lands and relocated under military supervision in extensive efforts to remove them as far as possible from the mainstream of American life. Nearly four hundred treaties with Indians were broken by the American government before the present century. Wave after wave of Western pioneers (and a sizable number of government agents) took advantage of many opportunities to undermine peaceful relations. Even parcels of land to which Indians had been consigned in the belief that the acreage was valueless were not immune from further encroachments if something valuable was discovered there later on.

Not just the Indians' land and the minerals it contained, but their means of livelihood as well, were the objects of the white man's greed. In 1865 approximately fifteen million head of buffalo—a major source of Indian livelihood—roamed the Great Plains. When buffalo hunting became a white man's sport, railroad expeditions were organized for the luxurious pleasure of white Americans. By 1885 buffalo were nearly extinct. The lack of concern about the consequences of these pastimes for Indian rights or Indian survival characterized the dominant attitude toward Indian culture.

Often the justification for this sustained program of genocide was racist, although there were numerous other factors which played a role. Indians were at best savages, perhaps even subhuman animals. They had no rights worth enumerating in the Constitution. Moreover, subjugation of a native population by an expansionist power was not unique. Americans were simply following the traditions of Western ethnocentrism and racism to justify their plans for territorial acquisition.

Some of the most vivid expressions of white racism are part of the official record of Indian relations. Consider the significance of the following statement which was made by Commissioner W. A. Jones in the *Annual Report of the Commissioner of Indian Affairs for 1903*:

It is probably true that the majority of our wild Indians have no inherited tendencies whatever toward morality or chastity, according to an enlightened standard. Chastity and morality among them must come from education and contact with the better element of the whites.

Three-quarters of a century before Indian Commissioner Jones was spouting off his racist notions, President Andrew Jackson stood firm in his refusal to enforce a Supreme Court decision which upheld Cherokee Indian rights in Georgia. The subsequent shocking mistreatment of the tribe which was being denied its rights by an American President revealed the extent to which the majority of Americans were willing to look the other way while bigotry prevailed.

Surely here was one crack in the Melting Pot that would not be easily ignored when Americans began to inspect the Melting Pot with two open eyes. In the late 1960s, when the Melting Pot myth was being challenged, Indian grievances were entering the field of majority awareness. Textbooks were beginning to be more forthright in their statements about Indian-American relations, as the following example shows:

All the nonwhite minorities in American California suffered from various kinds of unjust discrimination, but the mistreatment of the Indians began earliest and was far the worst. Between 1846 and 1900 about one-tenth of the California Indians were victims of outright genocide, while disease and starvation killed many more. In California, as in other parts of the United States, the history of American treatment of the Indians in the nineteenth century was too often a sickening record of racist murder and sanctimonious fraud.[3]

But if Americans are becoming more honest with themselves about the myth of the Melting Pot, and about the many examples of racism and discrimination which contradict the myth, there are still areas that have been covered up from general public awareness. The experience of Chinese and Japanese in America helps illustrate this clearly.

On the basis of their skin color and other "race-related" superficial features which serve to distinguish them from the Anglo-Saxon physical stereotype, Chinese and Japanese in America have been subjected to a long catalog of racist experiences. Fears of "coolie-labor" competition, mob ravages of Chinese sections of town, exclusion laws, court decisions, concentration camps, and constitutional provisions— the list is long and the message is crisp: neither Chinese nor Japanese have fit conveniently into the WASP mold. Immigrants from the Orient have been punished for not wanting to assimilate at the same time they were punished for trying to assimilate. The most elemental civil rights were denied them until very recently in our history.

Even in a nation which deliberately whitewashes its racist history, certain glaring anomalies have filtered out to the general public. Thus, most Americans do know something about the Gentlemen's Agreement in 1907 and the relocation camps in 1942. But the whole story of anti-Oriental racism is not a matter of common knowledge. The concentration camps were not just a single error, but were rather the culmination of a half-century of hatred between Americans, especially those in California, and Japanese.

The Chinese experienced an even longer history of anti-Oriental racism in this country. This was particularly true in California. For example, in *People* v. *Hall*, in 1854, the Chief Justice of the California Supreme Court, Hugh C. Murray, declared the Chinese to be legally Indians, since both were presumed to have descended from the same Asiatic ancestor. In practice, this prohibited the Chinese from testifying in court against a white man because in 1850 a California state law forbade Negroes and Indians from testifying in court for or against a white man. In 1863 the ban was removed for Negroes, but not until 1872 was it removed for Indians and Chinese.

How many Americans are aware that in *Gong Lum* v. *Rice,* in 1927, the United States Supreme Court upheld the right of local school districts to compel Chinese students to attend Negro schools out of their immediate neighborhood instead of white schools in their own neighborhoods?

How many Americans know that Article XIX of the California Constitution, which was in effect from 1879 to 1952, prohibited corporations from hiring Chinese and prohibited the hiring of Chinese on "any state, county, municipal, or other public work, except in punishment for crime"? Antimiscegenation statutes similar to those directed against white-Negro intermarriages specify "Chinese" or "Mongolian" or "Oriental" in several states.

The concept of "Yellow Peril" symbolized the white racist response to Oriental immigrants. It revealed another crack in the Melting Pot.

Today Americans have come to recognize that the roots of the present turmoil in race and ethnic relations go back deep into our history. Blacks, Indians, Chinese, Japanese are just a few of the examples of the breakdown of the Melting Pot. Many other groups have experienced, and are still experiencing, difficulty with the concept. Either they have believed in it, and have been rejected in their efforts to achieve assimilation; or else they have not wanted to reject their own cultural values, yet have had to fight off efforts to make them conform to the myth which those in the majority held.

Whether one is seeking to understand America's past, or its present, or its future, it is not all a wasted effort to attempt to examine the myth of the Melting Pot. In the selections which follow this introductory essay, noted authorities explore the subject further. They offer additional evidence which needs to be taken into consideration in attempting to answer one of the most critical questions of our day: "Is there still hope for the eventual realization of the American Melting Pot Dream?"

Notes

1   Paul Jacobs and Saul Landau, "To Serve the Devil," *The Center Magazine*, Vol. No. 2, March, 1969, p. 48.

2   Haywood Burns, "Equal—But Separate?" *Civil Liberties*, No. 260, February, 1969, p. 13.

3   Walton Bean, *California: An Interpretive History* (New York, McGraw-Hill, 1968), p. 508.

In this summary of late nineteenth-century racist rampages, Betty Lee
Sung enumerates the anti-Chinese riots that took place in California
and examines the reasons why sentiment against the Chinese
was so murderous.

Anti-Chinese Riots

Betty Lee Sung

In this explosive social, economic, and political climate, the heavy
concentration of Chinese in California made them a convenient
scapegoat for the relief of pent-up frustrations and emotions. In 1870
there were sixty-three thousand Chinese in the United States, ninety-
nine percent of whom were on the West Coast. Every tenth person in
California in 1860 was Chinese. Their large numbers, their physical
differences, the retention of their national dress, the custom of wearing their hair in pigtails, their habits and traditions, so incomprehen-
sible to the Occidental mind, made them an easy target to spot.

When employment with the railroad ceased, the Chinese sought
work in the mines, on the farms, in land reclamation, in domestic service, and in the cigar and woolen factories. These were jobs which the
white man scorned, for the white man was looking for a quick bonan-
za. Nevertheless, they were jobs that gave the Chinese employment
while the white man was out of work.

So whereas the Chinese had been praised for their industry, their
honesty, their thrift, and their peaceful ways, they were now charged
with being debased and servile coolies, clannish, dangerous, deceitful,
and vicious. They were accused of being contract laborers, although
there was not a shred of evidence to show that the Chinese were anything but Argonauts* of a different skin coloring. Degenerate traits
were ascribed to them, in direct contradiction of the praises heaped
upon them a few years earlier. The workingmen accused them of un-

From *Mountain of Gold* by Betty Lee Sung. Reprinted by permission of The
Macmillan Company. Copyright © 1970 by Betty Lee Sung.

*A term used to denote persons who went to California in 1849 in search of
gold. From the Greek legend of Jason and the Argonauts who sought the
Golden Fleece.

dermining the white man's standard of living. It was alleged they would work for less because they subsisted on next to nothing. The word was spread that the land and rail companies hired Chinese instead of white men because the Chinese accepted employment at any price. Yet the books kept by Charles Crocker of the Central Pacific showed that white men were paid at the rate of thirty-five dollars per month plus keep, and the Chinese were paid thirty-five dollars per month without keep, mainly because the Chinese preferred cooking their own food.

The charge of accepting slave wages was shortly disproved after the exclusion laws took effect. The drastic curtailment in immigration brought about a shortage of Chinese laborers. Quick to take advantage of the situation, Chinese laborers demanded and got higher wages for their services—this in spite of a surplus in white labor.

However, reason and fact could not prevail. Elmer Clarence Sandmeyer wrote: ['] . . . there would have been a depression in the 1870s if the entire population had been made up of lineal descendants of George Washington. . . . If the Chinese in California were white people, being in all other respects what they are, I do not believe that the complaints and warfare against them would have existed to any considerable extent. ['] [1] But once the charges were made, they spread like a prairie fire, fanned red-hot by Denis Kearney.*

Kearney invariably began his speeches with an attack upon the monopolies—the rich, huge corporate enterprises. He pointed out their owners' ornate mansions on Nob Hill and blamed these moguls for the plight of the workingmen. He accused the Chinese of working hand-in-hand with monopolies, of accepting slave wages, and of robbing the white man of his job. His wrath was directed against both the Chinese and the land and rail monopolies, but the latter were powerful, impregnable, organized, while the Chinese were docile, eager to avoid conflict, and ineffectual in court because their testimony could not be accepted as evidence. Kearney's speeches always ended with the slogan, "The Chinese must go!" So the blame fell upon the Chinese, and thus supplied with a hate object, the frenzied, incited mob would dash off to another orgy of attacks upon the defenseless Chinese.

During this period, the Chinese were stoned and robbed, assaulted and murdered. Hoodlums would organize attacks against the Chinese camps as sport, for they knew the Chinese could not obtain redress.

*The California labor agitator who organized the Workingmen's Party.

In the spring of 1876, the Chinese were driven from small towns and camps, their quarters burned. Some Chinese were killed or injured. In June of 1876, a violent attack was made upon them at Truckee.

In 1877, employers of Chinese labor in Chico received threatening letters. In March of that year, six tenant farmers were attacked and five killed. The murderer who was caught confessed to being under orders from the Workingmen's Party.

In July 1877, a great riot broke loose. Twenty-five wash houses were burned, and there followed an outbreak of riots. For months afterwards, no Chinese was safe on the streets. Arson and personal abuse spread to adjacent counties. Chinese laundries were burned, and when occupants tried to escape, they were shot or left to die in flaming buildings.

In 1878, the entire Chinese population of Truckee was rounded up and driven from town.

In 1885, the infamous massacre of twenty-eight Chinese in Rock Springs, Wyoming, occurred. Many others were wounded and hundreds were driven from their homes.

In 1886, Log Cabin, Oregon, was the scene of another brutal massacre.

Professor Mary Coolidge wrote: "During the years of Kearneyism, it is a wonder that any Chinese remained alive in the United States."

Murdering Chinese became such a commonplace occurrence that the newspapers seldom bothered to print the stories. Police officials winked at the attacks, and politicians all but incited more of the same. There were thousands of cases of murder, robbery, and assault, but in only two or three instances were the guilty brought to justice.

If murders were commonplace, the indignities, abuse, brutalities, and injustices practiced against the Chinese were outrageous. An old-timer told of the indignities he suffered at the hands of drunken white men:

> Every Saturday night, we never knew whether we would live to see the light of day. We operated a laundry near a mining camp. Saturday was the night for the miners to get drunk. They would force their way into our shop, wrest the clean white bundles from the shelves and trample the shirts which we so laboriously finished. If the shirts were torn, we were forced to pay for the damages. One night, one of the miners hit his face against the flat side of an iron. He went away, but we knew that our lives were now in danger so we fled, leaving all of our possessions and

money behind. The miner came back with a mob who ransacked our shop, robbed us of the $360 that was our combined savings and set fire to the laundry. We were lucky to escape with our lives, so we came east.

Whereas most Chinese had gone straight to San Francisco upon their arrival in the United States, they now began to disperse. Some had already gone north to work on the Northern Pacific and Canadian Pacific Railroads. Others sought work in the silver and coal mines of Nevada, Oregon, Wyoming, and Colorado. But prejudice and hatred confronted them everywhere. The anti-Chinese sentiments had spread like a cancerous growth to other parts of the West.

On February 11, 1870, a joint resolution passed the legislature of the territory of Colorado, affirming the desirability of Chinese immigration.

The preamble stated that the immigration of Chinese labor to Colorado was calculated to hasten the development and early prosperity of the territory by supplying the demand for cheap labor. It was, therefore, resolved that such immigration should be encouraged by legislation that would guarantee the immigrants security of their persons and property.[2]

Ten years later, the seeds of hatred sprouted in Colorado. Anti-Chinese feelings reached their pitch in Denver for the November elections, and these feelings soon gave way to open violence.

There were two versions to the story of how one riot started. The *Rocky Mountain News* version was that a Chinese laundryman charged ten cents more than a white customer was willing to pay. An argument ensued, whereupon the Chinese slapped the white man in the face with a knife. The injured man ran into the streets and a crowd gathered, so the Chinese fired a gun into the crowd.

The other version was revealed in a government publication as a result of an investigation to determine if indemnity was due the Chinese. The riots, said the government publication, began when a game of chance between two Chinese was broken up by a couple of drunken white men. Both versions then agreed about the crowd that gathered.

Because only fifteen policemen were on the Denver force, the mayor called out the fire department, promising the crowd a drenching if they did not disperse. The crowd became so angry that they began a destructive rampage lasting throughout the night. Every Chinese laundry, business, and home was destroyed. The mayor, with his pitiful law-enforcement staff, was helpless. An appeal was made to the governor for help. A light artillery battery and the governor's guards were dispatched to Denver. The Chinese were rounded up and locked in jail for their own safety. One Chinese was killed and several white men wounded, but the homes and property of the Chinese were completely destroyed.

Notes

1 Elmer Clarence Sandmeyer, *The Anti-Chinese Movement in California* (Urbana, Ill., University of Illinois Press, 1939), p. 88. [Sandmeyer was quoting Senator Morton.]

2 "The Chinese in Colorado," *Colorado Magazine,* October, 1952, p. 273.

The following selection discusses the importance of ethnicity in New York City and its relationship to the Melting Pot theory.

Ethnic Groups and the Melting Pot

Nathan Glazer and Daniel P. Moynihan

Perhaps the meaning of ethnic labels will yet be erased in America. But it has not yet worked out this way in New York. It is true that immigrants to this country were rapidly transformed, in comparison with immigrants to other countries, that they lost their languages and altered their culture. It was reasonable to believe that a new American type would emerge, a new nationality in which it would be a matter of indifference whether a man was of Anglo-Saxon or German or Italian or Jewish origin, and in which indeed, because of the diffusion of populations through all parts of the country and all levels of the social order, and because of the consequent close contact and intermarriage, it would be impossible to make such distinctions. This may still be the most likely result in the long run. After all, in 1960 almost half of New York City's population was still foreign-born or the children of foreign-born. Yet it is also true that it is forty years since the end of mass immigration, and new processes, scarcely visible when our chief concern was with the great masses of immigrants and the problems of their "Americanization," now emerge to surprise us. The initial notion of an American Melting Pot did not, it seems, quite grasp what would happen in America. At least it did not grasp what would happen in the short run, and since this short run encompasses at least the length of a normal lifetime, it is not something we can ignore.

It is true that language and culture are very largely lost in the first and second generations, and this makes the dream of "cultural pluralism"—of a new Italy or Germany or Ireland in America, a League of Nations established in the New World—as unlikely as the hope of a Melting Pot. But as the groups were transformed by influences in American society, stripped of their original attributes, they were re-created as something new, but still as identifiable groups. Concretely,

persons think of themselves as members of that group, with that
name; they are thought of by others as members of that group, with
that name; and most significantly, they are linked to other members of
the group by new attributes that the original immigrants would never
have recognized as identifying their group, but which nevertheless
serve to mark them off, by more than simply name and association, in
the third generation and even beyond.

The assimilating power of American Society and culture operated
on immigrant groups in different ways, to make them, it is true, something they had not been, but still something distinct and identifiable.
The impact of assimilating trends on the groups is different in part
because the groups are different—Catholic peasants from southern
Italy were affected differently, in the same city and the same time,
from urbanized Jewish workers and merchants from eastern Europe.
We cannot even begin to indicate how various were the characteristics
of family structure, religion, economic experience and attitudes, educational experience and attitudes, [and] political outlook that differentiated groups from such different backgrounds. Obviously, some
American influences worked on them in common and with the same
effects. But their differences meant they were open to different parts
of American experience, interpreted it in different ways, used it for
different ends. In the third generation, the descendants of the immigrants confronted each other, and knew they were both Americans, in
the same dress, with the same language, using the same artifacts,
troubled by the same things; but they voted differently, had different
ideas about education and sex, and were still, in many essential ways,
as different from one another as their grandfathers had been.

The initial attributes of the groups provided only one reason why
their transformations did not make them all into the same thing.
There was another reason—and that was the nature of American society itself, which could not, or did not, assimilate the immigrant
groups fully or in equal degree. Or perhaps the nature of human society in general. It is only the experience of the strange and foreign that
teaches us how provincial we are. A hundred thousand Negroes have
been enough to change the traditional British policy of free immigration from the colonies and dominions. Japan finds it impossible to
incorporate into the body of its society anyone who does not look
Japanese, or even the Koreans, indistinguishable very often in appearance and language from Japanese. And we shall test the racial attitudes
of the Russians only when there are more than a few Negroes passing
through as curiosities; certainly the inability of Russians to get over
anti-Semitism does not suggest they are any different from the rest of

mankind. In any case, the word "American" was an unambiguous reference to nationality only when it was applied to a relatively homogeneous social body consisting of immigrants from the British Isles, with relatively small numbers from nearby European countries. When the numbers of those not of British origin began to rise, the word "American" became a far more complicated thing. Legally, it meant a citizen. Socially, it lost its identifying power, and when you asked a man what he was (in the United States), "American" was not the answer you were looking for. In the United States it became a slogan, a political gesture, sometimes an evasion, but not a matter-of-course, concrete social description of a person. Just as in certain languages a word cannot stand alone but needs some particle to indicate its function, so in the United States the word "American" does not stand by itself. If it does, it bears the additional meaning of patriot, "authentic" American, critic and opponent of "foreign" ideologies.

The original Americans became "old" Americans, or "old stock," or "white Anglo-Saxon Protestants," or some other identification which indicated they were not immigrants or descendants of recent immigrants. These original Americans already had a frame in their minds, which became a frame in reality, that placed and ordered those who came after them. Those who were like them could easily join them. It was important to be white, of British origin, and Protestant. If one was all three, then even if one was an immigrant, one was really not an immigrant, or not for long.

Thus, even before it knew what an Italian or Jew or an Irishman was like, the American mind had a place for the category, high or low, depending on color, on religion, on how close the group was felt to be [to] the Anglo-Saxon center. There were pecularities in this placing. Why, for example, were the Germans placed higher than the Irish? There was of course an interplay to some extent between what the group actually was and where it was placed, and, since the German immigrants were less impoverished than the Irish and somewhat more competent craftsmen and farmers, this undoubtedly affected the old American's image of them. Then ideology came in to emphasize the common links between Englishmen and Germans, who, even though they spoke different languages, were said to be really closer to each other than the old Americans were to the English-speaking, but Catholic and Celtic, Irish. If a group's first representatives were cultured and educated, those who came after might benefit, unless they were so numerous as to destroy the first image. Thus, German Jews who arrived in the 1840s and 1850s benefited from their own characteristics and their link with Germans, until they were overwhelmed by the large number of East European Jewish immigrants after 1880. A new wave of German Jewish immigrants, in the 1930s, could not, regardless of culture and education, escape the low position of being "Jewish."

The ethnic group in American society became not a survival from the age of mass immigration but a new social form. One could not predict from its first arrival what it might become or, indeed, whom it might contain. The group is not a purely biological phenomenon. The Irish of today do not consist of those who are descended from Irish immigrants. Were we to follow the history of the germ plasm alone— if we could—we should find that many in the group really came from other groups, and that many who should be in the group are in other groups. The Protestants among them, and those who do not bear distinctly Irish names, may now consider themselves, and be generally considered, as much "old American" as anyone else. The Irish-named offspring of German or Jewish or Italian mothers often find that willy-nilly they have become Irish. It is even harder for the Jewish-named offspring of mixed marriages to escape from the Jewish group; neither Jews nor non-Jews will let them rest in ambiguity.

Parts of the group are cut off; other elements join the group as allies. Under certain circumstances, strange as it may appear, it is an advantage to be able to take on a group name, even of a low order, if it can be made to fit, and if it gives one certain advantages. It is better in Oakland, California, to be a Mexican than an Indian, and so some of the few Indians call themselves, at certain times, for certain occasions, "Mexicans." In the forming of ethnic groups subtle distinctions are overridden; there is an advantage to belonging to a big group, even if it is looked down upon. West Indian Negroes achieve important political positions, as representatives of Negroes; Spaniards and Latin-Americans become the representatives of Puerto Ricans; German Jews rose to Congress from districts dominated by East European Jews.

Ethnic groups then, even after distinctive language, customs, and culture are lost, as they largely were in the second generation, and even more fully in the third generation, are continually recreated by new experiences in America. The mere existence of a name itself is perhaps sufficient to form group character in new situations, for the name associates an individual, who actually can be anything, with a certain past, country, race. But as a matter of fact, someone who is Irish or Jewish or Italian generally has other traits than the mere existence of the name that associates him with other people attached to the group. A man is connected to his group by ties of family and friendship. But he is also connected by ties of *interest*. The ethnic groups in New York are also *interest groups*.

This is perhaps the single most important fact about ethnic groups in New York City. When one speaks of the Negroes and Puerto Ricans, one also means unorganized and unskilled workers, who hold poorly paying jobs in the laundries, hotels, restaurants, [and] small factories or who are on relief. When one says Jews, one also means small shopkeepers, professionals, [and] better-paid skilled workers in the garment industries. When one says Italians, one also means homeowners in Staten Island, the North Bronx, Brooklyn, and Queens.

If state legislation threatens to make it more difficult to get relief, this is headline news in the Puerto Rican press—for the group is affected—and news of much less importance to the rest of the press. The interplay between rational economic interests and the other interests or attitudes that stem out of group history makes for an incredibly complex political and social situation. Consider the local laws against discrimination in housing. Certain groups that face discrimination want such laws—Negroes, Puerto Ricans, and Jews. Jews meet little discrimination in housing in New York but have an established ideological commitment to all antidiscrimination laws. Apartment-house owners are against any restriction of their freedom or anything that might affect their profits. In New York, this group is also largely Jewish, but it is inhibited in pushing strongly against such laws by its connnections with the Jewish community. Private homeowners see this as a threat to their homogeneous neighborhoods. These are largely German, Irish, and Italian. The ethnic background of the homeowners links them to communities with a history of anti-Negro feelings. The Irish and Italian immigrants have both at different times competed directly with Negro labor.

In the analysis, then, of the conflict over antidiscrimination laws, "rational" economic interests and the "irrational," or at any rate non-economic, interests and attitudes tied up with one's own group are inextricably mixed together. If the rational interests did not operate, some of the older groups would by now be much weaker than they are. The informal and formal social groupings that make up these communities are strengthened by the fact that Jews can talk about the garment business, Irish about politics and the civil service, Italians about the state of the trucking or contracting or vegetable business.

In addition to the links of interest, family and fellow feeling bind the ethnic group. There is satisfaction in being with those who are like oneself. The ethnic group is something of an extended family or tribe.

And aside from ties of feeling and interest, there are concrete ties of organization. Certain types of immigrant social organization have declined, but others have been as ingenious in remolding and recreating themselves as the group itself. The city is often spoken of as the place of anonymity, of the breakdown of some kind of preexisting social order. The ethnic group, as Oscar Handlin has pointed out, served to create a new form of order. Those who came in with some kind of disadvantage, created by a different language, a different religion, a different race, found both comfort and material support in creating various kinds of organizations. American social services grew up in large part to aid incoming immigrant groups. Many of these were limited to a single religious or ethnic group. Ethnic groups set up hospitals, old people's homes, loan funds, charitable organizations, as well as churches and cultural organizations. The initial need for a separate set of welfare and health institutions became weaker as the group became more prosperous and as the government took over these functions, but the organizations nevertheless continued. New York organizational life is in large measure lived within ethnic bounds. These organizations generally have religious names, for it is more acceptable that welfare and health institutions should cater to religious than to ethnic communities. But of course religious institutions are generally closely linked to a distinct ethnic group. The Jewish (religious) organizations are Jewish (ethnic); Catholic are generally Irish or Italian, now with the Puerto Ricans as important clients; the Protestant organizations are white Protestant—which means generally old American, with a smaller German wing—in leadership, with Negroes as their chief clients.

Thus many elements—history, family and [fellow] feeling, interest, formal organizational life—operate to keep much of New York life channeled within the bounds of the ethnic group. Obviously, the rigidity of this channeling of social life varies from group to group. For the Puerto Ricans, a recent immigrant group with a small middle class and speaking a foreign language, the ethnic group serves as the setting for almost all social life. For Negroes too, because of discrimination and poverty, most social life is limited to the group itself. Jews and Italians are still to some extent recent immigrants, and despite the growing middle-class character of the Jewish group, social life for both is generally limited to other members of the group. But what about the Irish and the Germans?

Probably, many individuals who by descent "belong" to one of these older groups go through a good part of their lives with no special consciousness of the fact. It may be only under very special circumstances that one becomes aware of the matter at all—such as if one wants to run for public office. The political realm, indeed, is least willing to consider such matters a purely private affair. Consciousness of one's ethnic background may be intermittent. It is only on occasion that someone may think of or be reminded of his background, and perhaps become self-conscious about the pattern formed by his family, his friends, his job, his interests. Obviously, this ethnic aspect of a man's life is more important if he is part of one group than if he is part of another; if he is Negro, he can scarcely escape it, and if he is of German origin, little will remind him of it.

Conceivably the fact that one's origins can become only a memory suggests the general direction for ethnic groups in the United States—toward assimilation and absorption into a homogeneous American mass. And yet, as we suggested earlier, it is hard to see in the New York of the 1960s just how this comes about. Time alone does not dissolve the groups if they are not close to the Anglo-Saxon center. Color marks off a group, regardless of time; and perhaps more significantly, the "majority" group, to which assimilation should occur, has taken on the color of an ethnic group, too. To what does one assimilate in modern America? The "American" in abstract does not exist, though some sections of the country, such as the Far West, come closer to realizing him than does New York City. There are test cases of such assimilation in the past. The old Scotch-Irish group, an important ethnic group of the early nineteenth century, is now for the most part simply old American, "old stock." Old Dutch families have become part of the upper class of New York. But these test cases merely reveal to us how partial was the power of the old American type to assimilate—it assimilated its ethnic cousins.

Anti-Irish prejudices reached epidemic proportions during the mid-nineteenth century, as shown by the following discussion of nativist reactions to Irish immigration.

The American Irish

William Shannon

The natives responded [to the Irish] in convulsive bursts of violence and prolonged withdrawals. A native mob burned a convent in Charlestown, Massachusetts in 1831; another mob sacked a Catholic Church in Philadelphia in 1846; respectable ministers and civic leaders endorsed the comic opera "disclosures" of Maria Monk in the late 1830s; and reputable politicians flirted with organized bigotry on and off for thirty years, culminating in the brief Know-Nothing upheaval of 1854–1858. Meanwhile, Yankee employers everywhere in the seaboard cities published advertisements, "No Irish Need Apply." It is not easy to distinguish to what extent the nativist crusade of these three decades was directed against Catholicism as such or against the Irish, but it appears that the prevailing motive was an antipathy to the Irish as an alien group. They threatened the patterns of job and trade competition, the old values, the homogeneity of the once-small cities. Religious sentiment was probably an available, respectable pretext rather than the motive for action. The old community, particularly its lower-middle class and working class, feeling threatened, found the religious differences an easy rationale, sanctioned by the anti-Catholic tradition of the colonial era. The Irish workingman in the next block and not the Pope in Rome was the real enemy.[1]

The raid on the Charlestown convent represented the first *démarche* of the Boston workingmen against the Irish. It was also a gesture of defiance against a darkening future. Boston in 1830 was economically a sick city; only half of the persons born there in 1790 still dwelt in the city by 1820. Only emigration from the farming hinterland prevented the city from suffering an absolute shrinkage in population. The old trade with the Far East, the glittering superstructure of

From *The American Irish* by William Shannon. Reprinted by permission of The Macmillan Company. © 1963 by William V. Shannon.

the city's former maritime supremacy, had declined. New York, even before the opening of the Erie Canal in 1825, had pulled ahead in prosperity. The growth of factory towns along nearby rivers where electric current was cheap provided Boston entrepreneurs with new wealth, but afforded native craftsmen a glimpse of a dark future in which the factory system would be triumphant.[2] Hemmed in by these pressures, the workingmen searched for a scapegoat.

The imposing red-brick convent conducted by the Ursuline Nuns on the crest of Mount Benedict Hill in Charlestown across the Charles River from Boston was a convenient symbol. Ironically, the pupils in this convent, established in 1818, were drawn largely not from Catholic but from wealthy liberal Protestant homes. The hold of orthodox Congregationalism was breaking down under the impact of liberal Unitarian and Transcendentalist ideas about religion. A number of parents who desired a more cosmopolitan kind of education for their daughters than could be obtained in the female seminaries run by the Congregational Church entered them in the Ursuline Convent. All the hatreds born of the struggle then going on between liberal and Fundamentalist religion in Massachusetts thus became centered on the Charlestown convent. "To the lower classes, with whom Congregationalism was a sacred creed, Catholics and Unitarians seemed to be combining against their religion."

On Sunday evening, August 11, 1831, after weeks of rising tension, a mob gathered before the convent. The mother superior pleaded with the crowd to go away. When her entreaties failed, she tried intimidation. "The bishop has twenty thousand Irishmen at his command in Boston," she cried.

Her threat was not only injudicious but also inaccurate (it is doubtful if there were that many Irish adults in Boston in that year). By prearranged signal, mob leaders ignited barrels of tar in a neighboring field. Fire bells began ringing. Hundreds of persons streamed up the hill to join the crowd and watch the fun. As midnight approached, a gang of forty or fifty men forced their way into the convent. The mother superior, the dozen nuns, and some sixty frightened pupils fled by the rear entrance. The gang set fire to the building and a neighboring farmhouse owned by the order. The crowd stood and cheered as the two buildings went down in flames.

Eight men were ultimately accused of arson in connection with the burning of the convent, but their trial was an orgy of anti-Catholic prejudice. All but one was swiftly acquitted, and the latter was pardoned soon after when leading Boston Catholics, in a gesture of conciliation, signed a petition asking clemency. The nuns resumed teaching a year later in another Boston suburb, but few pupils cared to risk studying with them. In 1838 the Ursulines abandoned their work in Boston and withdrew to Canada.[3]

The burning of the convent brought the smoldering fires of anti-Catholic, anti-Irish feeling to the surface of national life. Equally incendiary in its own way was the publication in 1836 of Maria Monk's *Awful Disclosures*. In this inspired work of fiction, the author told of her education in a Catholic convent in Montreal, her conversion to Catholicism, her decision to become a nun, and her subsequent shocking discoveries. The mother superior of the convent instructed her, she reported, to "obey the priests in all things," and this, she discovered, meant "to live in practice of criminal intercourse with them." The children born of these liaisons were, she reported, baptized and immediately strangled. Nuns who refused to cooperate were murdered. Hers was a colorful picture of convent life complete with mass graves in the basement, a secret passageway to the priest's quarters, and midnight orgies. Maria explained that having become pregnant after relations with a priest, she had fled to New York to save the life of her unborn child.

Awful Disclosures, which apparently was ghosted by a professional writer, had a tremendous vogue. Maria was taken up by a sponsoring committee of Protestant clergymen and enjoyed a brief personal success. But then her mother in Montreal disclosed that Maria had never been a resident in the convent described in the book, that she had instead been in a Catholic asylum for delinquent girls, and had run away with the help of a former boyfriend, the probable father of her child. Maria's associates in the writing of the book cheated her out of most of the profits. When she gave birth to a second fatherless child, she did not bother to name him after a priest. One Protestant journal insisted her second pregnancy was arranged by crafty Jesuits to discredit her revelations, but the explanation did not catch on. Her respectable defenders deserted her, and she disappeared into obscurity. Years later she was arrested for picking the pockets of a man in a house of prostitution, and she died in prison. But the book outlived its nominal author. It went through twenty printings, sold three hundred thousand copies, and down to the Civil War served as the "Uncle Tom's Cabin" of the Know-Nothing movement.[4]

The most serious outburst of violence came in Philadelphia, the City of Brotherly Love. In 1843 Bishop Francis Kenrick persuaded the school board to permit Catholic children to read the Douai rather than the King James Version of the Bible in the public schools. Catholic children were also excused from the religious instruction that was then a customary part of the curriculum. Nativists attacked the decision as interference by a "foreign prelate" in American education. Mass meetings were held in Independence Square to denounce the change. In May, 1844, a Protestant group invaded the Philadelphia suburb of Kensington, an industrial section where the Irish predominated, to hold a protest meeting. This gesture of defiance produced street fighting in which the Irish drove off their antagonists. The nativists then called a mass meeting for the following Monday, May 6, in the same neighborhood and appealed to their supporters to turn out in force. The second meeting resulted in a far more serious melee in which one man was killed. This pitched battle touched off three days of general rioting. Protestant mobs roamed the streets of Kensington, setting blocks of houses in flames, and burning two Catholic churches.

An uneasy quiet reigned for several weeks. Then, on July 4, the holiday was converted into a testimonial to those nativist dead who had fallen in the May rioting. Seventy thousand persons paraded behind the carriages of the widows and children of these men in downtown Philadelphia. The next day street fighting broke out again. This time the focus of attack was St. Philip de Neri Church in Southwark, another suburb, where the pastor had stored guns in the basement of the church as a precautionary measure. When the rumor of the existence of this cache spread, hostile crowds gathered. Separate searches by the sheriff and by a committee of twenty drawn from members of the crowd turned up eighty-seven guns and a quantity of ammunition. When the crowd still did not disperse, the governor sent militia to protect the church. By nightfall of the second day, "a company of troops had turned the square on which the church was located into an armed fortress with barricades erected and cannon commanding the principal avenues of approach." The rioters obtained a cannon of their own and fired into the soldiers massed before the church doors. The troops returned the attack, and the sound of cannon and musket fire rang across the square for several hours.

Meanwhile, gangs roamed the streets looking for Irishmen. Priests and nuns went into hiding. Thousands of Catholics fled the city. Before these days of open civil war had passed, thirteen persons had been killed and more than fifty were wounded, most of them nativists who had engaged the militia in combat.[5]

The burning of churches and the open war in the streets in Philadelphia caused a strong backlash of public disapproval of the nativists.

The middle and upper classes drew back in fear from a movement that seemed to be reenacting the horrors of the French Revolution. The diary entries of a wealthy New Yorker, George Templeton Strong, record the change in opinion in respectable circles during that tumultuous spring and early summer. On April 10 he rejoiced in the victory of the nativists in the New York municipal elections:

"Hurrah for the natives!" he wrote. "Such a blow hasn't fallen on the Hibernian race since the days of Earl Strongbow."

On May 8, when news reached New York of the first outbreak of rioting, he wrote: "Great row in Philadelphia. . . . This'll be a great thing for the natives, strengthen their hands amazingly if judiciously used."

Two months later when the fighting broke forth again, he took a darker view. "Civil war raging [in Philadelphia]," he wrote on July 8. "Mob pelting the military, not with paving stones, but with grapeshot and scrap iron out of ten-pounders; the state of things in that city is growing worse and worse every day."

"I shan't be voting for a 'native' ticket again in a hurry," he concluded.[6]

The nativist movement rose and fell in successive waves of passion. In reaction to the episodes in Philadelphia, the movement ebbed for nearly a decade. It did not, however, go out of existence. By the 1840s a broad network of native societies, religious propaganda organizations, magazines, and newspapers was in existence. Books attacking Catholics had become staples in the publishing industry. One writer observed as early as 1835 that the abuse of Catholics "is a regular trade and the compilation of anti-Catholic books . . . has become a part of the regular industry of the country, as much as the making of nutmegs or the construction of clocks."

The last great surge of nativism came in 1854 with the emergence of the American, or Know-Nothing, party. (The party drew its name from the fact that members of the Order of the Star-Spangled Banner, a secret nativist organization, when asked about their activities said, "I know nothing.") In the elections of 1854–1855, the Know-Nothings scored unexpectedly sweeping victories. The party and its allies carried Maryland, Delaware, Kentucky, and most of New England and showed strength in other parts of the country. About seventy-five congressmen were elected, pledged to do battle against the Pope and his American adherents. The size of the victory was deceptive. In retrospect, it is clear that the Know-Nothing party was a halfway house for voters seeking a new political home. The ravaging struggle over slavery was tearing apart the dying Whig party and transforming the Democratic party. The new Republican party, pledged to halt the extension of slavery, had just been born. In this period of rapid political flux, the Know-Nothings represented an effort to divert attention away from the slavery issue to the "safer" issues of anti-Catholicism and anti-immigration about which the native community could more easily agree.

Massachusetts was the stronghold of the Know-Nothings. There they captured the governorship, all state offices, and huge majorities in both houses of the legislature. The election represented a real coming to power of the embittered lower classes of the native community. Of the 378 members of the lower house of the legislature, only 34 had ever served in office before. The great majority were "mechanics, laborers, clerks, school teachers, and ministers who understood nothing of the governmental processes and were ill-equipped to learn." The disorganized, disorderly legislative session passed little important legislation. A committee appointed to investigate convents became the butt of jokes in the newspapers. On a visit to Lowell, members of the committee charged to the state their liquor bills and also expenses incurred in their off-duty relations with a lady "answering to the name of Mrs. Patterson." The scandal became so great the legislature canceled the rest of the investigation and expelled the chairman of the committee from the legislature. Before adjourning, the members voted themselves a pay increase. At the next election, only one-sixth of the members were reelected.[7]

The fiasco in Massachusetts and the ineffectiveness of Know-Nothing legislators in other states contributed to the party's rapid decline. By 1860 it had dwindled to an inconsequential faction. Life in the cities, however, retained its violent tone. In the years just before the Civil War, a nativist mob of fifteen hundred persons rioted in the Irish districts of Lawrence, Massachusetts, burning homes and churches; in Baltimore eight men were killed in election-day battles between Know-Nothings and Democrats; and in New York, Philadelphia, and other cities violence flared sporadically.

Throughout these strife-torn decades of the 1840s and 1850s, however, each week during the spring and summer months vessels arrived in Atlantic Coast seaports carrying more Irish to America. While the battle raged intermittently in the streets between the Irish and the natives, the reinforcements poured forth from steerage. The Irish were slowly winning the battle for the city against the Protestant lower classes by sheer force of numbers.

Notes

1   John Higham, *Strangers in the Land: Patterns of American Nativism 1860–1925* (1955), chap. i.

2   Oscar Handlin, *Boston's Immigrants, 1790–1880* (1959), pp. 14–15.

3   Ray A. Billington, *The Protestant Crusade, 1800–1860* (1938), pp. 72–76.

4   The book was again in circulation on a small scale in the presidential campaign of 1960.

5   Billington, *op. cit.,* pp. 220–31.

6   Allan Nevins and Milton H. Thomas (eds.), *The Diary of George Templeton Strong* (1952), pp. 228, 232–33, 240.

7   Billington, *op. cit.,* pp. 412–416.

Unlike the pogroms of Eastern Europe or the genocidal policies of Nazi
Germany, collective violence against American Jews has not occurred.
However, anti-Semitism is not alien to America, as the following
selection points out.

Recent Trends in Anti-Semitism

Howard M. Sachar

As late as 1880 it did not appear as if the American-Jewish community needed to give more than nominal attention to the problem of
anti-Semitism. It was true that a distorted image of Jews existed in
many American minds—the image of the German-Jewish peddler
with the thick accent, hooked nose, and derby hat. But such a stereotype seemed hardly more offensive than the stage symbol of the
drunken Irishman, the chicken-pilfering Negro, or the parsimonious
Yankee. The caricature became somewhat less casual a decade later,
in the era of the greenback and free silver movements, and the
agrarian Populist revolt. During the 1890s the hated money changer,
the manipulator of hard currencies, was often associated with such
prominent Jewish financiers as the Levis, the Montefiores, the Roths-
childs—or, in America, the Belmonts and the Lehmans. The hard-
pressed Protestant farmer did not find it difficult to believe that the
Jews were members of a "great international conspiracy" to prevent
cheap money from reaching the market, and to keep American farm
families in chronic debt. When men like Governor Tom Watson of
Georgia and William Jennings Bryan of Nebraska drew attenion to
the "mysterious, invisible money powers" of the world, they unwit-
tingly lent credence to the emergent Jewish stereotype of a "Shylock"
or "octopus" of the world's finances. *Caesar's Column*, a Utopian
novel written in 1890 by the Populist Ignatius Donnelly, painted a
vivid picture of the future domination of Europe by "the Israelites,
the great money-getters of the world who rose from dealers in old
clothes and peddlers of hats to merchants, to bankers, to princes."
The novel's ominous reference to "international Judaism" was lent
verification, in some minds, by the Zionist Congress in Basel in 1897.

From *The Course of Modern Jewish History* by Howard Morley Sachar. Reprinted by permission of The World Publishing Company. Copyright © 1958
by Howard M. Sachar.

Yet the attitude toward the Jews of most Americans was, at the worst, merely vague suspicion; men like Donnelly still spoke primarily for the lunatic fringe of American life. The first serious change came with the spectacular growth of America's cities after the turn of the century. The rise of the American "Mammon" was a terrifying phenomenon for southern and midwestern farmers, people who found their credit and markets, their very livelihoods, governed by far-off metropolises. Bryan expressed their fear in his description of "Babylon the great, the mother of the harlots and of the abominations of the earth . . . drunken with the blood of the saints, and with the blood of the martyrs of Jesus." The cities were filled with more than harlots and dance halls, however, more than bankers and creditors. After 1900 they were filled with foreigners, with immigrants speaking strange tongues, worshiping the Pope in cathedrals, or denying the Trinity in synagogues. In time, it was primarily the Jew whom rural Americans identified with the city. Returning to the United States in 1907, as civilized and cultivated a person as Henry James could profess shock at the "Hebrew conquest of New York," which, he insisted, was transforming that city into a "new Jerusalem." To rural Americans, every Jewish storekeeper was the advance guard of the new commercial civilization, and bore the standard of the dread forces that threatened their security.

This suspicion was buttressed by a recrudescent race doctrine which made its appearance in the United States early in the twentieth century: the theory that men were divided into biological breeds, each incapable of "wholesome" fusion with the other. In the South the doctrine had long been applied to Negroes, and on the Pacific Coast to Orientals; and now, for the first time, it was applied to the "alien" Slavic-Jewish-Italian "islands" in the East. Prescott Hall and William Z. Ripley professed grave concern that the "Anglo-Saxon breed" was about to be inundated by the "hordes" of the big cities. Their fears were given even more "respectable" literary formulation when the writings of Count de Gobineau and Houston Stewart Chamberlain began to reach the United States. By 1914 increasing numbers of Americans were conditioned to the view that the Jews were as a race apart, members of the "Semitic" as distinguished from the "Aryan" race. Even such distinguished intellectuals as John R. Commons, Edward A. Ross, and Henry Pratt Fairchild misapplied sociological and anthropological terminology to urge that society be structured along sound "eugenic" lines; in this manner, they explained, Anglo-Saxons would avoid admixture with "inferior" breeds. The weird pseudo-science of eugenics was widely popularized by Alfred P. Schultz's

Race or Mongrel? (1908), and Madison Grant's *The Passing of the Great Race* (1916)—two of the most colorful and effective apologias for Anglo-Saxon superiority. By 1920 an influential minority of Americans had swallowed whole the notion that the "great American race" was in danger of permanent contamination by Negroes, Latins, Slavs, and Jews.

These racist fantasies were intensified by the isolationism and xenophobia that followed the First World War. The high tariffs, the virulent nationalism, the rejuvenated religious fundamentalism of the 1920s, the revival of Ku Klux Klan terrorization in Catholic and Jewish neighborhoods of the South and Midwest—all were merely the outward manifestations of a deeply rooted fear of contamination by alien ideas. Certainly the most sinister of those imported ideas was "bolshevism"—or "anarchism" or "syndicalism": they were all of a piece in the mind of the typical provincial American. "Once lead this people into war," Woodrow Wilson had predicted, "and they'll forget there ever was such a thing as tolerance." Wilson's attorney-general, A. Mitchell Palmer, now proceeded to justify this prediction by conducting a series of lawless raids on private houses and labor headquarters, rounding up thousands of aliens, holding them incommunicado, and subjecting them to drumhead interrogations. Even the courts bowed before the wind, construing the wartime Espionage and Sedition Acts with inflexible harshness. It was the age of the Sacco-Vanzetti case, of an unreasoning fear of radicalism, of antipathy to foreigners, and especially of antipathy to Jews, who, after all, came from the land of the Bolshevik Revolution, and who were hardly conservative in their own political and economic orientation.

Into all of these combustible elements there was now dropped an evil little pamphlet which had originally been circulated throughout Eastern Europe and Germany as a calculated means of promoting Jew-hatred. The *Protocols of the Elders of Zion* first appeared in 1905, as an addendum to a hopelessly confused religious tract written by Serge Nilus, a czarist civil servant. According to Nilus, the wise men of Zion had entered into a "secret" plot to enslave the Christian world. The leaders of the Jewish world government, who were variously identified as the chiefs of the twelve tribes of Israel and the leaders of world Zionism, planned to employ the institutions of liberalism and socialism to ensnare and befuddle the simple-minded "goyim." In the event of discovery, the Jewish elders apparently had made plans for blowing up all the capitals of Europe. The implication was plain: that resistance to liberalism and socialism was vital if the world was to be rescued from a malevolent Jewish conspiracy.

In 1921 the London *Times* exposed the *Protocols* as a crude forgery of a lampoon on Napoleon III, written as far back as 1864. Notwithstanding the exposure, it was in the interest of reactionaries everywhere to promote the circulation of the Nilus pamphlet. In the United States, Boris Brasol, a czarist *émigré*, persuaded a group of American business leaders, among them the motor magnate Henry Ford, to publicize the *Protocols*. Ford was a capable enough manufacturer; but his understanding of world affairs was astonishingly limited, and even more profoundly illiberal and bigoted. For several years his private newspaper, the *Dearborn Independent,* quoted liberally from the *Protocols*, and issued repeated warnings against the "Jewish menace." Not until 1927, when a Jewish attorney, Aaron Sapiro, brought a libel suit against the *Dearborn Independent*, did Ford repudiate his anti-Semitism and issue a public apology.

The confluence of all these factors—American provincialism, rural suspicion of the cities, the eugenics theory, the fear of alien radicalism, even, perhaps, the *Protocols of the Elders of Zion*—had its cumulative impact. It was felt not simply in the steady growth of the Ku Klux Klan, nor even in the anti-immigration legislation of 1921 and 1924 which closed America's doors to the fugitives of southeastern Europe; it was felt, too, in the adoption of nationwide Jewish "quotas" by colleges and professional societies. In 1922 President Abbott Lawrence Lowell of Harvard gave these quotas "respectability" when he sought openly to introduce them at his own institution. Similarly, medical and law schools began limiting the admission of Jews to a small fractional percentage of the total enrollment. Eventually employment agencies and large corporations adopted the same practice. Soon the exclusionist policy was extended into the field of housing. Through voluntary covenants of real estate owners, large areas of many cities were abruptly closed to persons of "Hebrew descent."

During the depression period, anti-Semitism proved to be a ready-made defense for some of the bigoted vested interests that feared "that man" Franklin Roosevelt's sweeping social reforms. A number of demagogic politicians, most of them the hired spokesmen for large industrial concerns, stigmatized the New Deal as the "Jew Deal," and identified trade unionism with "Jewish bolshevism." Scores of organizations—the Silver Shirts, the Khaki Shirts, the Militant Christian Patriots, the Green Mountain Boys, and others—many of them creations of cranks and rabble-rousers, but some of them financed by well-known corporations, drenched the United States with an avalanche of appeals to racial and religious hate. Fingers were pointed at the unusual numbers of Jews in Washington, and especially the Jews close to Roosevelt. Even such respected figures as Theodore Dreiser, Representative Louis T. McFadden of Pennsylvania, the eloquent Catholic priest Father Charles Coughlin of Detroit, and the national hero Charles Lindbergh attacked the Jews variously as radicals, international bankers, Reds, materialists, or warmongers.

During the late 1930s American anti-Semitism was given further direction and financial support by Nazi Germany. Hitler's most dependable agents in this campaign were German-Americans, many of them recent immigrants to the United States, veterans of the kaiser's army, and now ardent partisans of the Third Reich. The Nazi propaganda bureau supplied them with organizational leadership, funds, and endless quantities of uniforms, insignia, and propaganda literature. In 1934 many of America's German culture *vereins* [clubs] were reorganized and centralized in the German-American Bund. Under the successive leadership of Heinz Spanknoebel, Fritz Gissible, Fritz Kuhn, and Wilhelm Kunze, the Bund set about popularizing the doctrine of Hitler's New Order. Of course, anti-Semitism was the most convenient propaganda device of all. The Nazis contributed large sums of money to nativist "hate" groups. They shrilled their anti-Semitic slogans at mass meetings in Madison Square Garden and at the Philadelphia Municipal Stadium. Anti-Semitic literature was distributed to the American team as it departed for the Berlin Olympic Games in 1936. German-born professors frequently served as Nazi agents on university campuses.

Despite the many sewers from which the filth flowed, it is doubtful if the systematic "hate" campaign made a significant impact except on those who were already inclined to anti-Semitism. For the most part, the coverage given by the American press to Nazi barbarism in Europe effectively counteracted the efforts of paid German propagandists in America. It was, in fact, the appropriation of the anti-Semitic movement by the Nazi which ultimately doomed organized Jewhatred in the United States. When America went to war against Hitler, anti-Semitism at last became clearly identified in the public mind with an alien and subversive ideology. After 1945, organized American anti-Semitism made little significant headway. For one thing, the economic boom of the postwar era left few racial tensions for hate groups to exploit. Most Americans, too, were deeply moved by the courageous struggle of the Jews, as "underdogs," to win statehood for themselves in Israel. They were impressed by Israeli military valor, and by the new Israeli Republic's devotion to the democratic way of life. Moreover, the rise of a Jewish sovereign state endowed the Jews with standing in the eyes of the Christian world; they were no longer "gypsies," begging crumbs of hospitality from others. The B'nai B'rith Anti-Defamation League was able to report, in 1950, that anti-Semitism in America had fallen to an "all-time" low. Yet it is doubtful if Jew-hatred, even at its peak, was ever a major threat to the essential security of the Jewish community in the United States. The problem was rather one of Jewish social acceptance—the opportunity of Jews to gain entrance to colleges, legal and professional societies, restricted areas of employment, exclusive neighborhoods. These were unfortunate survivals which were not to be easily eliminated even with the lifting of depression or the termination of war. But they were mainly in the category of irritants. They were not really an overwhelming menace to the security of the American-Jewish community.

The selection below explodes the myth of the Melting Pot. The authors cite examples of prejudice and point out the continuing significance of the various racial enclaves or ghettos in American life today. The America which they describe does not conform at all to the Dream of democratic harmony.

Today's Ghettos

Paul Jacobs and Saul Landau

Most Americans who lived outside the ghettos or enclaves knew so little of what was happening inside them that they were surprised and shocked when recent racial conflicts ripped their cities, when anti-Semitism affected an election in New Jersey, when Mexican-Americans became mountain guerrillas in New Mexico, when Indians in the Pacific Northwest went to jail rather than give up their rights to fish.

Americans are surprised and shocked because they live in a mythical country. In this mythical America, the conditions of Negroes, Indians, and Spanish-speaking Americans are assumed to be gradually but inevitably improving as court decisions, governmental efforts, and education break down the barriers of discrimination and prejudice. The injustices and crimes committed by frontier Americans against the Indians are described as regrettable but necessary—or part of another era—and the reservation system, through which the government made wards of the Indians, was an attempt to redress the wrongs. The wholesale theft of land from Mexico through the device of the Mexican War with the resulting degradation of the Spanish-speaking peoples is held to be another lamentable but necessary episode in the country's need to expand. The myth takes in the gradual movement of Negroes toward equality. Negro slavery is acknowledged as a moral wrong, and prejudice against Negroes linked with overt discrimination is, too. In mythical America the country slowly is coming to accept Negroes as equals. The grade-school textbooks say so, and President Johnson put the country on record: "We shall overcome."

In mythical America, each wave of immigrants clung together,

From "To Serve the Devil" by Paul Jacobs and Saul Landau. Reprinted by permission from the March, 1969, issue of *The Center Magazine*, Vol. II, No. 2, a publication of the Center for the Study of Democratic Institutions in Santa Barbara, California.

maintained their Old World customs, ate their own kind of food, practiced their own religion, and kept the language of their homeland alive. Then, goes the myth, the children and grandchildren of the immigrants became acculturated to the majority America. The old neighborhood then became a haven for a new group of immigrants, preparing themselves to be melted into a homogeneous nation. This mythical social process has a mythical economic parallel, too. In it, the immigrant groups begin at the bottom of the work ladder, performing the most difficult, most onerous, and worst-paid jobs. But along with the acculturation process, they move up the economic scale and the newer immigrant groups take their place on the lower rungs, to begin their upward progress.

Like all myths, the one that has grown up about America does have some basis in fact. It is true that a great many white immigrants and descendants of white immigrants have achieved political power, financial success, and even a measure of social equality. Some of the walls that once separated them from those who went ahead have been broken down. But a great many Americans still live in enclaves. In Milwaukee, Wisconsin, or Gary, Indiana, and in many other cities, the sense of Slavic identity is still so strong that the Negro cry of "Black Power" was met with the slogan of "Polish Power"; whole wards of Slavs lined up to vote against Negro candidates and attempts to break segregated housing patterns were met with fierce resistance.

On Long Island, in New York, the "Golden Ghettos" are towns in which virtually no one but wealthy middle-class Jews live, isolated in their social and cultural life from the Gentiles who surround them. In Los Angeles, crowds of Jews, young and old, throng Fairfax Avenue, a street with Jewish restaurants, kosher meat markets, fish stores, and bookstores featuring Hebrew books and records.

In almost all our cities, there are Negro ghettos and Spanish *barrios* which have held up through three, four, and even five generations. So closed in are some of the Spanish-speaking communities that demands are now being made that the schools of the Southwest and far West treat the Spanish language as equal to English.

New Little Tokyos are growing in the cities, where most of the Japanese-Americans live, while Chinese-Americans of San Francisco have begun to move out to the edges of the city, returning to the older and larger Chinatown on weekends. Here the young have taken a new interest in things Chinese and identify themselves openly and proudly as Asiatics.

What America is witnessing is a new kind of clustering together of ethnic groups, who are perhaps frightened of being isolated from that which is familiar and reassuring. In a society that seems to be spinning apart, one's own special identity becomes essential to survival.

And few people outside these enclaves know what happens inside them; each is separated from the others and people in them find comfort only in being with those either in their own ghetto or in ghettos just like it. When a Negro leaves New York's Harlem for Los Angeles, he goes quickly to the city's central district, leaving behind him the potentially hostile white world for the reassurance of black faces like his own, the "soul" food he has always eaten, and customs he has been familiar with all his life. To the Jewish stranger in a city, the synagogue or temple is much more than a place of worship; it is a place to meet other Jews with whom to visit and socialize, a place where no one need worry about what the Christians might say if they heard the conversation.

The real life of the Chinese in San Francisco's Chinatown, the life that goes on in the houses behind the shops and restaurants, is just as unknown to the Caucasians who walk the streets as it was when the Chinese were first brought to America to fill the vast need for cheap labor required to connect the country's frontiers. Few Caucasians listen to the Chinese children of San Francisco talking as they walk to public schools that are ninety-nine per cent Chinese; the children speak Chinese while carrying their Dick and Jane readers.

What is true for the Chinese has been true for white groups, too. Only lately have Catholic priests and nuns ever been inside synagogues and Protestant churches. The Irish wake in Boston is as foreign a ceremony to the New England Unitarians as the burial rites of a tribe in New Guinea. Few "strangers" ever venture into the store-front card rooms where Italian men sit for hours and anyone who is not an Italian is a *straniero*. But while more than twenty million blacks continue to live in ghettos, while Orientals, Mexicans, and Filipinos remain in their racial enclaves, while millions of white European descendants also cling to their neighborhoods and their old languages, Americans cling precariously to the idea that their country is truly a great melting pot, even though, from its very beginnings, what has been indissoluble is America's prejudice.

Questions

1 Why has the myth of the Melting Pot persisted in the face of so much evidence to the contrary?

2 What are the major contemporary examples of the success of the Melting Pot idea?

3 Recently, the term "salad bowl" has been suggested as a substitute for "Melting Pot." To what extent can you support the suggestion?

4 For many ethnic groups, and for black people in particular, the question of integration versus separation has been a lingering concern. Should the answer be the same for all ethnic groups?

5 Does the concept of "Melting Pot" carry with it the connotation of compulsory conformity? Is there room for diversity within a system of equal rights and opportunities?

6 What countries do not practice racism? Is racism a universal human trait?

7 "America is a racist country." What evidence can you offer to support or contradict this statement?

6

The Dream of Westward Expansion
in the Nineteenth Century

Essay

Rationalizations for Territorial Acquisition
Melvin Steinfield

Readings

Not Counting Mexicans
Carey McWilliams

Racial Oppression
Walton Bean

The Traps of Expansionism
Frederick Merk

Will the Indians Get Whitey?
John Greenway

America's Obligations
William Jennings Bryan

The Frontier That No Longer Exists
Walter Allen

Americans have always seemed to need a clear conscience when engaging in questionable practices. For example, they armed themselves with the rationale of the Puritan ethic in pursuing an incessant quest for material goods. With regard to westward expansion, the author of the following essay claims that Americans embarked on a similar course. First, they created high-sounding doctrines of "Mission" and "Manifest Destiny," and then they proceeded to expunge anything or anyone who stood in their path toward continental control. In the process, they developed a callousness toward others and a violent mode that remain central features of American life today. The roots of American arrogance and violence can be traced largely to the beginnings of westward expansion, and to the polluted dreams which nudged it along.

Rationalizations for Territorial Acquisition

Melvin Steinfield

An aura of romance is commonly attached to the Winning of the West. Often overlooked, however, is the price Americans paid in order to nourish their dreams of unlimited land and their goals of westward expansion. Though it is true that the frontier served as a useful safety valve for a potentially discontented population and that it helped create democratic attitudes, it must not be forgotten at whose expense the frontier was expanded. The story of nineteenth-century western expansion is a sad commentary on what Americans were willing to do to their land, and to others, in order to pursue the dream of imperial power, which was cloaked in such slogans as Manifest Destiny and Mission.

The despoliation of the American land was a pattern that began not in the pollution-conscious 1970s when aluminum cans, plastic cups, and glass bottles were in wide use, but in the nineteenth century, when buffalo hunting was a white man's sport and forests were mercilessly uprooted to make way for a railroad or a new settlement. It was not with Vietnam that the first doubts about the purity of America's high-sounding policies were generated, but with the nineteenth-century willingness to conquer Indians, Mexicans, and others. The continuing war against pollution of the American environment, as well as the war against pollution of the American Dream, were dealt staggering blows by the course of nineteenth-century westward expansion and by the rationalizations that accompanied it.

When the Treaty of Paris ending the Revolutionary War was signed in 1783, the territory of the fledgling United States extended from the Atlantic Coast to the Mississippi River and from the Great Lakes to Georgia. It seemed like an abundant supply of land for future needs, for it was twice as much as the area claimed by the thirteen states at the start of the Revolution. Seven years earlier the original thirteen states had extended only as far west as the Appalachian mountain range, which was halfway between the Atlantic Ocean and the Mississippi River.

During the nineteenth century Americans proceeded by various means to increase their control of land on the continent by an amount equal to twice that held in 1783, excluding Alaska. By 1900 America reached all the way to the Pacific Coast as far north as the 49th parallel and south to the Mexican state of Baja California in one contiguous mass; it extended to the fringe of Russia by means of Alaska; it stretched to the Western Pacific by means of the Philippines; it included islands in the Caribbean. In one century, America had become one of the largest countries in the world.

How did this happen? By purchase, by coercion, and by violent force. In his March 7, 1900, speech to the United States Senate, Henry Cabot Lodge stated his understanding of how America managed to expand so rapidly. He cited the long record of American forcible expansion, and urged that it be continued in the case of the Philippines:

> Under the guidance of Thomas Jefferson, and with a Congress obedient to his slightest behest, we took Louisiana without the consent of the governed, and ruled it without their consent so long as we saw fit.
>
> A few years more passed, and, in 1819, we bought Florida from Spain without the consent of the governed. Then came the Mexican War, and by the Treaty of Guadalupe Hidalgo we received a great cession of territory from Mexico, including all the California coast; and although we paid Mexico twenty millions as indemnity I think it has been held that the cession was one of conquest. There were many Mexicans living within the ceded territory. We never asked their consent. In 1867 we purchased Alaska from Russia, territory, people and all. It will be observed that to the white inhabitants we allow the liberty of returning to Russia, but we except the uncivilized tribes specifically. They are to be governed without their consent, and they are not even to be allowed to become citizens.
>
> If the arguments which have been offered against our taking

the Philippine Islands because we have not the consent of the inhabitants be just, then our whole past record of expansion is a crime. I do not think that we violated in that record the principles of the Declaration of Independence. On the contrary, I think we spread them over regions where they were unknown. . . .[1]

Despite his admission that American territorial acquisitions were made without the consent of the governed and usually by force, the Republican Senator from Massachusetts was actually justifying American methods. Lodge urged that the application of those same methods of coercion against the will of the conquered be applied in the case of the Philippines, which had just been conquered in the Spanish-American War of 1898.

How was such justification possible? Paradoxically, by means of two polluted American Dreams—Manifest Destiny and Mission. Just as the Puritan ethic authorized a religiously intense pursuit of wealth, the twin concepts of Manifest Destiny and Mission (rooted in the belief in Anglo-Saxon superiority) combined to authorize a zealous pursuit of territorial gains. Americans were ingenious at devising mythologies to justify their acquisitive goals. To justify their materialistic greed, they adapted the Puritan mythology to American ends. To justify their greed for other people's lands, they fashioned an American version of the Chosen People.

That version stated that America was a superior civilization which had the "mission" of spreading its lofty ideals to other less favorably endowed peoples. It was also "manifest destiny" for American influence to spread over the entire continent, and perhaps even beyond the oceans. The slogan capturing the mood of the expansionist mania originated with the journalist John L. O'Sullivan when he wrote, in 1845, that nothing must interfere with "the fulfillment of our *manifest destiny* to overspread the continent allotted by Providence for the free development of our yearly multiplying millions." The term was enthusiastically latched on to by expansionist forces and, coupled with the concept of America's Mission, was soon translated into the idea of an irresistible force blessed by religious sanction.

Although the two concepts were different, as Frederick Merk's article emphasizes later in this chapter, they served the same useful rationalizing purpose, and often were intermingled. At first, Manifest Destiny held a certain regard for states' rights. The concept emphasized that states formed from the new land would be granted the privilege of joining, on a voluntary basis when they were ready for it, the marvelous American Union. The idea carried a benign facade: generous Americans would graciously bring more people into the

compact of freedom. It was inevitable destiny that the superior example of democratic institutions set by America would be copied by
other peoples, all of whom on this continent would eventually come
into the American fold voluntarily.

In the late 1840s the expansionist mania grew so frenzied that
Manifest Destiny was transformed to allow for the forcible conquest
and integration of alien peoples into American life. As Bernard De
Voto points out, the taboo against the forcible spreading of American
institutions was gradually dissolving in 1846:

> The Americans had always devoutly believed that the superi-
> ority of their institutions, government, and mode of life would
> eventually spread, by inspiration and imitation, to less fortunate,
> less happy peoples. That devout belief now took a new phase: it
> was perhaps the American destiny to spread our free and admir-
> able institutions by action as well as by example, by occupying
> territory as well as by practicing virtue.[2]

The apologies and rationalizations that were devised to justify
American conquest and expansion were rooted in beliefs of Anglo-
Saxon superiority. As the following excerpt from a newspaper editorial
of 1847 indicates, Americans tried to think of Mexicans as something
less than human in order to subjugate them without having pangs of
conscience:

> The Mexicans are Aboriginal Indians, and they must share the
> destiny of their race.
>
> Now we ask whether any man can coolly contemplate the idea
> of recalling our troops from the territory we at present occupy,
> from Mexico . . . and thus, by one stroke of a secretary's pen,
> reconsign this beautiful country to the custody of the ignorant
> cowards and profligate ruffians who have ruled it for the last
> twenty-five years? Why humanity cries out against it. Civiliza-
> tion, Christianity, protest against this reflux of the tide of bar-
> barism and anarchy.
>
> How we are to maintain our control over the country—on
> what terms, under what contingencies—is a matter of detail, and
> subject to future events; but we do not believe there lives the
> American, with a true understanding of this country's interests
> and duties, who, if he had the power, would deliberately surren-
> der Mexico to the uncontrolled dominion of the mongrel bar-
> barians, who, for a quarter of a century, have degraded and
> oppressed her.[3]

Not everyone eagerly supported the idea of conquering and keeping
all of Mexico, however. Some suggested that there would be problems

of integrating the population. One of these opponents of forcible Mission was Senator John C. Calhoun. Perhaps, as a representative of the slave-holding state of South Carolina, he objected to the addition of a large population which had already outlawed slavery in their own republic. Perhaps he was transferring his racist views from the black slaves of his native South Carolina to the Mexicans south of the border. Perhaps there were political motives for his remarks, but at any rate, this is what he said on the floor of the United States Senate during the debate on the aims of the 1848 Mexican War:

> We make a great mistake, sir, when we suppose that all people are capable of self-government. We are anxious to force free government on all; and I see that it has been urged in a very respectable quarter, that it is the mission of this country to spread civil and religious liberty over all the world, and especially over this continent. It is a great mistake.[4]

Calhoun, in other words, took strong exception to the notion that America had a mission to spread civil and religious liberty over the entire continent. Of course, as a major spokesman for states' rights and slavery, it would hardly be consistent for him to advocate forcible expansion of Federal authority over a new territory—especially if it had already abolished slavery.

Despite opposition from Calhoun for his reasons, and from Thoreau and Lincoln and others for their particular reasons, Americans generally supported the Mexican War and its outcome. The underlying motive was greed for land; the excuse was Destiny or Mission. It was a shallow excuse. It has been condemned by those who have studied it, but perhaps not severely enough. Consider, for example, the following statement by John Blum:

> The very success of the national experience fed national confidence, and confidence, as so often in the affairs of men, occasioned some arrogance about the privileges of power. So it was that a host of Americans concluded that they had not only an exemplary but also a militant function. They viewed themselves as a people chosen to use force, if necessary, "to overspread and possess the whole of the continent which Providence has given us for the development of the great experiment of liberty and federated government." It was the presumed destiny of the United States to arrogate to itself the lands of Indians, Mexicans, and Spaniards, and to bring to those lands American concepts of freedom and American uses of property. So a sometimes facile conscience eased the path of conquest, and the promise of America, in most ways benign, put on at times a predatory mask.

And yet beneath the mask the rapacious spirit yielded, after conquest, to the principle of freedom and abundance, for no territory taken by arms or treaty was long excluded from full participation in the nation.[5]

The last sentence of Blum's analysis smacks of the same type of apology as the proponents of Manifest Destiny and Mission were themselves prone to use. Anyone who considers the abuses which Indians and Mexicans have suffered under the aegis of these polluted American Dreams could not possibly assert that ". . . no territory taken by arms or treaty was long excluded from full participation in the nation." Technically, Mr. Blum is correct: no *territory* was excluded from participation. But, the *people* who originally lived on the land that was stolen from them are being insulted if it is asserted that ". . . the rapacious spirit yielded, after conquest, to the principle of freedom and abundance. . . ."

Maybe that's the basic problem. We are all so willing to forget the harsh realities that characterized westward expansion. Perhaps the guilt and shame stemming from the American method of moving west was too great to be confronted by the perpetrators of expansionism themselves. Thus, they and their friends romanticized the winning of the west by means of a series of false pictures—pictures which we continue to immortalize today in our westerns, our novels, and our folklore. Is the guilt too much for us as well?

Isn't it time to admit that the bitter legacy of America's westward expansion can be rectified only when a more honest approach to the past is adopted?

Notes

1 Henry Cabot Lodge, *Congressional Record*, 60TH Congress, 1ST Session, Vol. 33, Part 3, pp. 2618–2630.

2 Bernard De Voto, *Year of Decision: 1846* (Boston, Houghton Mifflin, 1961), p. 9.

3 Editorial, *New York Evening Post,* December 24, 1847.

4 John C. Calhoun, United States Senate Speech, January 4, 1848.

5 John Blum, *The Promise of America* (Boston, Houghton Mifflin, 1966), pp. 15–16.

The following selection by a highly respected author and editor of
"The Nation" magazine discusses authoritatively the background to the
Mexican War. In the "malignant conflict of cultures" one finds little
that resembles the noble phrases of Manifest Destiny or Mission.
Rather, one sees the raw power tactics of the American colossus applied
viciously against a people who happened to live on land
Americans wanted.

Not Counting Mexicans

Carey McWilliams

When asked how many notches he had on his gun, King Fisher, the
famous Texas gunman, once replied: "Thirty-seven—not counting
Mexicans." This casual phrase, with its drawling understatement,
epitomizes a large chapter in Anglo-Hispano relations in the Southwest. People fail to count the non-essential, the things and persons
that exist only on sufferance; whose life tenure is easily revocable.
The notion that Mexicans are interlopers who are never to be counted
in any reckoning dies but slowly in the Southwest. To this day Mexicans do not figure in the social calculations of those who rule the
border states. As I write these lines, the Mexican consul-general in
Los Angeles has just entered a vigorous protest against the insulting
behavior of customs inspectors at the municipal airport.

A majority of the present-day residents of the Southwest are not
familiar with the malignant conflict of cultures which has raged in the
borderlands for more than a century. Blinded by cultural myths, they
have failed to correlate the major events in a pattern of conflict which
has prevailed from Brownsville to Los Angeles since 1846. Once this
correlation is made, it becomes quite apparent that the Mexican-
American War was merely an incident in a conflict which arose some
years before and survived long after the Treaty of Guadalupe Hidalgo. It is only within the framework of this age-old conflict that it is
possible to understand the pattern of Anglo-Hispano cultural relations in the Southwest today. In summarizing the history of this conflict, one necessarily starts with Texas, for there the first blood was
shed.

Los Diablos Tejanos

In Texas the Spanish-Mexican settlements were directly in the path of Anglo-American expansion. Unlike the rest of the borderlands, Texas was not separated from the centers of Anglo-American population by mountain ranges and desert wastes; geographically it invited invasion. In a series of belts or strips, its rich, alluvial plains stretched from the plateaus to the gulf. The rivers that marked these belts could be crossed, at all seasons, at almost any point, without much trouble. On the other hand, between the most southerly settlements in Texas and those in Mexico, there was, as Dr. Samuel Harman Lowrie has pointed out, "a great expanse of semi-arid land which at that time served as a more or less natural, though temporary barrier to the effective extension of Mexican influence and control." Texas was 1,200 miles removed from its capital, Mexico City.

By 1834 the Anglo-Americans outnumbered the Mexicans in Texas: thirty thousand to five thousand. Most of the Mexicans were concentrated in the old Spanish towns or along the border, while the Anglo-Americans were to be found on the farms and ranches. Mexican townspeople had few opportunities for acculturation for they saw very little of the Anglo-Americans. From the outset, moreover, relations between the two peoples were clouded by the fear of war. The Anglo-Americans bore the brunt of Mexico's hostile distrust of the United States and were, in turn, encouraged to take an unfriendly attitude toward the natives by the unconcealed, aggressive designs of the jingoes in Washington.

As might have been expected, each group formed a highly unfavorable initial impression of the other. To the early American settlers, the Mexicans were lazy, shiftless, jealous, cowardly, bigoted, superstitious, backward, and immoral. To the Mexicans, on the other hand, the Texans were "*los diablos Tejanos*": arrogant, overbearing, aggressive, conniving, rude, unreliable, and dishonest. The first Mexican ambassador to the United States had complained in 1882 of the "haughtiness of these republicans who will not allow themselves to look upon us as equals but merely as inferiors." Still another Mexican official had charged that the Americans in Texas considered themselves "superior to the rest of mankind, and look upon their republic as the only establishment upon earth founded upon a grand and solid basis." Full of brag, bluster, and spread-eagle chauvinism, the Americans of the 1800s were hardly the most tactful ambassadors of goodwill. The truth of the matter is that the border residents were not a credit to either group.

Under the most favorable circumstances, a reconciliation of the two cultures would have been difficult. The language barrier was, of course, a constant source of misunderstanding; neither group could communicate, for all practical purposes, with the other. The Mexicans knew almost nothing of local self-government, while the Americans, it was said, travelled with "their political constitutions in their pockets" and were forever "demanding their rights." Although tolerant of peonage, the Mexicans were strongly opposed to slavery. The Anglo-Americans, most of whom were from the Southern states, were vigorously pro-slavery. The Anglo-Americans were Protestants; the Mexicans were Catholic. Speaking of a Mexican, a Protestant missionary is said to have remarked: "He was a Catholic, but clean and honest." Both groups lacked familiarity with the existing Mexican laws, for there was no settled government in Texas. Anglo-Americans found it extremely difficult to respect the laws of Mexico in the absence of law-interpreting and law-enforcing agencies. Thus it was, as Dr. Lowrie writes, that "cultural differences gave rise to misconceptions and misunderstandings, misunderstandings to distrust, distrust to antagonism, and antagonism on a very considerable number of points made open conflict inevitable."

The first Anglo-Americans literally fought their way into Texas. While most of these early filibustering expeditions were defeated, they succeeded in laying waste to the country east and north of San Antonio. Both Mexicans and Americans were killed by these invading private armies. No sooner had the Mexicans driven out the filibusters, than the Comanches raided the entire stretch of country between the Nueces and the Rio Grande. According to one observer, the whole region was "depopulated, great numbers of stock were driven off, and the people took refuge in the towns on the Rio Grande." Preoccupied with revolutionary events in Spain and Mexico, the government could give little attention to the Texas settlements. After 1821, however, a measure of protection was provided against the devastating raids of the Comanches and many of the settlers moved back across the Rio Grande.

Alas! the Alamo

With the Texas Revolution came the embittering memories, for the Texans, of the slaughter of Anglo-Americans at the Alamo and Goliad; and, for the Mexicans, of the humiliating rout and massacre at San Jacinto. Prior bitternesses were now intensified a thousandfold. "Towards the Mexicans remaining within the limits of the Republic," writes Dr. Garrison, "the feeling of the Texans was scarcely better than towards the Indians." Memories dating from this period still poison relationships between Anglos and Hispanos in Texas. Some years ago a district judge told of how, as a child, he had heard an old man give an eye-witness account of the slaughter at the Alamo. "I never see a Mexican," he confessed, "without thinking of that." José Vasconcellos, the well-known Mexican educator and philosopher, tells in his autobiography of how these same memories poisoned his boyhood in Eagle Pass. After the Texas Revolution, as Erna Fergusson has pointed out, "Texans could not get it out of their heads that their manifest destiny was to kill Mexicans and take over Mexico."

Throughout the decade of the Texas Republic (1836–1846), the shooting war continued in "the Spanish country" south of the Nueces. Murder was matched by murder; raids by Texans were countered by raids from Mexico. Since a peace treaty was never negotiated, no boundaries could be fixed. Texas claimed to the Rio Grande, while Mexico insisted that its boundary rested on the Nueces. In the bloody zone between the two rivers an uninterrupted guerrilla warfare continued throughout the life of the Texas Republic. In 1839 General Don Antonio Canales launched a revolution on Texas soil against Santa Anna and raised the banner of the Republic of Rio Grande. Of the 600 men who rallied to his standard, 180 were Texans. Awakening to the fact that Texans were using his insurrection as a cover for an attack on Mexico, General Canales finally surrendered but not until his troops had fought several engagements along the border. At the head of a raiding party of five hundred men, General Vásquez captured San Antonio in 1842 and held it for two days. These are but two of many similar episodes that occurred during the hectic life of the new republic.

Throughout the period of this border warfare, the Texas-Mexicans were caught between opposing forces. "When the Americans have gone there," explained a delegate at the Texas constitutional convention, "they have preyed upon the Mexicans; they have been necessarily compelled by force or otherwise to give up such property as they had. So vice versa, when the Mexicans have come in, they have been necessarily compelled to furnish them the means of support. . . . Since 1837 they [the Texas-Mexicans] have been preyed upon by their own countrymen as well as by ours. The Texans constantly suspected the Mexicans of inciting the Indians against them and every Indian raid provoked retaliation against the *Tejanos*. The Mexicans naturally regarded the Texas Revolution as American-inspired and the prelude to the conquest of Mexico.

However all Mexicans were not equally affected by this complex warfare. A sizable number of the upper-class settlers quickly became

216

identified with the Texans. These Texanized Mexicans or "the good Mexicans" were called *Tejanos* and were invariably of the *rico* class. Two of the fifty signers of the Texas Declaration of Independence were native Mexicans and a third, born in Mexico, became the first vice-president of the republic. At a later date, Captain Refugio Benavides commanded a company of Texas-Mexicans which operated along the border against Mexican raiders and marauders.

The Mexican-American War

Provoked by the annexation of Texas in 1846, the Mexican-American War represented the culmination of three decades of cultural conflict in Texas. To the Mexicans, every incident in Texas from the filibustering raids to the Revolution of 1836 was regarded, in retrospect, as part of a deliberately planned scheme of conquest. To the Anglo-Americans, the war was "inevitable" having been provoked, in their eyes, by the stupidity and backwardness of the Mexican officials. Not only did Mexico forfeit an empire to the United States, but, ironically, none of the signers of the Treaty of Guadalupe Hidalgo realized that, nine days before the treaty was signed, gold had been discovered in California. That they had unknowingly ceded to the United States territories unbelievably rich in gold and silver—the hope of finding which had lured Coronado and De Oñate into the Southwest— must have added to the Mexicans' sense of bitterness and defeat.

Furthermore the way in which the United States fought the Mexican-American War added greatly to the heritage of hatred. A large part of our invading army was made up of volunteers who, by all accounts, were a disgrace to the American flag. General Winfield Scott readily admitted that they had "committed atrocities to make Heaven weep and every American of Christian morals blush for his country. Murder, robbery and rape of mothers and daughters in the presence of tied-up males of the families have been common all along the Rio Grande." Lieutenant George C. Meade, of later Civil War fame, said that the volunteers were "driving husbands out of houses and raping their wives. . . . They will fight as gallantly as any men, but they are a set of Goths and Vandals without discipline, making us a terror to innocent people."

How bitterly these outrages were resented is shown by a passage which Lloyd Lewis has culled from one of the Mexican newspapers of the period: "the horde of banditti, of drunkards, of fornicators . . . vandals vomited from hell, monsters who bid defiance to the laws of nature . . . shameless, daring, ignorant, ragged, bad-smelling, long-bearded men with hats turned up at the brim, thirsty with the desire to appropriate our riches and our beautiful damsels." The year 1844 had seen the rise of a Native American Party in the states and much anti-Catholic feeling found expression during the war. Mexicans charged that the volunteers had desecrated their churches, "sleeping in the niches devoted to the sacred dead . . . drinking out of holy vessels." Two hundred and fifty American troops, mostly of Catholic background, deserted and joined the Mexican army to form the San Patricio battalion. The barbarous manner in which eighty of these deserters were executed in San Angel, a suburb of Mexico City, was long cited by the Mexicans as further proof of Yankee cruelty.

Nothing was more galling to the Mexican officials who negotiated the treaty than the fact that they were compelled to assign, as it were, a large number of their countrymen to the Yankees. With great bitterness they protested that it was "not permissible to sell, as a flock of sheep, those deserving Mexicans." For many years after 1846, the Spanish-Americans left in the United States were known in Mexico as "our brothers who were sold." As late as 1943 maps were still used in Mexican schools which designated the old Spanish borderlands as "territory temporarily in the hands of the United States." It is to the great credit of the Mexican negotiators that the treaty contained the most explicit guarantees to protect the rights of these people, provisions for which they were more deeply concerned than they were over boundaries or indemnities. It should never be forgotten that, with the exception of the Indians, Mexicans are the only minority in the United States who were annexed by conquest; the only minority, Indians again excepted, whose rights were specifically safeguarded by treaty provision.

Just as the end of the Texas Revolution did not terminate hostilities in Texas, so the Treaty of Guadalupe Hidalgo failed to bring peace to the borderlands. Under the terms of the treaty, it became the obligation of the United States to police 180,000 Indians living in the territories which we acquired from Mexico. This obligation the United States failed to discharge for many years. Taking advantage of the confusion which prevailed, the Indians launched fierce raids on both Anglo and Hispano settlements, conducted marauding expeditions deep in Mexican territory, and cunningly exploited the hatred that had been engendered between Anglo and Hispano. The Anglos promptly attributed these raids to Mexican duplicity and instigation; the Hispanos as promptly charged them up to the malice or carelessness of the Americans. Hard-pressed on all sides, the Indians had come to live off the plunder seized in these raids which, with the confusion and demoralization which prevailed in Mexico, were conducted on a larger scale than ever before. It was not until about 1880 that the United States finally managed to bring the Indians of the Southwest under close police surveillance.

Nor were Indians the only troublemakers in the post-war decades. Between 1848 and 1853, various American filibustering expeditions violated Mexican territory in Sonora, Lower California, and at various points along the border. When word of the discovery of gold reached the Eastern states, swarms of emigrant gold-seekers passed along the southern routes to California, often travelling in Mexican territory without passports, and not infrequently helping themselves to Mexican food and livestock en route.

In 1850 José M. Carvajal organized a revolution in Mexico, sponsored by American merchants, which aimed at converting the State of Tamaulipas into the Sierra Madre Republic. Carvajal was a Texan by birth who had been educated in Kentucky and Virginia. Backed by Richard King and Mifflin Kennedy, two of the great cattle-barons of south Texas, the Carvajal revolution was supported by bands of armed Texans who crossed the Rio Grande. The American ambassodor reported that these raids, in which as many as five hundred Texans participated, had "awakened a feeling of intense prejudice against everything connected with American interest."

The fateful strip of territory between the Nueces and the Rio Grande once again became the home of numerous outlaw bands who preyed indiscriminately upon both Mexican and American settlers. In the face of these staggering blows,—filibustering expeditions, Indian raids, revolution, war, and constant guerrilla fighting,—the Mexicans in Texas constantly retreated and their retreat, of course, gave rise to the notion that their conquerors were pursuing a mandate of destiny. Major Emery, writing in 1859, said that the "white race" was "exterminating or crushing out the inferior race"; and an American soldier wrote home that "the Mexican, like the poor Indian, is doomed to retire before the more enterprising Anglo-Americans."

The following essay surveys the treatment of ethnic minorities in California during the second half of the nineteenth century. The brutalities enumerated contradict the promises of participation which Mission and Manifest Destiny carried. Instead of being included in the government, Mexicans, Indians, blacks, and Chinese were ignored or persecuted. For them, the American Dreams of Mission and Manifest Destiny meant "conquest" and "control."

Racial Oppression
Walton Bean

In the years after the gold rush a large majority of the American citizens of California, whether they had come from Northern or Southern states, cherished a fixed belief in the innate superiority of "whites" over other races. They also believed that Protestant Christians were better people than the followers of other religious faiths, and that persons of Anglo-American nativity were innately superior to those of other national origins.

Of the fears, the hatreds, and the various kinds of intolerance that accompanied this set of opinions, the deepest were probably associated with the idea of racial superiority. In part, this was because that idea was very closely associated with economic group interest; equally important, however, were the essentially irrational aspects of racial fears and hatreds.

Treatment of Mexican Miners

As Americans poured into the mining districts of California in 1849 and 1850, they found themselves in competition with substantial numbers of foreigners. The most numerous of these were Mexicans from the state of Sonora, as the naming of one of the largest towns in the southern mines attested. Feelings of hostility left over from the Mexican War were intensified because many of the Sonorans were experienced miners, skillful in locating good claims, while others were peons brought to California in labor gangs to work the claims of their wealthier Mexican masters. Americans feared that foreigners were removing too much of the readily available gold, and that there would soon be none left. Mining-camp codes, enforced by vigilance committees and soon ratified by the state legislature, excluded Mexicans and Orientals from many of the diggings.

Further evidence of antiforeign sentiment appeared when the California legislature of 1850 enacted a foreign miners' license tax. Introduced by Senator Thomas Jefferson Green, the act required miners who were not citizens of the United States to pay a fee of $20 a month. This levy was so high that the Mexicans, upon whom most of the burden would fall, were unable or unwilling to pay it, and a mass meeting in the town of Sonora announced their refusal. Hundreds of armed American miners, including many veterans wearing their old Mexican War uniforms, then gathered at Sonora to aid the collectors of the tax and to prevent Mexicans from mining without a license.

At this time there were about fifteen thousand Mexicans in the "southern mines"—Calaveras, Tuolumne, and Mariposa Counties. Under the pressures of the tax and of threats of violence, about ten thousand left the region in the summer of 1850, most of them to return to Mexico. Although the treaty of Guadalupe Hidalgo provided that Mexican citizens of California who chose to remain there for a year became American citizens automatically, many Americans, in ignorance or defiance of this provision, lumped all "Mexicans" together, and many native Californians were driven from the mines along with the Mexican nationals, in fear of their lives and with bitterness in their hearts. Their protests had little or no political effect. On the other hand, the protests of American merchants in the mining districts, who had lost so many customers, were strong enough to carry considerable weight in the legislature, especially when it became clear that the nearly prohibitive tax was bringing in only a small amount of revenue. The tax was repealed in 1851, but it was soon reenacted in more moderate form.

In the troubles at Sonora in 1850 several hundred Frenchmen had been involved on the side of the Mexicans, to such a degree that the episode was sometimes called "the French Revolution." Mob violence between French and American miners was again narrowly averted in the summer of 1851 near Mokelumne Hill. The earliest discrimination by American Californians against foreigners, however, was directed mainly against Mexicans and other Spanish Americans. Beginning in 1852, the prime target of xenophobia became the Chinese, who had replaced the Mexicans as the most numerous and the most obviously "alien" of the various foreign groups. The California Indians, not easily classified as foreigners, were in a separate and peculiar category.

Early Discrimination Against the Chinese

At the end of 1849 only a few hundred Chinese had come to seek the gold of California. In 1851, however, the outbreak of the great Taiping Rebellion against the Manchu dynasty plunged China into 15 years of civil war and general disorder that further depressed the poverty of most of its people. For more than two centuries, periods of extraordinary economic depression had induced many thousands of Chinese to emigrate, particularly from South China to several parts of Southeast Asia. Now rumors of easy wealth brought a great stream of Chinese emigrants to "the Golden Mountains," their name for California. Nearly all of them, like most of the American Argonauts, were young men who dreamed of acquiring a fortune and returning home to enjoy it with the families they had left behind. But whereas most of those Americans who were disappointed in this hope eventually reconciled themselves to becoming permanent residents of California, the Chinese tended to cling for the rest of their lives to the dream of returning to their homeland, even though pitifully few of them were ever able to do so. Having no desire to become a part of a foreign country, most of the early Chinese immigrants remained alien by their own choice as much as by that of the Americans.

Even worse than the discrimination that the Chinese suffered at American hands was their oppression by creditors and other exploiters among their own countrymen. Following a pattern long established in Chinese overseas migration, impoverished young men from Canton, Hong Kong, or the neighboring rural areas made contracts for the payment of their passage under the "credit-ticket" system. In California their labor was sold, through Chinese subcontractors, to Chinese mining companies which paid them very low wages. The American miners permitted these companies to acquire and to work only the claims which they themselves had abandoned, or those which had never contained enough gold to produce a sizable profit. The hapless Chinese workers were kept in a state of debt-bondage enforced by a Chinese creditor-employer network. This system operated without reference to American courts or other legal authorities, and was reenforced by various types of associations. The most important of these were the district companies, based on the several districts of Southeastern China from which nearly all of the California Chinese had come.

Indentured servitude, in which men labored for a period of years to repay the cost of their passage, was nothing new in American history. Indentured servants from England had made up more than half of the white population of several of the thirteen English colonies on the Atlantic seaboard in the 17th century and the first half of the 18th. As one observer put it, the progenitor of many a proud American family had originally come to colonial America because his person could be advantageously exchanged there for a quantity of tobacco or sassafras root. But most of the Chinese immigrants, harried both by Americans and by greedy and powerful men of their own race, found it far more difficult to rise out of debt-bondage and extreme poverty.

In 1852 the number of Chinese in California rose to about twenty-five thousand. Concentrated in the mining regions and in San Francisco, they were now by far the largest of the foreign minorities. They formed a tenth of the state's population other than Indians, and nearly a third of the population in several of the mining counties. An outburst of agitation against them began when a bill was introduced in the state senate to legalize the enforcement in California of labor contracts made in China. Throughout the mining camps there was such a rash of mass meetings and resolutions denouncing this "coolie bill" that the measure was decisively defeated. Later in the legislative session of 1852 the foreign miners' license tax was reenacted with the clear understanding that it would be enforced primarily upon the Chinese. The tax was set at $3 per month, later raised to $4.

Much to the irritation of the white miners, but greatly to the benefit of the state treasury, the tax failed to discourage the Chinese, who paid it willingly in the hope that it would reconcile the whites to their continued presence in the mines. Until 1870 when the state supreme court belatedly declared it unconstitutional, this tax, paid by the Chinese almost exclusively, brought in nearly a fourth of the state's entire revenue, even though thieving tax collectors, dissatisfied with the commissions allowed them, often let the Chinese miner off with a payment of $2 if he agreed not to demand a receipt. In addition, many Chinese were victimized by Americans impersonating tax collectors.

The Chinese almost always considered it useless and unwise to try to defend themselves against any action, even including violence and robbery, directed against them by Americans. This was true even before a peculiar decision of the state supreme court rendered them still more helpless. A state law of 1850 forbade Negroes and Indians to testify in court, either "in favor of, or against a white man." in *People v. Hall* in 1854, Chief Justice Hugh C. Murray (who was 29 years old) pronounced the doctrine that the Chinese were legally Indians, since both were probably descended from the same Asiatic ancestors. Thus nonwhites (and whites also) were denied legal protection from any outrage at the hands of a white man if the only witnesses were Chinese, or Negro, or Indian. This ban against giving evidence was removed from Negroes in 1863, but Chinese and Indians remained under it until 1872, when it was dropped from the California code in deference to the Federal Civil Rights Act.

In the meantime another legal weapon against the Chinese had been found in the Federal law which had provided since 1790 that only "free white persons" could be naturalized. This provision was a deep flaw in the application of American ideas of democracy. As for the Chinese immigrants in particular, it happened that most of them had no desire for the privilege of American naturalization. Hence they would not have suffered greatly from the denial of it, if that denial had not come to be used in a remarkable number of California laws as an excuse for other forms of discrimination. This shabby device would continue to be employed for nearly a hundred years. Turned primarily against land ownership by Japanese immigrants in California in the 20th century, its use would end only when discrimination on the ground of race as such was finally stricken from the Federal naturalization statutes in 1952. In California, state laws directed against "aliens ineligible to citizenship," as a euphemism for aliens of nonwhite ancestry, began to appear in 1855 when the legislature sought to impose a head tax of $50 on all immigrants "who cannot become citizens." This was soon declared unconstitutional because the state could not tax immigration; but another state law of 1855 made ineligibility for citizenship the main definition of those to whom the foreign miners' license tax applied, and thus ensured the enforcement of the tax more specifically against the Chinese. The latter law remained in effect for many years.

Fortunately, the Chinese were a people who had developed a remarkable combination of fatalism and adaptability, during many centuries of oppression in China itself. Their sufferings, and those of all the other racial minorities, were overshadowed by the disasters that befell the California Indians.

The "Indian Question"

Since the 1820s the Federal government had followed a "removal policy" as its general solution of "the Indian problem." A "permanent Indian frontier" had been created along the eastern edge of the Great Plains. That region, which extended from Texas to the Canadian border was then regarded as a "Great American Desert" where white men would never want to live. By a long series of treaties the Indian "nations" or tribes of the Eastern and Central parts of the country had been induced to move west of this line to new lands which the American government promised to reserve for them in perpetuity. But this process had scarcely been completed when in the 1840s the extension of the American boundary to the Pacific made the line obsolete.

In California, where it was no longer possible to remove the Indians to lands farther west, many American settlers argued that the only solution was to remove them from the face of the earth. Governor Burnett told the legislature that a "war of extermination will continue to be waged between the races until the Indian race becomes extinct," and that it was "beyond the power or wisdom of man" to avert the "inevitable destiny of this race." Among the American Californians this was the predominating view, and the overwhelming barbarousness of it was at the root of the tragic futility of all the attempts to solve the "Indian question."

Units loosely organized as state militia went on ineffectual and expensive Indian-hunting expeditions in 1850. In 1851 Governor John McDougal asserted in a letter to President Millard Fillmore that 100,000 Indian warriors were in a state of armed rebellion, and the following year one of California's United States Senators, John B. Weller, claimed that only a "master spirit" was needed to "confederate the tribes in a bloody and devastating war."

These statements were fantastically false. By this time there were less than 100,000 Indians of all ages and both sexes left in the whole state, and because of their inability to understand each others' dialects, and their lack of tribal organization, they were no more capable of "confederating" for war or for any other purpose than they had ever been. Yet the most terrifying assertions about them were widely believed in California.

The state's politicians demanded that the Federal government provide the funds to pay the expenses of campaigns conducted against the Indians by state militia volunteers. This, at first, the Federal authorities refused to do. Gen. Persifor F. Smith complained that the pay of a private in the latest Indian campaign of the California militia was equal to the salary of any officer in the Regular Army, except his own. Secretary of War C. M. Conrad wrote to Governor McDougal that the pay of California's volunteer Indian-fighters was "exorbitant and beyond anything ever known in this country"; that "in a population like that of California, where there are so many ardent young men, the love of adventure with some and the high pay with others" offered "inducement to perpetual collisions with the Indians"; and that this abuse was "as injurious to the State" as it was "revolting to humanity." Secretary Conrad maintained that the troubles resulted far more often from the aggressive behavior of the whites than from that of the

Indians, and that there was no genuine need for a perpetual war between them.

The policies of the Federal government toward the California Indians, though very different from the policies of the state, were equally unsuccessful in providing any effective solution. In 1850 Congress passed an act authorizing three Indian agents or commissioners to negotiate a series of treaties. The commissioners were Redick McKee of Virginia, George W. Barbour of Kentucky, and Dr. Oliver M. Wozencraft, a practicing physician from Louisiana, who had been a member of the constitutional convention at Monterey. Like Governor Burnett, who had lived in Tennessee and Missouri before coming to Oregon and California, the three commissioners were Southerners. But unlike Burnett, they were men of some humanitarian feelings, and they were shocked and alarmed by the belligerent attitude of the state government.

Placing their hope of insuring peace in the idea of segregating the Indians from the whites as completely as possible, the commissioners negotiated 18 treaties affecting 139 tribes or bands. These treaties would have removed the Indians from the mining districts and other areas of white settlement and concentrated them on large reservations totaling 11,700 square miles, or 7,488,000 acres. This was about 7½ percent of the entire land area of the state. Moreover, although Congress had appropriated only $50,000 for the work of the commissioners, they let contracts totaling nearly a million dollars for provisions and beef cattle for the reservations, on the theory that, as they reported to Washington, "it is *cheaper* to feed the whole flock for a *year* than to fight them for a *week*."

Obviously, the Federal commissioners overreached themselves, and their plan was unworkable. Only a small fraction of the California Indians moved even temporarily to their proposed reservations. The Federal government could neither have persuaded nor forced the American settlers to respect the boundaries of such large areas of potentially valuable land, and in the state legislature hostility to the treaties became intense. It was argued that Indians had no right to any land at all; that not even Mexico had recognized such a right on the part of the "wild" Indians of California; that removal to the reservations would deprive the towns and ranches in Southern California of their Indian laborers; and that the government ought to have continued its previously established policy of removing the Indians entirely outside the boundaries of states.

That the last two of these arguments were contradictory, and that they both appeared in the same list of state senate resolutions in denunciation of the treaties, suggest the irrational aspects of the state of feeling that prevailed. California's United States Senators, Gwin and Weller, opposed the treaties so vigorously that the Senate rejected all of them when they came up for ratification in 1852.

Beale and the Reservation System

There was widespread fear that the rejection of the treaties would lead the Indians to outbreaks of violence. Thus in 1853, as a palliative, Congress adopted a much more modest plan suggested by Edward F. Beale, the new superintendent of Indian affairs for California. Beale recommended a system of smaller reservations that would also serve as military posts for the United States Army. The Indians would be taught to engage in agriculture and handicrafts, much in the manner of the Spanish missions though without the religious emphasis. Ultimately, it was hoped, the Indians on these reservations might become self-sustaining. Five such establishments, of 25,000 acres each, were authorized under the act of 1853. The first, at Tejon in the Tehachapi foothills, attracted about twenty-five hundred Indians. Other reservations were soon established, notably the Nome Lackee in Colusa County, the Klamath on the Klamath River, and the Mendocino on the Pacific Coast.

Beale pushed his experiment with enthusiasm and vigor, but it had scarcely begun when he was removed from office, in 1854, partly because of his inefficiency in business matters and partly through the efforts of political enemies. The Office of Indian Affairs in Washington was peculiarly vulnerable to the abuses of the spoils system, and its personnel rotated with every new administration. In general, Beale's successors and their subordinates were incompetent and venal political appointees. In 1858 a Federal investigator reported that the reservations were a lamentable failure—mere almshouses for a trifling number of Indians.

Unsuccessful as this pitiful system was, however, the Federal government failed to devise a better one, and Beale's plan became the model for Federal Indian reservations all over the West for many decades afterward. In 1870, Indian agents began to be appointed on the recommendation of Christian churches, and the California Indians were placed under the care of the Methodists. But little or no improvement was possible within the limitations of the small-reservation system.

The Indian "Wars"

The two decades after the gold rush produced dozens of wretched episodes that can best be described as massacres, the great majority of them perpetrated on the Indians by the whites. Many of these "punitive expeditions" were financed by the state government, and during the 1850s more than a million dollars' worth of state bonds was issued to pay the expenses of local volunteer campaigns for "the suppression of Indian hostilities." The Federal government, overcoming its earlier reluctance, reimbursed the state for most of these expenditures under congressional appropriation acts of 1854 and 1861, although Federal auditors disallowed some of the most obviously exaggerated claims. In this dreary tale of legalized and subsidized murder, the Mariposa campaign and the "Modoc War" stand out as relatively colorful incidents.

In 1851 the Mariposa Battalion under James D. Savage, pursuing a band of Yosemites and Chowchillas under Chief Tenieya, rediscovered the Yosemite Valley, whose earlier discovery by Joseph Reddeford Walker's party had never been widely known. The Yosemites did not risk a battle with the Savage expedition, and in general very few of the California Indians offered any effective resistance to the military and quasi-military campaigns against them. The main exceptions came in the mountainous northern part of the state.

The most famous conflict in that region occurred after a band of Modocs left the reservation which they had been forced to share with the Oregon Klamaths, and returned without permission to their former country on Lost River. The conflict could have been prevented by allowing the Modocs to occupy a bit of land which was of very little value to the whites, and which would have been only a tiny fragment of the lands that had once been Modoc territory.

In 1873 a force of 400 soldiers, mostly of the Regular Army, drove the Modocs to take refuge in the lava beds. There, although heavily outnumbered and fighting only with old muzzle-loaders and pistols against rifles and artillery, the Modocs fortified themselves so well that they inflicted many casualties on the Americans while suffering very few of their own. At a peace conference where they were offered no better terms than a return to the reservation in Oregon, their chief Kientepoos ("Captain Jack") was goaded by some of his warriors into a plot in which they treacherously murdered Gen. E. R. S. Canby and a Methodist missionary, Dr. Eleazar Thomas, and wounded Indian Agent A. B. Meacham. Ultimately the Modocs were defeated and Captain Jack was hanged, but not until the war had cost the lives of about 75 Americans, and half a million dollars.

Decline of the Indian Population

Under Spain and Mexico there had been no more than a few dozen Spaniards, a few thousand Mexican Californians, and a few hundred Americans in California—and they had occupied only parts of it. Nevertheless the aboriginal population had dropped from more than 275,000 in 1769 to about 100,000 in 1846. Epidemics had been the largest factor in this decline.

With the coming of hundreds of thousands of Americans, the Indian death rate was tragically accelerated. By 1870 there were only about 30,000 Indians left. In 1900 there were less than 16,000. Disease continued to take the largest toll, probably accounting for about 60 percent of the deaths during the second half of the 19th century. As the incoming tide of Americans drove the Indians from the food-producing areas, starvation and malnutrition probably added about 30 percent of the death toll. Less than 10 percent resulted from purely physical assault, through formal military campaigns, informal expeditions, and various other forms of homicide.

Many of the surviving Indians could get food only by stealing it from the whites, and this led to constant and violent retaliation. To a limited extent the Indian could also obtain food by working for the white man, particularly in Southern California, and the Americans adopted various regulations which continued the Mexican system of Indian peonage. Under a military order of 1847 and an act of the state legislature in 1850, any unemployed Indian could be declared a vagrant and forced to labor on public works, while those not needed for this purpose could be auctioned off to the highest bidder as indentured servants. The flourishing illegal business of kidnaping Indians, especially children, for sale as household and farm servants, was continued. A white man could mistreat and even murder an Indian with virtual impunity. J. Ross Browne wrote that "If ever an Indian was fully and honestly paid for his labor by a white settler, it was not my luck to hear of it." The treatment of Indian laborers was in general so oppressive that it contributed more to their extinction than to their support, and particularly in agriculture, the feeling that the landowner had a right to a supply of cheap labor drawn from the people of some supposedly inferior race set an evil precedent for future generations.

As for the alternative of assimilating the Indians into the general population, this was made impossible in the early American period not only by the prejudices of the whites against the Indians but also by the deep and hopeless resentment which the Indians felt against the whites.

The "Free" Negroes

Although the efforts of Governor Burnett to secure legislation excluding free Negroes were no more successful than the similar efforts
in the constitutional convention, the coming of "persons of color" was
effectively discouraged in less direct ways, and in the late 1850s there
were only about twenty-five hundred of them in California. Several
state laws, such as the ban against their testimony in legal proceedings, infringed their civil rights and treated them as an inferior people.
In 1852 the state adopted a harsh fugitive slave law reflecting the
odious Federal statute that had been a part of the compromise under
which it was admitted to the Union. Only one actual fugitive slave is
known to have reached California; but the law was enforced against a
number of Negroes whose masters had brought them there and later
wished to return them to the South. The last and most famous of these
cases, that of Archy Lee, was tried in 1858. Peter H. Burnett was then
on the state supreme court. With the concurrence of the ex-Texan
Justice David S. Terry, he ruled that although the master had forfeited
his right to the slave by bringing him to a free state after its admission
to the Union, and by remaining for a substantial time, an exception
should be made in this instance because the master was young and in
poor health, and in need of his slave's services. This decision was
widely ridiculed, and Lee was freed shortly afterward by a United
States commissioner in San Francisco.

Are Americans as vicious and land-hungry as the preceding selections seem to indicate? Was the expansionism of the 1890s merely another form of the Manifest Destiny of the 1840s? According to Frederick Merk, distinguished Professor Emeritus of Harvard University, neither of the above conclusions is entirely correct. Continental and imperialist doctrines of expansion were never true expressions of the American spirit, he asserts. They were, instead, traps into which the nation was led, and from which it managed to extricate itself. Merk makes an interesting distinction between Manifest Destiny and Mission, as well as between the expansionism of the 1840s and 1890s.

The Traps of Expansionism

Frederick Merk

The imperialism of the 1890s is regarded by some historians as a variant merely of Manifest Destiny of the 1840s. This is an error. It was the antithesis of Manifest Destiny. Manifest Destiny was continentalism. It meant absorption of North America. It found its inspiration in states' rights. It envisaged the elevation of neighboring peoples to equal statehood and to all the rights and privileges which that guaranteed. Expansionism in 1899 was insular and imperialistic. Its inspiration was nationalism of a sort. It involved the reduction of distant peoples to a state of colonialism. It was what O'Sullivan had thundered against in his writings about Rome and England. It was what he had assured his readers America would never tolerate. Manifest Destiny had contained a principle so fundamental that a Calhoun and an O'Sullivan could agree on it—that a people not capable of rising to statehood should never be annexed. That was the principle thrown overboard by the imperialists of 1899.

After the Spanish-American War, as after the Mexican War, expansionism lost attractiveness. The theory that growth is necessary to national life, as it is to individual life, that it is indispensable to vigor, and is a people's duty, even if it involves swallowing other people, fell into disfavor. A desire for an opposite course gradually replaced it, a wish to liquidate most, if not all, of the new empire as soon as was.

decently possible. Too much swallowing had, as usual, the effect of surfeit, weariness, and lethargy.

Cuba is a case in point. It had long been a goal of expansionists. In the 1840s and 1850s it had become a compelling attraction to them. In the 1890s some expansionists still hoped for it, though the interventionists in 1898 usually denied that they had a desire to acquire it. Senator Henry M. Teller, of Colorado, was of this group. He had been an exponent of Manifest Destiny for years. But he was unusual in his devotion to the principle of consent. He adhered to it more stubbornly than had his great predecessor, O'Sullivan. When the congressional resolution to intervene in Cuba reached the voting stage in the Senate he feared that some of his colleagues rushing to rescue the oppressed might yield to the temptation to keep the Pearl of the Antilles as reward for their labors. He proposed an amendment to the intervention resolution, pledging the United States to transfer sovereignty of the island to its people as soon as order had been restored. The amendment was easily passed in both houses without a recorded vote, a revealing evidence that as late as April 1898 Congress was not in an imperialist mood. Teller was hopeful that the Cuban people would have sense enough to ask admission to the Union after the war. They never had that sense.[1]

In 1901, Congress, preparing for the withdrawal of the Army from the island, inserted stipulations in the Army appropriation bill. Cuba was to enter into no treaty, when once free, with another power which might impair her independence. She was to lease naval bases to the United States. The United States was to have a right to intervene in Cuba to maintain orderly government. These were the provisions of the Platt amendment, which Cubans perforce accepted. In later years these provisions were used to give validity to several interventions. But in 1934, in the days of Franklin D. Roosevelt, in line with his "Good Neighbor" policy, they were replaced by a treaty canceling all special rights of the United States in Cuba, with the exception of a lease of the naval base at Guantánamo Bay. Thus, at last, in the liquidation of an empire, freedom came to the island which had been one of the earliest goals of Manifest Destiny.

The Philippine archipelago, which had been acquired as an afterthought of the war, was also kept in a status wherein its release was possible. It never was admitted into the bosom of the family with quite the warmth shown Hawaii. It was not made part of the United States by Congress in the sense in which the term "United States" is used in the Constitution. It was a possession of, an unincorporated part of, the United States. The restrictions placed on Congress in legislating for the United States proper did not apply to it. At least this is what the United States Supreme Court held in a major decision in 1904. In the decision use of the term "overseas colony" was avoided. The term used was "unincorporated territory," but it had a colonial look to it.[2]

Democrats began demanding the liberation of the Philippines as early as the ratification of the treaty. They never did become reconciled to the view that national maturity inexorably required colonialism. In successive party platforms they urged that the islands go the way of Cuba. In the administration of Woodrow Wilson the Jones Act was passed, which gave dominion status to the islands as a first step toward independence. In 1933, over the veto of Herbert Hoover, Congress passed an independence act. But independence accompanied by the loss of trade privileges with the United States was not accepted by the legislature of the archipelago. However, satisfactory arrangements were eventually made, and on July 4, 1946, the Philippine Republic entered the community of free nations.

Others of the accessions of the period 1898–9 have had a different history. Hawaii, the most attractive of them, became linked to the mainland by ties of mutual interest and kindred population so close as almost to make her part of it. She had been "incorporated" into the United States by Congress as early as 1900.[3] Her population kept up a persistent agitation for admission to statehood in the Union. In 1959 she was offered statehood, and by an overwhelming vote accepted it. Puerto Rico, with a large Negro element in her population, became in 1952, with the consent of her people, a commonwealth associated with the United States. Guam, an advanced Pacific base, was administered by the Navy for a time. In 1950 the island obtained a civil government with a measure of local autonomy. Her function was that of defense, as was also that of other islands acquired at other times.[4]

In this remodeling of empire, there emerged a pattern indicative of the true temper of the American people. A few islands—those necessary for defense—were retained. Those that were useful chiefly for commercial exploitation, such as the Philippines, were freed. Commercial exploitation had lost favor. It had proved injurious to some interests on the mainland, even if advantageous to others. For instance, the agitation for the independence of the Philippines was led by some of the sugar interests in the United States. The archipelago may be said to have been shown the door by sugar barons. In separating functions which colonies served—commerical from defense— and renouncing the first, Americans were repudiating their imperialists of 1899 who had merged the two for the greater glory of both. The stage was finally reached where Americans boasted, in a war of propaganda, of not being a colonial power at all, and looked askance at expansionists of their past who had conceived of the possessions of their neighbors as apples to be gathered in a basket.

Mission

It may be safe now to venture an opinion that continentalist and imperialist doctrines were never true expressions of the national spirit. They were the very opposite. In their espousal of the "outward look" in the Mahan* sense of acquiring the property of others without consultation of the wishes of the owners; in their insistence on growth, regardless of the nature and manner of the growth; and in their reliance on divine favor for procedures that were amoral, they misrepresented the nation. They fooled a small part of the American people much of the time, another part some of the time, but never the mass all the time. A thesis that continentalist and imperialist goals were sought by the nation regardless of party or section, won't do. It is not substantiated by good evidence. A better-supported thesis is that Manifest Destiny and imperialism were traps into which the nation was led in 1846 and in 1899, and from which it extricated itself as well as it could afterward.

A truer expression of the national spirit was Mission. This was present from the beginning of American history, and is present, clearly, today. It was idealistic, self-denying, hopeful of divine favor for national aspirations, though not sure of it. It made itself heard most authentically in times of emergency, of ordeal, of disaster. Its language was that of dedication—dedication to the enduring values of American civilization. It was the language of Abraham Lincoln in the Civil War, on a great battlefield of the war, at a time when new meaning had been given to the war and to American democracy by the Emancipation Proclamation. It appeared in the immortal phrases of the Gettysburg Address:

> It is rather for us to be here dedicated to the great task remaining before us—that from these honored dead we take increased devotion to that cause for which they gave the last full measure of devotion; that we here highly resolve that these dead shall not have died in vain—that this nation, under God, shall

*In 1890 Alfred Mahan wrote *The Influence of Sea Power Upon History*. As a result of that and subsequent publications, he became known as one of the foremost advocates of imperialism in America.

have a new birth of freedom; and that government of the people, by the people, for the people, shall not perish from the earth.[5]

Mission was a force that fought to curb expansionism of the aggressive variety. It did so with a measure of success at the time of the All Mexico movement. At the height of that movement Albert Gallatin sent to the press the first of his articles on the Mexican War, a section of which was a moving definition of "The Mission of the United States":

Your mission is to improve the state of the world, to be the "model republic," to show that men are capable of governing themselves, and that the simple and natural form of government is that also which confers most happiness on all, is productive of the greatest development of the intellectual faculties, above all, that which is attended with the highest standard of private and political virtue and morality.

Your forefathers, the founders of the republic, imbued with a deep feeling of their rights and duties, did not deviate from those principles. The sound sense, the wisdom, the probity, the respect for public faith, with which the internal concerns of the nation were managed made our institutions an object of general admiration. Here, for the first time, was the experiment attempted with any prospect of success, and on a large scale, of a representative democratic republic. If it failed, the last hope of the friends of mankind was lost, or indefinitely postponed; and the eyes of the world were turned towards you. Whenever real or pretended apprehensions of the imminent danger of trusting the people at large with power were expressed, the answer ever was, "Look at America!" . . .

Your mission was to be a model for all other governments and for all other less-favored nations, to adhere to the most elevated principles of political morality, to apply all your faculties to the gradual improvement of your own institutions and social state, and by your example to exert a moral influence most beneficial to mankind at large. Instead of this, an appeal has been made to your worst passions; to cupidity; to the thirst of unjust aggrandizement by brutal force; to the love of military fame and false glory; and it has even been tried to pervert the noblest feelings of your nature. The attempt is made to make you abandon the lofty position which your fathers occupied, to substitute for it the political morality and heathen patriotism of the heroes and statesmen of antiquity.[6]

Again, in the 1890s Mission fought imperialism. It held its own in the fight until war brought an overwhelming force against it. It held the imperialists who sought Hawaii at bay until then. From the stronghold of Mission, old-school Republicans fought the imperialists in the Senate. So did the stalwart "Czar," Thomas B. Reed, in the House. Imperialists seemed to him betrayers not merely of a sacred American tradition but of the very life of the Constitution. Reed fought them till war overwhelmed him. He never recovered from the shock of the defeat.[7] Democrats fought from the same citadel. The annexation of the Hawaiian Islands seemed to Grover Cleveland in 1898 "a perversion of our national mission. The mission of our nation is to build up and make a greater country out of what we have instead of annexing islands."[8] Animating all defenders of the old faith was the sentiment of Daniel Webster admonishing expansionists of his day: "You have a Sparta; embellish it!"

Mission appeared in the twentieth century as a national sense of responsibility for saving democracy in Europe. It was an important force, among others, in inducing Congress in 1917 to vote entrance into the First World War. It did for democracy in the world, then, what it had not done for the newborn European republics in 1848. It inspired Woodrow Wilson, during the war and at its close, to take the lead in forming the League of Nations, which was designed to save the future from wars precipitated by nationalistic states pursuing aggressive ends. The League had the support, probably, of a majority of the American people. But American membership in it was blocked in the Senate by a collision over the "reservation issue." Among individuals who blocked entrance the most influential were Republicans who had been nationalists and imperialists in 1899, the elements led by Henry Cabot Lodge, Theodore Roosevelt, and Albert J. Beveridge. Even louder and more fanatical were the isolationists, such as William E. Borah, Hiram W. Johnson, and James A. Reed, who had appeared in national politics after 1898.

In the tempestuous era following the First World War, Mission was a steadying force in an age of disaster. Disaster swept over the world in a succession of waves in the 1930s and 1940s. An economic tempest almost toppled the old order; then, before it had subsided, came the Second World War; and after that, the continuing crises of the cold war. In this era the hemispheric policy of the "Good Neighbor" was given effect; it was a truer expression of the American spirit than Manifest Destiny ever had been, and it quieted memories in Latin America which had persisted from the Mexican War. The concept of the Four Freedoms was framed by Franklin D. Roosevelt early in 1941, as the nation drifted toward involvement in the Second World

War. The freedoms named were those imperiled by the war and the continuing depression—freedom of speech, freedom of religion, freedom from want, and freedom from fear. In defense of these freedoms Great Britain was given aid, the Fascist powers were checked, and were finally overthrown. Victory was followed by the framing of a new organ of internationalism, the United Nations, this time approved by the United States Senate and set on a course of peace.

National ideals are not simple. They are complex, and sometimes combined in mixtures as incompatible as oil and water. Manifest Destiny was sometimes mixed with a form of Mission of its own. It would be reckless to say that zealots of Manifest Destiny in the 1840s and in the 1890s had no sense of Mission. They battled for possession of the public mind armored in their own coats of idealism. They knew that in the United States a program armored in unrelieved materialism would lose the battle before a blow was struck or a shot fired. The public was usually able to detect differences between varieties of idealism, however, and to choose between them. The tests applied were the proportions found, in each variety, of aid to others and gain for self, of generous spaciousness and narrow parochialism, of enduring values and momentary appeal.

From the beginning programs of public welfare were identified with Mission. Programs of political, social, and economic change for the benefit of the underprivileged were fought for throughout the nineteenth century as phases of Mission. So were religious programs in which refreshment of the soul was sought in service to others. Philanthropy for public purposes was encouraged as part of the image of America. It reached dimensions in the United States unprecedented in the history of the world. At the end of the Second World War the same spirit appeared in the Marshall Plan for rebuilding the devastated areas of the world. It has appeared in recent programs, vast in scale, to help the peoples of underdeveloped areas.

Manifest Destiny, by contrast, seemed, despite its exaltation of language, somehow touched by a taint of selfishness, both national and individual. The sacrifices it asked were to be from others. Territory was to be taken, and all that was to be given in exchange was the prospect of American citizenship.

Manifest Destiny, moreover, seemed, on close examination, despite its breath-taking sweep, to be parochial. Its postulates were that Anglo-Saxons are endowed as a race with innate superiority, that Protestant Christianity holds the keys to Heaven, that only republican forms of political organization are free, that the future—even the predestined future—can be hurried along by human hands, and that the means of hurrying it, if the end be good, need not be inquired into too closely. Undeniably, some Americans were satisfied with such ideals. But a large majority appraised them—at least in periods when the nation was at peace—at their true worth.

Manifest Destiny and Mission differed in another respect—durability. Manifest Destiny, in the twentieth century, vanished. Not only did it die; it stayed dead through two world wars. Mission, on the contrary, remained alive, and is as much alive at present as it ever was. It is still the beacon lighting the way to political and individual freedoms—to equality of right before the law, equality of economic opportunity, and equality of all races and creeds. It is still, as always in the past, the torch held aloft by the nation at its gate—to the world and to itself.

Notes

1   Elmer Ellis: *Henry Moore Teller* (Caldwell, Id., 1941), 308. Teller became an anti-imperialist after a break with his party over the silver issue.

2   *Dorr* v. *United States,* 197 U.S. Reports, 138 ff.

3   *Hawaii* v. *Mankichi,* 190 U.S. Reports, 197 ff.

4   Other island possessions of the United States are eastern Samoa, taken as a protectorate in 1889 and annexed in 1899 in the imperialistic climate of that year, and the Virgin Islands, purchased in 1916. Guam, Samoa, and the Virgin Islands were transferred from the Navy Department to the Department of the Interior in 1950, 1951, and 1954, respectively. Local legislatures have been set up in Guam and the Virgin Islands, and are proposed for Samoa.

5   The evolution of the phrasing of the address is recounted briefly in Basler (ed.): *Collected Works of Abraham Lincoln,* VIII, 16–23.

6   Gallatin: *Peace with Mexico,* Section VII.

7   William A. Robinson: *Thomas B. Reed* (New York, 1930), 357–71; Samuel W. McCall: *Life of Thomas Brackett Reed* (Boston, 1914), ch. 20.

8   Allan Nevins (ed.): *Letters of Grover Cleveland* (Boston, 1933), 491–2. A mixed concept of mission is described in Edward M. Burns: *The American Ideal of Mission* (New Brunswick, N.J., 1957).

The following essay, originally published in the March 11, 1969, issue of the
"National Review," presents an interpretation that is diametrically opposed
to most of the other views expressed in this chapter.

Will the Indians Get Whitey?

John Greenway

When 36 out of 81 superior American college students can look at
a photograph of American soldiers removing piles of emaciated Jewish corpses from a liberated Nazi horror camp and identify the scene
as Americans committing atrocities in Vietnam—well, is it not to be
expected?

The unnatural eagerness of Americans to believe themselves to be
monsters is not a biological imperative, despite its constancy from the
earliest period of American history. It is learned behavior, implanted
neither by genes nor by experience, but by the teachings of the
strangest class of intellectuals any nation has ever been damned with.
With few significant exceptions, America's professional thinkers have
been anomic dropouts from their own culture, burning the American
spirit as their bearded acolytes burn the American flag. They find
some unrepented sin in themselves and take up whatever scourge lies
at hand to visit its punishment upon their forefathers. Now more than
ever before, the American Indian is a favorite scourge—as a study of
ten popular, non-scholarly books[1] on the Indian demonstrates.

To the authors of these books the Indians are a stick to beat the
American soul, as sympathizer William Eastlake ingenuously disclosed in a review in *Book Week*. "The Nez Perce Indians," Eastlake
began, ". . . set out to get Whitey on Wednesday, June 13, 1877. The
war lasted 117 days, and cost Whitey over $1 million, an expense
probably considerably less than Watts, which shows that Whitey's
wars with the Hostiles are not only costing more now but we are
learning less. . . . Learn, Whitey, Learn."

All of these books are stern indictments of Our Treatment of the
Indians, though the authors have little more qualification to write
books about the Indians than a plumber has to practice brain surgery.

From "Will the Indians Get Whitey?" by John Greenway. Reprinted by permission from the March 11, 1969, issue of *National Review*, 150 East 35th
Street, New York, N.Y. 10016.

Historical value is claimed for most of them by the dust jackets and as to that point, what A. E. Housman once said under similar provocation can be said here; history as practiced by these writers is not a game—an exercise requiring skill and heed, like marbles, or skittles or cats' cradles—but a pastime, like leaning against a wall and spitting. They write about the Indian because the Indian in the American mind is as imaginary as Sandburg's Lincoln, a creation of fantasy, guilt and ignorance, on which everyone is his own authority. Edward Hicks should have painted the scene: in the background a massacre of Indian women and children; in the foreground a young Indian lad and his Indian lass, hand in hand, about to hurl themselves off a Lovers' Leap while singing "By the Waters of Minnetonka." The illusion is always more romantic than the reality; in real life Running Bear would have been less likely to seduce Little White Dove than to rape her.

The Indian As Dionysus

The lay reader should have a hardcore course in what the real Indian was like before exposing his raw conscience to books like these. He should know that the real Indian was ferocious, cruel, aggressive, stoic, violent, ultra-masculine, treacherous and warlike, though these are anemic adjectives to describe the extent of his Dionysiac extremism. As for Our Treatment of the Indians, never in the entire history of the inevitable displacement of hunting tribes by advanced agriculturists in the 39,000 generations of mankind has a native people been treated with more consideration, decency and kindness. The Mongoloids in displacing the first comers of Asia, the Negroes in displacing the aborigines in Africa, and every other group following the biological law of the Competitive Exclusion Principle thought like the Polynesian chief who once observed to a white officer: "I don't understand you English. You come here and take our land and then you spend the rest of your lives trying to make up for it. When my people came to these islands, we just killed the inhabitants and that was the end of it." It could be argued that the only real injury the white man ever did the Indian was to take his fighting away from him. Indians did not fight to defend their land, their people or their honor, as these writers apparently believe; like the Irish, they fought for the fighting. Without war and raiding and scalping and rape and pillage and slave-taking, the Indian was as aimless as a chiropractor without a spine. There was nothing left in life for him but idleness, petty mischief and booze.

Some two million people who have read Ruth Benedict's classic of just-so anthropology, *Patterns of Culture,* suppose that there were

Apollonians on this earth, and that they were the Pueblo Indians. The only flaw in the Pueblos' angelic character was their effeminate peacefulness, Dr. Benedict suggested. But she did say that the Pueblos killed the first Spaniard to visit them (ironically, the first "white" man killed by the Pueblos was a Negro), that they killed and scalped missionaries, and that they conducted the most successful of all violent Indian rebellions against the whites.

The Indian As Democrat

While the *lumpenproletariat* cherished the image of the romantic Indian, the *lumpenintelligentsia* clutched the noble Indian to the body politic. Our universities today swarm with men who truly believe that both the Constitution specifically and American democracy generally were copied from Indian originals. Some of these men have been seen to laugh at the New Fundamentalists for believing that Christ ascended to heaven in a space ship.

The Indians indeed did put up imitations of civilized institutions when it seemed profitable to do so, but they were the most palpable travesties. Dale Van Every's contribution to the Black Pages of White History, *Disinherited,* is an unintentional illustration of how academic folklore on the Indians is constructed. He meets the stringent standards of authority established by his peers, having once written a history entitled *The AEF in Battle* (which I have not read, fearing it might take the side of the Germans) and making movies for thirteen years. He deals with the central illusion, on which most of the others depend: that the Indians in the forest primeval were gathered into mighty nations. There were, he says, "twenty great Indian nations" in the Southeast alone, of which the greatest in civilization and suffering was the Cherokee. (Fact: From a population of two thousand in 1761, this great Cherokee empire was reduced by the white man's oppression, diseases, wars and massacres, to *fifty* thousand the last time they came into court to sue for the return of the Southeastern states.)

Within these nations pure democracy flourished. At the top of page 82 Mr. Van Every tells of the "instinctive sympathy" between Negroes and Indians, and of the "ingrained Indian abhorrence of slavery as an institution." At the bottom of page 82 Mr. Van Every gives us a census of the Cherokee Nation in 1825: 15,563 Indians; Negro slaves, 1,277. These were not refugee slaves; these were real slaves. In 1824 the Cherokee National Committee prohibited any of their Negroes from owning stock, voting or marrying Indians. Still, one must consider the iron law of economics; Van Every could make neither a book nor a movie on the Cherokee as they really were—intruders into the land the United States paid them for, important only because they were the victors in a bloody war to extermination or exile with other tribes—the Yamasee, Creek, Choctaw, Shawnee, Catawba, Tuscarora and Chickasaw—over which tribe should have the monopoly of selling slaves to the South. The only Indians in these books that did not hold slaves were those too poor to afford to keep them. Even the Quechans, about whom Jack D. Forbes has written a kind of book, *Warriors of the Colorado,* had slaves when they had very little else. It is not pertinent to say much about the book, for only literate Quechans would be tempted to read it, but it has the same sort of weird ideas about the Indians as the others. "Their hearts were good and strong, and the Quechans have survived," effuses Forbes. In reality, the Quechans survived because the whites came in and saved them from the Maricopas and Gila Pimas and Halchidomas and Walapais and Havasupais and Cahuillas and Paipais and Kiliwas and Halyika-wamais and Kohuanas, all of whom were fighting for slaves.

When Van Every's heart is not weeping for the Cherokee, it is hemorrhaging for the Seminoles, who established a claim to Florida that the Indian Claims Commission has offered to pay off in a 1965 decision. How did the Seminoles establish ownership to Florida? By fleeing over the Georgia line with Negro slaves they stole from the whites. The Seminoles have been granted a cash settlement for the state, but they still want the state. We may get off easy by giving them Miami.

Edmund Wilson, an Indian expert in the tradition of that Boston booby, Ralph Waldo Emerson, long ago finished writing learnedly on everything he knows anything about and has recently begun writing learnedly on everything he knows nothing about, e.g. the Indians, and the income tax. *Apologies to the Iroquois* was commissioned by the *New Yorker.*[1] Read it and learn all about the Seneca Republic (population 3,792; not to be confused with the rival Seneca Nation) and our responsibilities to it in the question of title to New York State. Read it and learn that the Senecas and their neighbors shared their Southern cousins' abhorrence of slavery, though they retained some whites "adopted" during raids on settlements.

Wilcomb Washburn is a different kettle of fish. He resides in the Indian territory of Washington, D.C., and he feels enough guilt about Our Treatment to give up his own real estate to the original owners, the Manahoac, if there were any left. He is an objective historian writing "from a point of view strongly sympathetic to the American Indian," an apologia that permits him to distort history in his anthology of primary materials, *The Indian and the White Man.* The selections are genuine enough, but they are rigorously chosen for his special pleading, and each is prefaced by an officious analysis setting the primary writer straight whenever he is in danger of straying into the truth. Washburn informs us, for example, that the term "tribe" was a dysphemism for "nation," introduced by the whites when they decided to reduce the Indians. He is right, of course; the word "tribe" was brought in by the whites. And so was the concept.

The real Indian was only most tenuously a member of a tribe. His ecological unit was the nomadic band, either hunting-gathering or primitive agricultural, with little cohesion beyond an approximation to a common language and some weak psychological unity. These marauding social fragments cohered only when profitable raiding was visible.

Tribes have to have chiefs, so the white man invented that concept also. In the old days, the nearest any Indian tribe got to a chief was somebody who could persuade a few young braves to accompany him in a sneak raid on the neighbors' horses. Several such expeditions would authorize a warrior to sign treaties with the whites and eventually visit Washington for a real raid (Red Cloud made fifteen personal assaults on the Treasury). Later, candidates for chiefhood did not even have to steal horses—they just applied to the Great White Father for certification. In 1891 the Acting Agent for the Pine Ridge Sioux endorsed a dozen such applications for chief from sundry Indians with this comment: "Furnishing these papers can have no effect except to please the vanity of the recipients and keep them in good humor." From 1860 on, politics among the Indians was a situation of too many chiefs and not enough Indians.

Imagination abhors a factual vacuum, and so in these books chiefs are made out of nothing more substantial than euphonious names. The real leader of the Nez Perce flight was Poker Joe, hopeless as a potential eponym, so "Chief Joseph" becomes the Great Red Father. Chief Moses, another naturally named leader, is apotheosized by another expert on the Indians not terribly well known in anthropological circles, Dr. Robert H. Ruby. Ruby has his doctorate in medicine, which would seem to limit his authority to sick Indians, but he published a previous book through a vanity press, and that makes a difference. His biography of Moses, *Half Sun on the Columbia* (one of Moses' aliases) unfortunately says little about the ethos of Moses' people, the Sinkiuse-Columbia. Other writers have found them to be like the rest of the Northwest Coast tribes—obsessed with a paranoid status competition, slavery, warfare and cannibalism. So Moses, like Joseph, must have been a phenomenon, for Ruby offers him as a man of peace. "The peacemaking of our subject," writes Ruby, "assured him a place not among the blazoned, but among the blessed." In reality's dull record, Moses attained his chiefly status by slaughtering lone travelers. On one of his later peacemaking expeditions his warriors killed a party of fifty miners, but excused themselves by saying they thought the miners were soldiers. If Dr. Ruby gets away with his refurbishment of this rascal, he should be able to write Stokely Carmichael into a Nobel Peace Prize.

The Indian As Victim

When sneak attacks on horses escalated into massive and murderous raids on settlements, people would sometimes get hurt. But Washburn speaks for his peers when he forbids the term "massacre" to describe such incidents; such invidious expressions, he says, were designed to put the Indian into bad repute "and to provide good reason why he should be treated the way he was treated by that society." It is just as unfair, he adds, as accusing the Indian of cannibalism merely because he ate people.

So James C. Olson pours out his heart's blood for the Sioux in nearly 400 pages of *Red Cloud and the Sioux Problem* without ever finding it pertinent to mention the Minnesota Massacre, in which at least 800 whites were killed and 10,000 square miles of Minnesota cleared of settlers. About the only consistent use of the word "massacre" in these books appends to the Sand Creek and Wounded Knee massacres.[3]

It is, by the way, almost impossible to find a book giving the white side of the Sand Creek affair; authors ignore the voluminous testimony of the congressional investigation and accept the testimony instead of one Robert Bent, a survivor. This Bent makes an interesting witness; he was a renegade halfbreed who with his two brothers lived and raided with the Cheyenne. They were a precious trio; one of them captured a white settler, staked him to the ground, cut out his tongue, castrated him, and built a fire on his stomach.

In *The Long Death* Andrist mentions the Minnesota Massacre, but his interest is in the Indians who were captured, tried and executed for the murders—39 Indians went to the gallows. Andrist (who is also the author of *Heroes of Polar Exploration*) chooses as the most regrettable part of the episode the second hanging of Rattling Runner, on whom the rope broke—"but the traditional ritual of legal life-taking had to be gone through in its entirety . . . his body was hoisted again, to dangle yet a while for the edification of the spectators." Rattling Runner's hangman, who so edified the crowd, had three children lying dead out on the plains, and his wife and two other children still in the tender hands of the uncaught Indians. Still, as the dust jacket judges, "Mr. Andrist writes with such passion that the reader hears the roar of guns and the rumble of hooves, the whistle of whips, the creak of wagon wheels, and always, and everywhere, the screams of dying and dispossessed . . . the most fitting tribute ever written to the noblest victims Destiny ever had." The jacket is talking about the Indians.

Least funny of all these books is *The Shoshoneans—The People of the Basin-Plateau,* by two beatniks who toured the desert country of Idaho, Utah and Nevada stirring up mischief for a non-book. Its deception begins with the title, which might lead the unwary to think it was a work of dull but reputable ethnography. It is nothing of the sort; it is an undisciplined screed against the whites of the area illustrated by photographs by a man who confuses underexposure with art. Mainly the photographs are of sullen young Indians in sunglasses staggering out of bars. All the degeneration, of course, is attributable to the "fascism" of the cowboy culture that corrupted the pristine Indian. A typical passage describes an old Indian lying in filth and asks why "the pasty doctors of the agency did not come and bathe him." Edward Dorn's photographer companion might have washed him, but he was out in the field dancing the Sun Dance with the Indians for peace in Vietnam.

The Indian As Cop

The idea of Indians policing Indians was a simultaneous self-invention on several reservations in the late 1860s. Its purpose was to perpetuate the old way of life rather than to conclude it. Some raiding bands now became police, and other bands fought them, and the only significant difference for the whites was their notion that one side was better than the other, so they paid the one in money and the other in rations. There was a more significant difference for the Indians: those who joined the police or the accompanying judiciary knew where the action was. Before Bob Dalton decided it was more profitable to rob banks, he worked as a chief of the Osage police. While the displaced generation of Red Cloud, Kicking Bear, Moses, Joseph, and the several Sitting Bulls sat around sulking like tired Union League Republicans talking about Roosevelt, Sammy Running Bear Glick put down his tomahawk and took up the gavel.

Judge B. H. Sixkiller, one of the well-known Cherokee, showed how the old ways remained the same the more they changed. He went too far one day and sat in judgment of the wrong Indian. Before the trial was over, Judge Sixkiller and ten other people in the courtroom lay dead on the floor, and the jury, so to speak, was hung.

Another member of the Sixkiller family of law enforcers, Sheriff Sam, was twice tried for murder for defending himself against a raiding band that was shooting at him. He beat the rap, but was wounded later by an Indian who successfully pleaded in his defense that he was just "shooting at police." Three months after that affray Sam was killed, and his successor as captain of the agency police was also knocked off. Everybody has heard of the sadistic Hanging Judge Parker, who strung up an Indian from time to time at Fort Smith, but there are a few who do not know that during Parker's tenure of office 65 of his deputies were killed. Judge Abraham No Heart was perhaps a wiser jurist; he collected the guns of convicted Indians in lieu of monetary fines. These incidents are typical, and one can find more of them in a fine book by William T. Hagan, *Indian Police and Judges* (Yale, 1966, $6.50).

Our books all stop short of the final subject in the sequence of Our Treatment of the Indian: the Indians' Treatment of Us. In 1960 the arrest rate for whites in the United States was 2,739 in 100,000. For Negroes it was 8,703. But for Indians it was 51,090. This inequity of iniquity has persuaded some racist commentators to explain excessive criminality as a Mongoloid characteristic—but Chinese and Japanese in the United States have the lowest arrest figure of any group, lower even than for the most law-respecting WASPs.

The Indian As Litigant

As civilization displaces savagery, raiding becomes litigation. The year of 1946 will be remembered not only as the year ballpoint pens sold for $15.98, but as the year the United States was given back to the Indians. It was then that the Indian Claims Commission was quietly established by Congress as a device to simplify suits against the government for compensation for land usurpation. In fact liability was admitted, with the only issue to be determined in most cases being which Indians should get the money. Five years were allowed for the filing of claims, and by the 1951 deadline, 852 claims were entered for 70 per cent of the United States.

This is not to say that the American conscience did not awaken until 1946. Indians have been suing the whites for more than a century and swindling them for much longer than that. The first real estate fraud on the American continent was that famous purchase of Manhattan by Peter Minuit—but the tale has been twisted over the years. It was the Dutch who were swindled; the Scaticook Indians were the occupying owners, but the deal was pulled by a mob of Canarsie Indians who were visiting Manhattan for the day. The Scaticooks, by the way, have their claim in for the island, and they are not about to take any junk jewelry for it this time.

Jefferson paid Napoleon $15 million for the Louisiana Territory in another well-publicized bargain—a sum that did not include a further $300 million under the blanket to the Indians. Some Indians were paid as many as six times for the same land, each time returning to complain that the white man was an Indian giver.

And so from tribe to tribe (a tribe now is defined as comprising any Indians the tribe council wishes to include in the loot). The Cherokee, who were themselves invaders and usurpers of the land they occupied, have received $14 million.

Their contending neighbors sued for $22 million and settled for $1,769,940 in 1952. The Nez Perce received $3 million for their expenses in massacring settlers, with their suit for 100,000 square miles of Idaho still in litigation. Edmund Wilson's Seneca Nation was given $12,128,917 out of court two years ago. The Utes got $31,938,473.43 as a starter for the land they stole from the Pueblos, and then made their expert anthropological witness, Dr. Omer C. Stewart, wait nine years for his $100-a-day fee (he was finally persuaded to settle for half what was owed him).

An important point in this saga of masochistic largesse is how many Indians all this is going to. The Creeks number eighteen thousand. Six hundred Quapaws are claiming $54,397,110.34. Altogether there are 550,000 Indians asking for $10 billion.

These claims do not include all the money going free from the taxpayer to the Indian. On the 397 federal reservations (eleven of which are over a million acres) no taxes are paid on either the land or its usufruct—and the usufruct ran to $70 million in 1965 for rental to whites alone, not counting the uncountable hundreds of millions for primary use. And then there are the continuing service subsidies from the Bureau of Indian Affairs—$221,482,405 in the last official report, with many more millions hidden in other areas of budgetry.

Even the Office of Economic Opportunity is shotgunning poverty funds into the Indians; in just one caper the OEO spent $208,741 to show the Zuni how they could mass-produce their handcrafted jewelry for a guaranteed annual income of $150,000—unaware that the Zuni already market more than $2 million worth of jewelry every year in New Mexico alone. The idea is known as "the Zany Zuni Plan."

The Zuni are nearly unique in that they work. Most reservation-bound Indians agree with what Chief Moses once said: "We do not want to work and don't know how. Indians are too old to learn that when five years old." The Utes are mentioned from time to time in the menopause magazines as successful agriculturists, but what farming is done on the Ute reservation is done by hired white labor.

A random deskload of books all arguing the profundity of American guilt in our injustice to the Indians, and a class of students confusing American immolation with Nazi atrocities suggests a situation worth observing for the sheer insanity of it. How far can it all go? Will the 22 million Negroes in the United States sue the Government for all that free labor before 1865? Will the descendants of Adam enter a claim against the United States (God being safely dead) for their ancestor's unjust expulsion from the Garden? Will Sioux citizen William Hawk succeed in his incredible compensation claim against the government for wounding his uncle, Gall, the Hunkpapa chief, when Gall led his warriors against Custer at Little Big Horn? Will the Americans ever find out where to go to surrender for the crime of being Americans? Not even the Indians are safe from the implicit absurdities of the claims game. A year ago, a suit was filed in federal court in Denver, Colorado, against the United States and its derivative usurpers, *including* the Indians, by 28 descendants of early Mexican grant holders. This deprived minority claims all of California, Utah, Oregon, Louisiana, Missouri, Arkansas, Iowa, North and South Dakota, Nebraska, and Oklahoma, and parts of Kansas, Colorado, Wyoming, Montana, Minnesota, New Mexico, Florida, Texas, Arizona, Georgia, North and South Carolina, Maryland, Virginia, Washington, and Idaho. Their lawyer, a former United States Attorney for Colorado, is no ordinary nut. A practical and reasonable man, he has indicated a willingness to settle with the United States, the Indians and the Civil Rights Commission for one trillion dollars.

Notes

1 *The Long Death: The Last Days of the Plains Indians,* by Ralph K. Andrist. Macmillan, $8.95. *The Flight of the Nez Perce: A History of the Nez Perce War* by Mark H. Brown. Putnam, $8.95. *The Shoshoneans: The People of the Basin-Plateau* by Edward Dorn and Leroy Lucas. Morrow, $6.95. *Warriors of the Colorado: The Yumas of the Quechan Nation and their Neighbors* by Jack D. Forbes. Oklahoma, $5.95. *The Nez Perce Indians and the Opening of the Northwest* by Alvin M. Josephy Jr. Yale, $12.50. *Red Cloud and the Sioux Problem* by James C. Olson. Nebraska, $5.95. *Half Sun on the Columbia: A*

Biography of Chief Moses by Robert H. Ruby and John H. Brown. Oklahoma, $5.95. *Disinherited: The Lost Birthright of the American Indian* by Dale Van Every. Morrow, 95¢ (paper). *The Indian and the White Man* by Wilcomb E. Washburn. Doubleday Anchor, $1.95 (paper). *Apologies to the Iroquois,* by Edmund Wilson. Random House, $1.95 (paper).

2 Wilson's book is so naive that one cannot analyze it. Nearly every point he makes about Indian culture demonstrates a near-total ignorance of anthropological principles and solid knowledge about Indians. It's rather like a gardener discussing deoxyribonucleic acid in plant genetics.—J.G.

3 A typical distortion of the facts. The assemblage of Indians at Wounded Knee were hostiles dancing the Ghost Dance, which among the Sioux demanded genocide of the whites. The fighting—which indeed ended with the total slaughter of the Indians by soldiers harboring long infuriation for unavenged killings by the Indians—began when a shaman blew the eagle whistle and Indians pulled concealed rifles from under their blankets. The Wounded Knee Massacre put an end to Indian wars.—J.G.

In 1900 William Jennings Bryan argued passionately against annexation of the Philippines. He attacked the rationalizations for expansion on several counts. Morality was the central core of his argument. By what right does the United States presume to govern others? he asked. Certainly the Declaration of Independence does not justify our annexation, he argued. Do you agree with his views?

America's Obligations
William Jennings Bryan

The Title to the Philippines

What is our title to the Philippine islands? Do we hold them by treaty or by conquest? Did we buy them, or did we take them? Did we purchase the people? If not, how did we secure title to them? Were they thrown in with the land? Will the Republicans say that inanimate earth has value and when that earth is molded by the Divine hand and stamped with the likeness of the Creator it becomes a fixture and passes with the soil? If governments derive their just powers of the consent of the governed it is impossible to secure title to people either by force or by purchase. We could extinguish Spain's title by treaty, but if we hold title we must hold it by some method consistent with our ideas of government. When we made allies of the Filipinos and armed them to fight against Spain, we disputed Spain's title. If we buy Spain's title we are not innocent purchasers. But even if we had not disputed Spain's title, she could transfer no greater title than she had, and her title was based on force alone. We cannot defend such a title, but as Spain gave us a quit claim deed, we can honorably turn the property over to the party in possession. Whether any American official gave the Filipinos moral assurance of independence is not material. There can be no doubt that we accepted and utilized the services of the Filipinos and that when we did so we had full knowledge that they were fighting for their own independence, and I submit that history furnishes no example of turpitude baser than ours if we now substitute our yoke for the Spanish yoke.

Let us consider briefly the relations which have been given in support of an imperialistic policy. Some say it is our duty to hold the Philippine islands. But duty is not an argument; it is a conclusion. To ascertain what our duty is, in any emergency, we must apply well-settled and generally accepted principles. It is our duty to avoid steal-

250

ing, no matter whether the thing to be stolen is of great or little value. It is our duty to avoid killing a human being, no matter where the human being lives, or to what race or class he belongs. Every one recognizes the obligation imposed upon individuals to observe both the human and moral law, but as some deny the application of those laws to nations it may not be out of place to quote the opinion of others. Jefferson, than whom there is no higher political authority, said: "I know of but one code of morality for men, whether acting singly or collectively."

Franklin, whose learning, wisdom and virtue are a part of the priceless legacy bequeathed to us from the revolutionary days, expressed the same idea in even stronger language when he said: "Justice is as strictly due between neighbor nations as between neighbor citizens. A highwayman is as much a robber when he plunders in a gang as when singly; and the nation that makes an unjust war is only a great gang."

Morals and Numbers

Men may dare to do in crowds what they would not dare to do as individuals, but the moral character of an act is not determined by the number of those who join in it. Force can defend a right, but force has never yet created a right. If it was true, as declared in the resolution of intervention, that the Cubans "are and of right ought to be free and independent" (language taken from the Declaration of Independence), it is equally true that the Filipinos "are and of right ought to be free and independent." The right of the Cubans to freedom was not based upon their proximity to the United States, nor upon the language which they spoke, nor yet upon the race or races to which they belonged. Congress by a practically unanimous vote declared that the principles enunciated at Philadelphia in 1776 were still alive and applicable to the Cubans.

Who will draw a line between the natural rights of the Cubans and the Filipinos? Who will say that the former have a right to liberty and the latter have no rights which we are bound to respect? And if the Filipinos "are and of right ought to be free and independent," what right have we to force our government upon them without their consent? Before our duty can be ascertained, and when their rights are once determined, it is as much our duty to respect those rights as it was the duty of Spain to respect the rights of the people of Cuba, or the duty of England to respect the rights of the American colonists. Rights never conflict; duties never clash. Can it be our duty to kill those who, following the example of our forefathers, love liberty well enough to fight for it? Some poet has described the terror which overcame a soldier who, in the midst of battle, discovered that he had slain his brother. It is written, "All ye are brethren." Let us hope for the coming of the day when human life—which when once destroyed cannot be restored—will be so sacred that it will never be taken, except when necessary to punish a crime already committed, or to prevent a crime about to be committed.

The Highest Obligation

If it is said that we have assumed before the world obligations which make it necessary for us to permanently maintain a government in the Philippine islands. I reply, first, that the highest obligation of this Nation is to be true to itself. No obligation to any particular nation or to all nations combined can require the abandonment of our theory of government and the substitution of doctrines against which our whole national life has been a protest. And, second, that our obligations to the Filipinos who inhabit the islands are greater than any obligation which we can owe to foreigners who have a temporary residence in the Philippines or desire to trade there.

It is argued by some that the Filipinos are incapable of self-government and that therefore we owe it to the world to take control of them. Admiral Dewey in an official report to the Navy Department declared the Filipinos more capable of self-government than the Cubans and said that he based his opinion upon a knowledge of both races. But I will not rest the case upon the relative advancement of the Filipinos. Henry Clay in defending the rights of the people of South America to self-government said:

> It is the doctrine of thrones that man is too ignorant to govern himself. Their partisans assert his incapacity in reference to all nations; if they cannot command universal assent to the proposition, it is then remanded to particular nations; and our pride and our presumption too often make converts of us. I contend that it is to arraign the disposition of Providence himself, to suppose that he has created beings incapable of governing themselves, and to be trampled on by kings. Self-government is the natural government of man.

Clay was right. There are degrees of proficiency in the art of self-government, but it is a reflection upon the Creator to say that He denied to any people the capacity of self-government. Once admit that some people are capable of self-government, and that others are not, and that the capable people have a right to seize upon and govern the incapable, and you make force—brute force—the only foundation of government and invite the reign of the despot. I am not willing to believe that an all-wise and an all-loving God created the Filipinos, and then left them thousands of years helpless until the islands attracted the attention of the European nations.

The possibilities of the American frontier as a romantic, escapist Dream
are discussed in the cogent excerpt below. As the author points out,
"Huckleberry Finn" and "The Grapes of Wrath" and "The Catcher
in the Rye" all have a common bond. That bond is the American
Dream.

The Frontier That No Longer Exists

Walter Allen

The frontier, the movement westward, remains the great image of
the American sense of possibility. As such, it is one of the main components of the American dream, one might say of America as dream.
It is summed up in a peculiarly American book, a seminal book,
Mark Twain's *The Adventures of Huckleberry Finn,* especially in its
last sentences: "I reckon I got to light out for the territory ahead of
the rest, because Aunt Sally she's going to adopt me and sivilize me,
and I can't stand it. I been there before." The dream of the frontier,
then, from one point of view, is the dream of the escape from Aunt
Sally, from respectability, the constraints of civilisation and society,
indeed from civilisation and society itself into the life of uninhibited
freedom. Twain was not the first to state it in American fiction: it is
embodied in the figure of Natty Bumppo, 'Deerslayer', 'Pathfinder',
'Leather-Stocking', in Fenimore Cooper's sequence, *The Pioneers,
The Last of the Mohicans, The Prairie, The Pathfinder* and *The
Deerslayer*. Published between 1826 and 1841, they reflect among
other things, through the idyllic, chivalrous character of Bumppo,
their patriotic author's disenchantment with what seemed to him the
materialism and narrowness of American society.

The dream of the frontier as expressed by Twain and Cooper, is no
doubt a romantic dream, even an adolescent or neurotic dream. For
many years it has been contradicted by the facts of the real situation.
The Okies of John Steinbeck's novel, *The Grapes of Wrath,* when
dispossessed of their farms in Oklahoma by soil-erosion or by the
banks that own the land, pile their belongings into their battered, all

but broken-down cars and drive the thousand miles across the desert to the promised land of California, flowing with milk and honey. But California is already owned and occupied; there is no welcome for them there. There is in fact no place for them to go.

The Grapes of Wrath, written out of Steinbeck's passionate indignation against the miseries caused by the economic depression of the Thirties, was published in 1939. Twelve years later, another equally famous novel was published, on the face of it very different from Steinbeck's: J. D. Salinger's *The Catcher in the Rye.* But it too is concerned with flight. *The Grapes of Wrath* describes flight motivated by economic misery towards more prosperous lands. *The Catcher in the Rye* describes a more hopeless flight, the flight from what seems to the boy-hero the crippling evasions and hypocrisies, the absence of generosity, of adult American life. Like the Okies, but unlike Huck, who is in many respects his exemplar, he finds nowhere to fly to, no place to go. There is no escape for young Holden Caulfield except the psychoanalyst's couch, after which, one must assume, follows conformity with the society rebelled against.

These two novels in their different ways are seemingly criticisms of the American dream in that they show its inadequacy in the face of the brute facts of American life. It could also be said that the dreamers themselves are inadequate: Steinbeck's Okies are illiterates, some of them indeed almost morons, and Salinger's Holden is a boy in early adolescence; neither he nor the Okies are in a position to know the reality of their situations. Yet there can be no question at all where the authors' sympathies lie: they are with the dream, against the brute facts of reality, and their criticism works both ways. And this criticism of the nature of American life, made as it were from the standpoint of the dream itself is, as we shall see, a constant element in American literature.

The movement westward of the Okies of *The Grapes of Wrath* is towards a frontier that no longer exists. Yet the movement westward itself duplicates one made by the ancestors of all Americans, whether of old families or of recent origin. All, whether they came in hope or were driven by persecution or by the threat of starvation at home, crossed a frontier, the frontier of the Atlantic. They made a leap into a country where it seemed to them a better life was possible. The leap is what differentiates them from the men who remained at home, is what makes them American. And even though the frontier is no more, the possibilities it represents are still there as powerful elements in the American mind.

Questions

1 Were Americans justified in their treatment of Mexicans and Indians occupying western lands?

2 How much did the rationalizations for territorial expansion actually influence the **desire** to expand? What were the underlying motives for expansion?

3 Professor Merk praises America's sense of Mission. In view of the American role in Vietnam today, do you think that this praise was shortsighted?

4 Is there any significance in the fact that America began to turn its eyes across the seas about the time the frontier vanished?

5 What are the most legitimate acquisitions of territory America has made? What are the least justifiable?

6 Is the American Dream of unlimited land responsible for this country's aggressive expansionist record?

7

Civil War,
Hot and Cold

Essay
The House Is Divided, Mr. Lincoln
Frederick Gentles

Readings
Lincoln's House Divided Speech
Abraham Lincoln

South Carolina Declaration of Causes of Secession
South Carolina Convention

The Emancipation Proclamation
John Hope Franklin

The Radicals and Lincoln
David Donald

The Negro in American Life: 1865–1918
C. Vann Woodward

Report of the National Advisory Commission on Civil Disorders
Otto Kerner, Chairman

The Black Nation
James Burnham

Man's continuing needs of security and identity, especially as they related
to race, politics, and economics, were among the causes for the nation
being torn asunder by civil war over one hundred years ago. It is
abundantly clear that the Civil War did not nullify civil tensions because
a cold war continues, and the American Dream of equality and a
house united remains unfulfilled. Former Chief Justice Earl Warren, speaking
as late as October 1970 on the bitter conflict in America, said: "If Americans
do not, individually, change their attitudes and concede equality—chaos
will follow. . . . It would take only a change of attitude on the part of
millions of Americans. If this can be done, perhaps we can achieve the
promise of America."[1] There is still time to reform in the American
tradition. But the unrest in America today poses the question: How much
time do we have? Reading of Civil War problems may help us to see
ourselves engulfed in the same security-identity complex that plagued
the nation a hundred years ago and thus speed the day when all
Americans are willing to concede the equality Earl Warren says is necessary.

The House Is Divided, Mr. Lincoln

Frederick Gentles

The House is still divided, Mr. Lincoln. Hot and cold civil war has
been a condition in America at least since your famous speech in
1858. It was once believed that a reconstruction period would put the
nation back together again, but the turmoil of the present, partly a
consequence of the Civil War, proclaims the nation is still divided.
Why? Because men have been conditioned throughout history to distrust people different from themselves? Because it is man's nature to
hate and to fight, as well as to love? Because self-interests—whether
social, political, economic—have always influenced man's actions
more than moral or humanitarian considerations?

Self-interests are many and complex, but certainly among the important needs most men are selfish about are those of security and
identity. Men want not only to be safe and comfortable but also to be
recognized as somebody by their fellow men—they want a framework
in which they can feel secure and with which they can identify. Those
with security and identity want to keep their status, even enhance it;
those without such status want to obtain it and often challenge the
Establishment of the society in which they live. War hot or cold may
result from the threats and the competition. It happened before, during, and after the Civil War.

Security identity needs got mixed up with two of the basic causes of the Civil War, slavery and the tariff. The slavery issue first became a problem for the new nation at Philadelphia in 1787, when the conferees modified their differences in two of the three great compromises of that Constitutional Convention. One compromise permitted the slave trade to continue for twenty years after ratification of the Constitution, and the other provided for counting three in every five slaves for purposes of both representation and taxation. The Northern delegates wanted to discontinue the trade in Africans immediately, and they did not want to count slaves as part of the population for many reasons, one being that more congressmen would be elected from the South if they were counted. The South, of course, wanted to continue the slave trade indefinitely and wanted to count all the slaves in order to give them a power base in Congress which could defend and further their selfish interests.

Sectional controversies were rather low key during the first thirty years of the new American government, but when Missouri applied for admission to the Union in 1819, the nation was split along national and states'-rights lines, free and slave, North and South. Senator Rufus King of New York warned of the danger of Missouri extending slavery into the previously free Louisiana Territory: "Such increase of the states," he said, "whatever other interests it may promote, will be sure to add nothing to the security of the public liberties." The South took the position, however, that any efforts by Congress to curtail a new state's rights would lead to tyranny of the Federal government. Henry Clay maneuvered both sides to agree to a compromise that would admit Maine as a free state in return for Missouri which would obviously be a slave-holding state. There was to be no other slavery in the Louisiana Territory north of 36 degrees 30 minutes latitude.

The security and identity of both sides was temporarily preserved —the South's by the *extension* and the North's by the *limitation* of slavery in that vast territory. But threats to national harmony continued. The decade of the 1830s witnessed Nat Turner's rebellion, which left a trail of nearly sixty whites dead in Virginia, and the rise of the Abolitionist movement with the publication of William Lloyd Garrison's *Liberator*. Garrison said he would be uncompromising on the slavery issue, and abolitionists gained momentum in both North and South during this and succeeding decades. Many Southerners responded to the threats posed by abolitionists by assembling arguments from the Bible, which they said condoned slavery; from history, which they used to cite the example of civilized Greeks and Romans profiting from slavery; from economic necessity, in which they found slavery tied to the survival and prosperity of Southern agriculture. Furthermore, they contended, it was none of the North's business what the South did about the slaves. The Constitution provided for all kinds of states' rights, and it did not prohibit slavery. Setting the slaves free would certainly threaten the whole Southern way of life.

The decades of the 1840s and 1850s were fraught with the strife of the slavery issue. Slave owners moved in large numbers into Texas, which was applying for admission into the Union; some Southerners hoped to extend the land base for what was called their "peculiar institution" by war with Mexico; the Compromise of 1850, besides admitting California as a free state, provided for a stronger fugitive slave law. In addition, the Kansas-Nebraska Act appeased the South but at the same time infuriated the North by providing for "popular sovereignty." That would permit people to determine for themselves whether or not they should have slavery—this despite the fact that Kansas and Nebraska were in the original Louisiana Territory and north of 36 degrees, 30 minutes. In effect, the Missouri Compromise of 1820 was null and void. Slave owners from Missouri were encouraged to come to Kansas and vote on election day. John Brown's abolitionists objected, and "bleeding Kansas" resulted. And the Dred Scott Decision, the Lincoln-Douglas Debates, and John Brown's raid on Harper's Ferry only regenerated emotions already hot on both sides of the Mason and Dixon Line. The cold war was heating up. Lincoln's election in 1860 was, in the minds of many Southerners, the last straw of Northern oppression; the new President was looked upon as "the black Republican" because of his statements opposing the extension of slavery.

But slavery was not the only issue that threatened the security and identity of both North and South. Bitterness developed over the protective tariff that John C. Calhoun of South Carolina had supported in 1816 with the hope it would benefit the whole country. Twelve years later, however, Calhoun issued the *South Carolina Exposition and Protest* repudiating the nationalistic view he once held and taking up a strong states'-rights position in opposition to the Tariff of 1828, the so-called Tariff of Abominations. Since the South did not develop industry as rapidly as the North, and since cheaper foreign manufactures were virtually excluded from America, that section was paying premium prices for Northern industrial goods. In protest, some South Carolinians began wearing rough homespun garments rather than buying the "damn Yankee goods." The tariff is not fair, Calhoun contended; furthermore, it is not constitutional because the Constitution provides that certain powers are reserved to the states. He patterned his argument of states' rights after the Virginia and Kentucky Resolutions of Jefferson and Madison earlier in the century.

Four years later (1832) Congress passed another tariff which modified some of the "abominations" of 1828, yet it still did not meet the demands of Southerners for a more equitable law. A powerful movement began in South Carolina to nullify the tariff. A convention called by the state legislature declared the existing tariff null and void, called for military preparations, and threatened to leave the Union if the Federal government tried to use force in collecting duties in South Carolina. The cold war was about to erupt into a hot one as President Andrew Jackson dispatched military and naval reinforcements to the Palmetto State and called for an increase in the size of the army. Moderates prevailed over the extremists on both sides, however, and a civil war was averted for the time being.

The tariff continued to be an issue with anti-protectionist Southerners always fighting for lower duties. In February 1861, President James Buchanan signed the Morrill Tariff which increased rates for the first time in many years. The South was already moving toward secession from the Union at this time, because of the slavery issue. Now incident was piled upon incident in both North and South until the nation's fearful emotions were set aflame. The newly born Confederacy had seized most United States property in the South before Lincoln's inauguration in March. Although the President's inaugural address was conciliatory, it was firm; the Union *must* be preserved. South Carolina's answer to what she considered a Northern threat to her security was the firing on Fort Sumter after Lincoln had decided to send food to the beleaguered garrison. Cold war had turned hot; an American tragedy of gigantic proportions was about to be enacted.

The American South has always had a marked identity that has been at the same time unique, exciting, romantic, proud, almost feudal, and certainly vigorous, especially in the "manly arts" of combat on the field of battle (or on the gridiron today). Southerners rallied around the Confederate flag and thrilled to "Dixie," the rebel yell, and the boys in grey, all to protect everything dear to the Southern way of life. Traditionally, Southerners have opted to identify with their states first, their section next, and *then* with the Union. But this strong states'-rights attitude weakened the Confederate government as it had previously weakened the Union.

Both sides during the Civil War appealed to God and to the higher morality, interpreting that higher morality in terms of their own welfare. Millions were willing to die for their cause, North or South, if only because the wheel of fortune had placed them on a particular spot of earth at a particular time in history. They identified with those around them, defending their security in what historian Bruce Catton in *A Stillness at Appomattox* called the insane logic of war. For four long years they suffered, and only stopped because one side was too exhausted to go on; otherwise they might still be fighting. Actually, both sides are fighting still, except that it is a cold war now (and much more diffuse throughout the country). It has been a cold war ever since the Reconstruction that did not reconstruct the nation.

In 1865 the Thirteenth Amendment freed the slaves, but multitudes of blacks believe that being second-class citizens in a country that mouths a beautiful Dream of equality is little better than slavery. The Fourteenth Amendment provided that no state shall deprive any person of life, liberty, or property without due process of law, nor deny to any person within its jurisdiction the equal protection of the laws. One has only to read the history of Jim Crow, the Black Codes, and separate but not equal schools, restaurants, hotels, ghettos, and suburbs to realize that this amendment has been tattered and torn on both sides of the Mason and Dixon Line. The Fifteenth Amendment states that one shall not be denied the vote on account of race, color, or previous condition of servitude. Deceptions on voting rights are familiar to everyone with only a little knowledge of history. Why the deceptions? To preserve white identity and security despite the intent and spirit of the law and the American Dream?

Although there were many gains for the black man during Reconstruction, as Professor Woodward explains in a reading later in this chapter, the period has been called "the tragic era" because many of the fundamental social, political, and economic problems festered to become chronic sores: states' rights, due process, equal protection, white power. The nation remained divided, not only North-South, but black-white, liberal-conservative, and that bizarre division of the 1960s and 1970s, human rights versus "law and order."

The Civil War probably represents the nadir in the pursuit of the American Dream—the house was divided; sectional self-interests took precedence over the national good; hatreds flared because of racial questions. War did not solve the tensions that disrupted the nation in 1860, and the Dream of unity and equality is in as precarious a balance today as it was a hundred years ago. No laws or court decisions will solve the problems of inequality, said Chief Justice Warren; Americans must voluntarily change their attitudes and concede equality. One qualification, however: Morality can be legislated; it always has been and probably always will be as long as society exists. From the Ten Commandments on down, laws, written and unwritten, have usually reflected moral values. The problem is that people do not always obey such laws. Those calling for law and order in one situation may break the law in another when they deny civil rights to a fellow man. American citizens have come a long way toward granting civil rights to blacks and other minorities in the last twenty years, due to laws, written and unwritten, and due to Earl Warren, the Reverend Martin Luther King, Jr., and countless others. But Americans still have some distance to go.

Note

1 "Earl Warren Fears U.S. Racial Chaos," *San Diego Union,* October 17, 1970, p. B-1.

Lincoln's Speech at the Republican State Convention at Springfield, Illinois, June 17, 1858, expressed concern that the ideals of the American Dream of union were being undermined by agitators in both the North and the South. Lincoln obviously recognized the cold war atmosphere of the country, yet he was unable to prevent the Dream from disintegrating into actual war. It is disconcerting to discover—if we only substitute "segregation" or "racism" for "slavery"—that much of this first paragraph could apply equally to the United States today.

Lincoln's House Divided Speech

Abraham Lincoln

MR. PRESIDENT AND GENTLEMEN OF THE CONVENTION: If we could first know where we are, and whither we are tending, we could better judge what to do, and how to do it. We are now far into the fifth year since a policy was initiated with the avowed object and confident promise of putting an end to slavery agitation. Under the operation of that policy, that agitation has not only not ceased, but has constantly augmented. In my opinion, it will not cease until a crisis shall have been reached and passed. "A house divided against itself cannot stand." I believe this government cannot endure permanently half slave and half free. I do not expect the Union to be dissolved; I do not expect the house to fall; but I do expect it will cease to be divided. It will become all one thing, or all the other. Either the opponents of slavery will arrest the further spread of it, and place it where the public mind shall rest in the belief that it is in the course of ultimate extinction, or its advocates will push it forward till it shall become alike lawful in all the States, old as well as new, North as well as South. . . .

According to the Declaration of Causes of Secession issued by South
Carolina on December 24, 1860, it was Mr. Lincoln and Northern
agitators who were dividing the nation. The South had its own
version of the American Dream and a strong union was not included
among its ideals, especially in light of the discrimination Southerners
felt they had suffered at the hands of Northerners. The Declaration
speaks of twenty-five years of increasing agitation by the North
on the slavery issue and refers to the Constitution to support
its reasons for secession.

South Carolina Declaration of Causes of Secession

South Carolina Convention

The people of the State of South Carolina in Convention assembled, on the 2d day of April, A.D. 1852, declared that the frequent violations of the Constitution of the United States by the Federal Government, and its encroachments upon the reserved rights of the States, fully justified this State in their withdrawal from the Federal Union; but in deference to the opinions and wishes of the other Slaveholding States, she forbore at that time to exercise this right. Since that time these encroachments have continued to increase, and further forbearance ceases to be a virtue.

And now the State of South Carolina having resumed her separate and equal place among nations, deems it due to herself, to the remaining United States of America, and to the nations of the world, that she should declare the immediate causes which have led to this act.

In 1787, Deputies were appointed by the States to revise the articles of Confederation; and on 17th September, 1787, these Deputies recommended, for the adoption of the States, the Articles of Union, known as the Constitution of the United States.

. . . Thus was established by compact between the States, a Government with defined objects and powers, limited to the express words of the grant. . . . We hold that the Government thus established is subject to the two great principles asserted in the Declaration of Independence; and we hold further, that the mode of its formation subjects it to a third fundamental principle, namely, the law of compact. We maintain that in every compact between two or more parties, the obligation is mutual; that the failure of one of the contracting parties to perform a material part of the agreement, entirely releases the obligation of the other; and that, where no arbiter is provided, each party is remitted to his own judgment to determine the fact of failure, with all its consequences.

In the present case, that fact is established with certainty. We assert that fourteen of the States have deliberately refused for years past to fulfil their constitutional obligations, and we refer to their own statutes for the proof. The Constitution of the United States, in its fourth Article, provides as follows:

"No person held to service or labor in one State under the laws thereof, escaping into another, shall, in consequence of any law or regulation therein, be discharged from such service or labor, but shall be delivered up, on claim of the party to whom such service or labor may be due."

This stipulation was so material to the compact that without it that compact would not have been made. The greater number of the contracting parties held slaves, and they had previously evinced their estimate of the value of such a stipulation by making it a condition in the Ordinance for the government of the territory ceded by Virginia, which obligations, and the laws of the General Government, have ceased to effect the objects of the Constitution. The States of Maine, New Hampshire, Vermont, Massachusetts, Connecticut, Rhode Island, New York, Pennsylvania, Illinois, Indiana, Michigan, Wisconsin and Iowa, have enacted laws which either nullify the acts of Congress, or render useless any attempt to execute them. In many of these States the fugitive is discharged from the service of labor claimed, and in none of them has the State Government complied with the stipulation made in the Constitution. The State of New Jersey, at an early day, passed a law in conformity with her constitutional obligation; but the current of Anti-Slavery feeling has led her more recently to enact laws which render inoperative the remedies provided by her own laws and by the laws of Congress. In the State of New York even the right of transit for a slave has been denied by her tribunals; and the States of Ohio and Iowa have refused to surrender to justice fugitives charged with murder, and with inciting servile insurrection in the State of Virginia. Thus the constitutional compact has been deliberately broken and disregarded by the non-slaveholding States; and the consequence follows that South Carolina is released from her obligation. . . .

We affirm that these ends for which this Government was instituted have been defeated, and the Government itself has been destructive of them by the action of the non-slaveholding States. Those States have assumed the right of deciding upon the propriety of our domestic institutions; and have denied the rights of property established in fifteen of the States and recognized by the Constitution; they have denounced as sinful the institution of Slavery; they have permitted the open establishment among them of societies, whose avowed object is to disturb the peace of and eloin the property of the citizens of other States. They have encouraged and assisted thousands of our slaves to leave their homes; and those who remain, have been incited by emissaries, books, and pictures, to servile insurrection.

For twenty-five years this agitation has been steadily increasing, until it has now secured to its aid the power of the common Government. Observing the *forms* of the Constitution, a sectional party has found within that article establishing the Executive Department, the means of subverting the Constitution itself. A geographical line has been drawn across the Union, and all the States north of that line have united in the election of a man to the high office of President of the United States whose opinions and purposes are hostile to Slavery. He is to be intrusted with the administration of the common Government, because he has declared that "Government cannot endure permanently half slave, half free," and that the public mind must rest in the belief that Slavery is in the course of ultimate extinction.

This sectional combination for the subversion of the Constitution has been aided, in some of the States, by elevating to citizenship persons who, by the supreme law of the land, are incapable of becoming citizens; and their votes have been used to inaugurate a new policy, hostile to the South, and destructive of its peace and safety.

On the 4th of March next this party will take possession of the Government. It has announced that the South shall be excluded from the common territory, that the Judicial tribunal shall be made sectional, and that a war must be waged against Slavery until it shall cease throughout the United States.

The guarantees of the Constitution will then no longer exist; the equal rights of the States will be lost. The Slaveholding States will no longer have the power of self-government, or self-protection, and the Federal Government will have become their enemy.

Sectional interest and animosity will deepen the irritation; and all hope of remedy is rendered vain, by the fact that the public opinion at the North has invested a great political error with the sanctions of a more erroneous religious belief.

We, therefore, the people of South Carolina, by our delegates in Convention assembled, appealing to the Supreme Judge of the world for the rectitude of our intentions, have solemnly declared that the Union heretofore existing between this State and the other States of North America is dissolved, and that the State of South Carolina has resumed her position among the nations of the world, as a separate and independent state, with full power to levy war, conclude peace, contract alliances, establish commerce, and to do all other acts and things which independent States may of right do.

Much has been written on the reasons why Lincoln issued the Emancipation Proclamation. John Hope Franklin, eminent black historian at the University of Chicago, presents a sympathetic history of the developments leading to its issuance on January 1, 1863. This high-sounding humanitarian document had political, military, social, and economic motives underlying it, and Lincoln had to weigh all the factors. Does Lincoln's vacillation about the Proclamation, due to the circumstances in which the Union found itself at this time, detract from the ideals of the American Dream which that document expresses?

The Emancipation Proclamation

John Hope Franklin

The road that led to the issuing of the Preliminary Emancipation Proclamation was a long and difficult one. It was marked by an incredible amount of pressure on Abraham Lincoln, pressure that began the day Sumter fell and that did not relent until his decision was announced on September 22, 1862. It is not possible to weigh the effects of the pressures created by hardheaded generals who would set slaves free in order to break the back of the Confederacy. One cannot know what impressions the procession of the Charles Sumners, the Orestes Brownsons and the religious deputations made on the President as they came by day and by night to tell him what he should do about slavery. Did a Greeley editorial or a Douglass speech sway him? One cannot know the answers to these questions, for Lincoln, the only one who could do so, never gave the answers. He was doubtlessly impressed by all arguments that were advanced, and he took all of them "under advisement." But the final decision was his.

Lincoln needed no convincing that slavery was wrong, and he had been determined for many years to strike a blow for freedom if the opportunity ever came his way. As a young man he told a New Orleans group in 1831, "If I ever get a chance to hit that thing, I'll hit it hard." He fully appreciated, moreover, the disastrous effect of slavery on national development and on the national character. He told a

Cincinnati audience in 1842 that "Slavery and oppression must cease, or American liberty must perish."[2]

Lincoln was irritated by any suggestion that he was "soft" on the question of slavery. "I am naturally antislavery," he wrote a friend shortly after the beginning of his second term. "If slavery is not wrong, nothing is wrong. . . . And yet I have never understood that the Presidency conferred upon me an unrestricted right to act officially on this judgment and feeling. . . . And I aver that to this day [April 4, 1864] I have done no official act in mere deference to my abstract judgment and feeling on slavery."[3]

Thus Lincoln was troubled by unanswered questions regarding the legality as well as the effect of emancipation on the course of the war and on the peace and well-being of the country. Who could know if the soldiers of Kentucky would lay down their arms if Lincoln set the slaves free? Greeley replied, "Let them do it. The cause of Union will be stronger, if Kentucky should secede with the rest, then it is now." It was not quite so simple, when one had the responsibility for shaping the course of the war and preserving the life of the Union. What would happen to the Negroes once they are free? Who would take care of them? These were questions that Lincoln asked over and over. Frederick Douglass, the runaway slave who had been a resounding success on two continents, had the answer. "Let them take care of themselves, as others do." If the black man could take care of his master and mistress, he could take care of himself. Should the freed Negroes be allowed to remain in the United States? "Yes," Douglass replied, "they wouldn't take up more room than they do now." Facile, even witty answers were not enough for the troubled Lincoln. . . .

The character of the Civil War could not possibly have been the same after the President issued the Emancipation Proclamation as it had been before January 1, 1863. During the first twenty months of the war, no one had been more careful than Lincoln himself to define the war merely as one to save the Union. He did this not only because such a definition greatly simplified the struggle and kept the border states fairly loyal, but also because he deeply felt that this was the only legitimate basis for prosecuting the war. When, therefore, he told Horace Greeley that if he could save the Union without freeing a single slave he made the clearest possible statement of his fundamental position. And he was holding to this position despite the fact that he had written the first draft of the Emancipation Proclamation at least six weeks before he wrote his reply to Greeley's famous "Prayer of Twenty Millions."

Lincoln saw no contradiction between the contents of his reply to

Greeley and the contents of the Emancipation Proclamation. For he had come to the conclusion that in order to save the Union he must emancipate *some* of the slaves. His critics were correct in suggesting that the Proclamation was a rather frantic measure, an act of last resort. By Lincoln's own admission it was, indeed, a desperate act; for the prospects of Union success were not bright. He grabbed at the straw of a questionable victory at Antietam as the occasion for issuing the Preliminary Proclamation. If anything convinced him in late December that he should go through with issuing the final Proclamation, it was the ignominious defeat of the Union forces at Fredericksburg. *Something* needed to be done. Perhaps the Emancipation Proclamation would turn the trick!

The language of the Proclamation revealed no significant modification of the aims of the war. Nothing was clearer than the fact that Lincoln was taking the action under his authority "as Commander-in-Chief of the Army and Navy." The situation that caused him to take the action was that there was an "actual armed rebellion against the authority and government of the United States." He regarded the Emancipation Proclamation, therefore, as "a fit and necessary war measure for suppressing said rebellion." In another place in the Proclamation he called on the military and naval authorities to recognize and maintain the freedom of the slaves. Finally the President declared, in the final paragraph of the Proclamation, that the measure was "warranted by the Constitution upon military necessity." This was, indeed, a war measure, conceived and promulgated to put down the rebellion and save the Union.

Nevertheless, both by what it said and what it did not say, the Proclamation greatly contributed to the significant shift in 1863 in the way the war was regarded. It recognized the right of emancipated slaves to defend their freedom. The precise language was that they should "abstain from all violence, unless in necessary self-defence." It also provided that former slaves could now be received into the armed services. While it was clear that they were to fight to save the Union, the fact remained that since their own fate was tied to that of the Union, they would also be fighting for their own freedom. The Negro who, in December 1862, could salute his own colonel instead of blacking the boots of a Confederate colonel, as he had been doing a year earlier, had a stake in the war that was not difficult to define. However loyal to the Union the Negro troops were—and they numbered some 190,000 by April 1865—one is inclined to believe that they were fighting primarily for freedom for themselves and their brothers in the months that followed the issuance of the Emancipation Proclamation.

Despite the fact that the President laid great stress on the issuance of the Proclamation as a military necessity, he did not entirely overlook the moral and humanitarian significance of the measure. And even in the document itself he gave some indication of his appreciation of this particular dimension that was, in time, to eclipse many other considerations. He said that the emancipation of the slaves was "sincerely believed to be an act of justice." This conception of emancipation could hardly be confined to the slaves in states or parts of states that were in rebellion against the United States on January 1, 1863. It must be recalled, moreover, that in the same sentence that he referred to emancipation as an "act of justice" he invoked "the considerate judgment of mankind and the gracious favor of Almighty God." This raised the Proclamation above the level of just another measure for the effective prosecution of the war. And, in turn, the war became more than a war to save the integrity and independence of the Union. It became also a war to promote the freedom of mankind.

Throughout the previous year the President had held to the view that Negroes should be colonized in some other part of the world. And he advanced this view with great vigor wherever and whenever possible. He pressed the Cabinet and Congress to accept and implement his colonization views, and he urged Negroes to realize that it was best for all concerned that they should leave the United states. It is not without significance that Lincoln omitted from the Emancipation Proclamation any reference to colonization. It seems clear that the President had abandoned hope of gaining support for his scheme or of persuading Negroes to leave the only home they knew. Surely, moreover, it would have been a most incongruous policy as well as an ungracious act to have asked Negroes to perform one of the highest acts of citizenship—fighting for their country—and then invite them to leave. Thus, by inviting Negroes into the armed services and omitting all mention of colonization, the President indicated in the Proclamation that Negroes would enjoy a status that went beyond mere freedom. They were to be free persons, fighting for their *own* country, a country in which they were to be permitted to remain.

The impact of the Proclamation on slavery and Negroes was profound. Negroes looked upon it as a document of freedom, and they made no clear distinction between the areas affected by the Proclamation and those not affected by it. One has the feeling that the interest of the contrabands in Washington in seeing whether their home counties were excepted or included in the Proclamation was an academic interest so far as their own freedom was concerned. After all, they had proclaimed their own freedom and had put themselves beyond the force of the slave law or their masters. The celebration of the issuance of the Proclamation by thousands of Negroes in Norfolk illustrates the pervasive influence of the document. President Lincoln had said that Norfolk slaves were not emancipated by his Proclamation. Norfolk Negroes, however, ignored the exception and welcomed the Proclamation as the instrument of their own deliverance.

Slavery, in or out of the Confederacy, could not possibly have survived the Emancipation Proclamation. Slaves themselves, already restive under their yoke and walking off the plantation in many places, were greatly encouraged upon learning that Lincoln wanted them to be free. They proceeded to oblige him. There followed what one authority has called a general strike and another has described as widespread slave disloyalty throughout the Confederacy.[4] Lincoln understood the full implications of the Proclamation. That is one of the reasons why he delayed issuing it as long as he did. Once the power of the government was enlisted on the side of freedom in one place, it could not successfully be restrained from supporting freedom in some other place. It was too fine a distinction to make. Not even the slaveholders in the excepted areas could make it. They knew, therefore, that the Emancipation Proclamation was the beginning of the end of slavery for them. Many of them did not like it, but the realities of the situation clearly indicated what the future had in store for them.

Notes

1   William H. Herndon, *History and Personal Recollections of Abraham Lincoln.* Springfield, n.d., p. 76.

2   Emanuel Hertz, *Abraham Lincoln.* New York, 1931, vol. II. p. 531.

3   Lincoln to Albert G. Hodges, Frankfort, Kentucky, April 4, 1864, *Collected Works,* vol. VII, p. 281.

4   W.E.B. Du Bois, *Black Reconstruction.* New York, 1935, pp. 55–83; Wiley, *Southern Negroes,* pp. 63–84; and Harvey Wish, "Slave Disloyalty under the Confederacy," *Journal of Negro History,* XXIII (October 1938), 435–50.

The stereotype is so easy to create, and historians have created their stereotypes of the Radical Republicans for decades. To some, they were dedicated leaders striving to bring freedom to black men with justice, education, and social, political, and economic equality for all. To others, they were rebel baiters, power hungry, and extremist villains.
Professor Donald of Columbia University challenges these easy generalizations and shows that the Radical Republicans were not united on any positive social and economic programs. Mainly, they were opposed to slavery and to the President. Whatever they were individually, some historians suggest that their reconstruction program only worsened relations between North and South and that we are still reaping the whirlwind today. Do you agree?

The Radicals and Lincoln

David Donald

What the Civil War historian needs is a good villain. In Abraham Lincoln he has the ideal hero, but the purity of the President's character can best shine in contrast with the blackness of others' motives. As all good historians are frustrated dramatists, there have been many attempts to supply the necessary villainous relief. For a biographer like William H. Herndon there was no problem, for he pictured Jefferson Davis as Milton's Satan summoning up his Confederate hordes:

> *He call'd so loud, that all the hollow deep*
> *Of Hell resounded, Princes, Potentates,* [etc.] . . .
> *Awake, arise, or be for ever fall'n.*

But after Robert E. Lee and Stonewall Jackson were admitted to the national pantheon, and after the Lost Cause won in the history books what it never could on the battlefield, it was necessary to seek a new villain for the piece. The Republican laureates, John Hay and John G. Nicolay, found a substitute in the Northern Democratic party. It was under a Democratic President, they wrote, that the nation divided; it was Northern Copperheads who impeded the prosecution of the war; it was the Peace Democrats who nominated McClellan in 1864 in the great "Chicago surrender" to the forces of secession; it was the Democratic party that consistently opposed Lincoln's plans. Their theory was both dramatically satisfying and politically useful in the 1890s, but today it seems hopelessly dated. Contemporary Civil War historians, nearly all of whom are firm Democrats, are not inclined to view the triumph of the Republican party as an example of wonder-working Providence, and they have looked elsewhere for villains.

The recent writers, in fact, have given an ironical twist to the Nicolay-Hay story. Nearly every major contemporary writer on the Civil War period now finds the most serious opponents of Lincoln in the Radical wing of the Republican party. This "revisionist" interpretation runs somewhat as follows: Abraham Lincoln was an astute, far-seeing statesman who would have won the war with expedition and ended it without bitterness. For the North he proposed malice toward none and charity for all; for the Negro, freedom, a gradual emancipation, possibly continuing till 1900; for the Southern whites, compensation for their slaves and amnesty for their rebellion in return for future loyalty. Preserving the Union and painlessly readmitting the reconstructed states, he would have bound up the nation's wounds, so that Americans could live in peace.

But these plans were frustrated, not so much by the Southerners, not even by the Democrats, but by a small yet articulate and potent group within the President's own party. These were the antislavery extremists, the "Jacobins," the Radicals. The true villains of the piece, they looked the part. There was malevolent and sharp-tongued old Thaddeus Stevens, whose uncertainly placed wig, protruding lower lip, and club foot made him "the perfect type of vindictive ugliness." Equally unlovely were the corrupt Ben Butler, with his "small, muddy and cruel eyes," perpetually crossed, and the constantly inebriated Zach Chandler, "that Zantippe in pants." The florid and arrogant Charles Sumner was of this group, as were pompous Salmon P. Chase, profane Benjamin F. Wade, and the "oleaginous" Edwin M. Stanton.

The abolitionist principles that these Radicals so piously announced were only a front for their real purposes. "Their main characteristics," according to J. G. Randall, "were antislavery zeal as a political instrument, moralizing unction, rebel-baiting intolerance and hunger for power." "They loved the Negro less for himself," T. Harry Williams adds, "than as an instrument with which they might fasten Republican political and economic control upon the South." For these unsavory Radicals were the advance agents of industrialism, which was about to take over the government of the United States and pervert it for selfish ends. Some of the Republicans openly admitted their economic objectives. John Sherman of Ohio said bluntly: ". . . those who elected Mr. Lincoln expect him . . . to secure to free labor its just right to the Territories of the United States; to protect . . . by wise revenue laws, the labor of our people; to secure the public lands to actual settlers . . . ; to develop the internal resources of the country by opening new means of communication between the Atlantic and the Pacific." Translated from politician's idiom, this meant that the Radicals intended to enact a high protective tariff that mothered monopoly, to pass a homestead law that invited speculators to loot the public domain, and to subsidize a transcontinental railroad that afforded infinite opportunities for jobbery.

Secession and the withdrawal of Southern Congressmen from Washington gave the Radicals a chance to enact their program, but an early end of the fighting might imperil their schemes. Ben Wade was, therefore, willing to see the war continued for thirty years, and Charles Sumner proclaimed: "I fear our victories more than our defeats. There must be more delay and more suffering. . . . We are too victorious." When peace did come, it must be under terms that would never permit Southern and Western agrarians to challenge the Radical-fostered industrial supremacy. Abolition of slavery became not merely a humanitarian striving but a desperately needed political requirement, for only thus could the Wendell Phillipses be sure that "the whole social system of the Gulf states is . . . taken to pieces; every bit of it." Emancipation alone was not enough, for the freedmen, loyal to the party that set them free, must have the ballot. ". . . I see no substantial protection for the freedmen except in the franchise," Sumner declared. "And here is the necessity for the universality of the suffrage: every vote is needed to counter-balance the rebels." . . .

Such, then, are the new villains of the piece. Civil War historians agree upon so few matters that one hesitates to start another controversy by questioning this universally held interpretation, but there seem to be valid reasons for challenging the stereotype of Lincoln-versus-the-Radicals.

After all, these "Jacobins" have received rather unfair treatment from the historians. The men, rather than their principles, come in for condemnation. Radicals are characterized as ugly, vain, pompous, power-grabbing, dictatorial, inflexible, oleaginous, arrogant, and unctuous—all at the same time! Because Thaddeus Stevens is said to have cherished a mulatto mistress and Salmon P. Chase presidential aspiration, because Ben Butler had a cocked eye and Charles Sumner a passion for Latin quotations, all right-thinking readers are supposed to condemn Radicalism. In all justice it should be pointed out that physical attributes do not make a statesman. Abraham Lincoln never won a beauty contest. Is it not possible for a Senator to be vain, ambitious, and even unctuous—and still be perfectly correct in his views? The historian who indulges in name-calling makes his point by innuendo rather than by argument.

But if one grants that these Radicals were antislavery zealots, unlovely in body and in spirit, it is hard to see that they have entirely merited the abuse heaped upon them. The charge that they were spokesmen for the business interests of the North presupposes a degree of unity among these antislavery leaders which did not, in fact, exist. Most of them favored a high tariff, it is true—but so did most Conservative Republicans and many Northern Democrats, too. Other economic issues found the Radicals badly divided. It was Charles Sumner who introduced the first bill for Federal regulation of railroads ever proposed in Congress, and he was supported by Radical Horace Greeley, but other Radicals killed his measure in committee. Some Radicals spoke for the creditor classes in financial affairs, abhorred inflation, and demanded a return to a specie basis of currency, but Radicals Ben Wade, Thad Stevens, and Ben Butler all championed greenback inflation. Most Radicals—and, indeed, most Congressmen —stood for the sanctity of private property, yet Stevens and Sumner proposed to create economic democracy in the South by dividing plantations among the freedmen—a proposal that other Radicals condemned as "a piece of political vengeance wreaked without the intervention of courts of justice, in defiance of the forms of law and to the ruin of the innocent and helpless."

If these Radical antislavery men were not united upon any positive social and economic program, they more nearly agreed about the things they opposed. But their dislike of slavery, of fumbling generalship, of presidential slowness, was shared by millions of Conservatives. It is true that a Charles Sumner was bent on converting the war into an antislavery crusade, but so was his principal rival, the leader of the Massachusetts Conservative Republicans, Charles Francis Adams, who declared in 1861: "We cannot afford to go over this ground more than once. The slave question must be settled this time once for all." Radicals were unhappy when Lincoln overruled General Frémont's proclamation freeing the slaves in his military district, but they were no more angry than was Orville H. Browning, one of the most Conservative of Illinois Republicans, who protested that the President's act was "damaging both to the administration and the cause" since Frémont's proclamation embodied "a true and important principle."

The American Dream of civil and political equality, the promise and
implementation of that equality during the Reconstruction period, are
evaluated by Professor Woodward of Yale in a conversation with
John A. Garraty of Columbia. Woodward says Reconstruction was overall
a failure in that it did not achieve its professed goals and aims of
bringing about social, political, and economic union. The inability of the
Reconstructionists to successfully integrate blacks into American life is an
important instance in which the ideals of the Dream have not
corresponded to reality.

The Negro in American Life: 1865–1918
C. Vann Woodward

John A. Garraty Professor Woodward, one common assumption
about the period of the Civil War and Reconstruction is that it was a
time of progress for the American Negro. Would you summarize the
gains made by the black people during those years?

C. Vann Woodward I think of the era as a period of promise
rather than of progress. The expectations aroused were far in excess
of the fulfillment. It was a time of change, but primarily of legal
change, of changes potential rather than actual. The legal foundations
of slavery were of course destroyed, but not the psychological or economic foundations. The legal foundations of civil and political equality
were laid down, but the enjoyment of these rights was tenuous,
temporary, limited. Many of the freedmen were worse off materially
than they had been under slavery. Many of the older generation of
blacks never broke through the internalized psychological bondage of
a servile existence, and some even sought to pass these old values on
to the next generation.

This contrast between promise and reality, between the potential
and the actual, has been used by cynics and conservatives to discredit
Reconstruction as a stumbling collection of blunders and frauds, in-
sincere in purpose, business-guided and futile. What the cynics have
overlooked are two results of Reconstruction: the long-term significance of the constitutional and legal changes, and the genuine gains

From *Interpreting American History: Conversations with Historians*, Vol. II,
by John A. Garraty. Reprinted by permission of The Macmillan Company.
Copyright © 1970 by The Macmillan Company.

that were made to the freedmen as a direct result of the Reconstruction process.

Men still argue about the relative importance of the gains and their durability, but one of them certainly was religious freedom. There was a conscious withdrawal of Negroes from the white churches. They established their own churches, their own clergy, and this was of special importance. The leaders of the Negro churches were far more than religious leaders. They became leaders of all kinds. A second category of gains, more limited, was educational. Hundreds of schools, thousands of them for a while, were founded, and a sizable group of literate blacks began to develop. A considerable number of what were called colleges and universities were founded. Often they were mere academies, but from them evolved a great many durable colleges and universities.

J.A.G. If it is safe to assume that illiteracy was almost universal among slaves, how much progress had been made by the end of Reconstruction?

C.V.W. We don't have exact figures. Reconstruction fell between census years, and the census of 1870 was notoriously inadequate. We know the number of blacks who attended school, but not how many learned to read or write. The archives of these schools indicate that many possessed an overwhelming urge to learn, so undoubtedly many did master reading and writing. The difficulty is that some of the schools functioned only for a couple of months during the year. At least, however, some school experience was very widespread among the freedmen. Whether it resulted in literacy is a question.

J.A.G. Is it just a romantic myth that large numbers of the older blacks made serious efforts to learn to read once it became legal for them to do so?

C.V.W. No, that was not a myth. This urge for literacy cut across the generations. Older people wanted to read the Bible first of all. Literacy was a social aspiration religiously motivated.

J.A.G. What was the white reaction to the Negroes' leaving the white churches?

C.V.W. Many resisted it, and some churches officially fought it. Religion was a means of control. One of the phobias of the ante-bellum era was that Negro religious leaders might use the church subversively, and those fears didn't end with the end of slavery.

Aside from the religious and educational advantages of freedom, the end of slavery opened access to the professions to Negroes. They became lawyers and doctors, for example. And they won access to public services like transportation and to places of entertainment.

On the economic side, they did not often obtain the land that they aspired so to own. But a black middle class of shopkeepers and preachers and peddlers and politicians gradually emerged. It was small, but it provided the leadership that the Negro masses needed. Reconstruction also made political experience possible for the American Negro. The resistance to slavery in other Western cultures often took political forms, as in Brazil and in parts of the Caribbean region. Resistance in the South had been not primarily political, but individual: the expression of individual discontent and frustration and resentment. During Reconstruction for the first time the Negro was acting politically. He voted, held office, campaigned, bargained, took some small part in self-government.

I don't think this list would be complete without reference to certain intangible, psychological gains. The black man grew in self-esteem; he could talk back, speak for himself, resist collectively and openly, not merely covertly and indirectly and individually. Then there was the Negro soldier, whom other Negroes could see and share experiences with. Guns had been a symbol of white dominance in slavery times. Blacks had never been permitted to have weapons. Now, military service symbolized the fact that they could exercise power and authority and responsibility.

Now I'm not arguing that Reconstruction was a great success, a golden age of Negro history. There was too much tragedy in Reconstruction to make it anybody's golden age, white or black. Nor do I endorse the concept of black Reconstruction. It was overwhelmingly a white Reconstruction, though this is not to disparage the Negroes' achievement. The white man was in control.

J.A.G. Among the religious or psychological gains, surely the right of legal marriage was one of the most important. Do we know anything about the durability of sexual relations among slaves, and among the former slaves after legal marriage became possible?

C.V.W. This is one of the frontiers of research in the field. Two of my students are doing some extremely interesting work with statistics and church and court records and manuscript census reports. Their research already indicates that family relationships were more enduring than was generally supposed, even in slavery times. Apparently, there was very little difference between black and white in this regard in the North before 1860. Whether that was true in the South, however, is yet to be determined.

J.A.G. Did the changes of the Reconstruction period cause any basic shift in white opinion, either in the North or in the South, about the character and the ability of the black man?

C.V.W. Let's talk about the North first. I once said that the Union fought the Civil War on borrowed moral capital. By that I meant that it committed Northern people to principles and goals that exceeded their moral resources, their capacity and will to pay the debts that they were piling up morally. The consequence was that they defaulted on their debt and went into moral bankruptcy, legalized by the Supreme Court. The have only recently begun to refund the debt. It's still mostly unpaid, of course.

Ante-bellum Northern society was thoroughly segregated on racial lines, much more segregated in the formal sense than that of the South. This situation was not changed by the Civil War. The grand moral purposes of the Civil War were an afterthought, designed to give a noble front to a power struggle. The Union had to justify the slaughter of 600,000 men (about one man was killed for every six slaves liberated) to the people. Thus, men died in the belief that they were fighting for the cause of justice and freedom, as well as union, for equality and the rights of man. The result was the depletion, instead of the accretion of moral capital. The war exhausted rather than restored the people's moral fervor, as men like Emerson and Walt Whitman were quick to point out. The professed goals of the war didn't endow the average American with moral grandeur, or destroy centuries-old racial attitudes. We are just beginning to realize how deeply embedded those attitudes were.

The work of the historians Winthrop Jordan and David Davis shows how white supremacy was used as a foundation for European identity in the New World in early colonial times. The Negro was a counter-image; he defined what the white man was *not* going to be in the wilderness. He was not going to be savage, or sensual, or primitive, or degraded. This stereotype was as common in the northern colonies as in the southern. The South, of course, had additional incentives for building and strengthening these attitudes. And the Civil War and Reconstruction didn't eliminate or deeply change them. In many ways, they intensified white belief in race supremacy, which seemed more necessary when the discipline of slavery was removed.

J.A.G. Then the concrete achievements that the Negro made in running his own affairs and establishing his own institutions had no effect on white opinion of his potential?

C.V.W. It had an effect, certainly. It proved that some of the grosser conceptions of Negro inferiority had no foundation. The Negro could learn to read and write, could speak up and defend himself. But deeper attitudes were not fundamentally changed.

J.A.G. What, then, were the motives of the Republican Radicals in insisting on the granting of legal rights to Negroes, if they still believed the Negro to be congenitally inferior?

C.V.W. When I generalized about Northern opinion, I was talking about mass opinion; there were always exceptions, and the exceptions included many prominent Radicals. But when one speculates about motives, one tackles a very elusive and controversial question. In the last decade, a renewed sympathy for the professed aims of the Radicals has developed. The old picture was cynical and derogatory. The new one is quite the reverse. The tendency is to absolve the Radicals of selfish partisan and economic motives, and to stress their perseverance, idealism, and sincerity.

Another revisionary tendency is to point out that the extreme defense of Negro rights often cost the Radicals a great deal politically. In many parts of the North, their views were unpopular. But while the revisionists have served to correct the old picture of Radical cynicism, I don't think that they prove that the Radicals were devoid of the normal political-economic motives. It's perfectly clear that the Republican party had something to gain from the establishment of a large constituency of blacks in the South, and that in narrowly divided Northern states like Indiana, New York, and Connecticut, there was political capital to be made by securing the votes of Negroes. The Radicals identified the cause of idealism with the Republican party.

But granting even the maximum of disinterestedness and idealism on the part of the Radicals, it must be remembered that they sought to substitute Northern paternalism for the Southern type in their approach to the freedmen. Their paternalism was of a missionary sort. The planter's paternalism was a basic part of the slave society, whatever you think of it and its effect. The Northern paternalism was more shallow, and not nearly as durable. It was episodic and quickly faded away.

J.A.G. I'm not sure that I understand the difference.

C.V.W. The Northern paternalism was humanitarian, liberal, eighteenth-century rights-of-man paternalism. The Southern variety had little of these concepts. It was Christian but not humanitarian. Southerners were responsible, they said, for their people.

J.A.G. You have said nothing about vindictiveness as a motive of Northern Radicals. Were they not, at least to some extent, motivated by a desire to punish the South?

C.V.W. I think that the idea has been exaggerated. Certainly there were bitter feelings and talk of revenge, but the Radicals weren't trying essentially to debase or degrade white Southerners. No doubt some took satisfaction in the troubles of the former slaveholders. That was only human. But it's unfair to the Radicals to dismiss their motivation as that of vengeance and vindictiveness.

J.A.G. On balance, was Reconstruction a success or a failure?

C.V.W. In the sense of the realization of the professed aims and goals it has to be called a failure, the first great collective failure of our national (not Southern) experience. Americans have "a thing" about failure. We think of our society as successful, indomitable, ever-victorious. In coping with this failure, both Northerners and Southerners have resorted to a great deal of fancy evasion. Southerners have romanticized the "lost cause," but Northerners have treated Reconstruction with the same kind of evasiveness. One tendency has been to stress the positive gains of Reconstruction; another is to justify it in terms of the present, by pointing out that laws which we are now trying to enforce were passed at that time, and by arguing that without that period of intensive constitutional revision and law-making, recent gains would have been impossible.

Before we can arrive at a definitive assessment of this whole experience, we're going to have to move beyond the national context and take a look at comparative history. The only comparisons that are traditionally made are with the North. The important comparisons should be with other slave societies in the New World, which also went through a process of emancipation and reconstruction. How did the English, the Dutch, the French, the Portuguese, and the Spaniards make this adjustment? The United States was the only slave society that had a bloody civil war. Is that the whole story? What problems did other societies have as a result of emancipation? Until we know the answers, it's quite misleading to assume unique American depravity and failure in this field.

J.A.G. I gather from the tone of your answer that you think comparative analyses will improve our opinion of our own Reconstruction.

C.V.W. It will put it in a different perspective. The evidence indicates that in all postemancipation situations around the world some type of involuntary servitude followed slavery. It took various forms, and lasted for different periods, but it was always a follow-up of emancipation. The freedmen were put back to work by force, sometimes in a formalized way, as with the apprenticeship system of the British West Indies, sometimes through black codes, as in the United States. If it happened everywhere, it was not an American peculiarity.

J.A.G. It's traditional to associate the formal ending of Reconstruction with the removal of the last federal troops from the South by President Hayes. Was this removal really very significant? After all, only a handful of soldiers were involved.

C.V.W. One must distinguish between the symbolic and the real importance of the removals of April, 1877. By that time, the troops in Florida, South Carolina, and Louisiana were mere token units, but they were of genuine political significance. In these states two contesting governments claimed to be legitimate, one conservative and one radical. The question of which was going to prevail was unsettled until the troops were removed. As soon as they were pulled out, the radicals gave up and the conservatives took over. That would have happened sooner or later, given the political situation. The deeper significance of Hayes's withdrawal was the symbolic statement to the country and the world that the use of force to maintain Republican governments was now abandoned.

J.A.G. I've never really understood the inconsistency of federal policy in this matter before 1877. Why were the troops removed from other Southern states sooner? Why the inconsistency?

C.V.W. In many states, the conservative take-over was of quite a different sort. It was political. The radicals simply didn't have the votes. But in South Carolina and in Louisiana, the Republican governments had held power continuously.

J.A.G. It's clear from President Hayes's diary and from other sources that he had received assurances from Southern leaders that the rights of Negroes would be protected after the 1877 compromise. Hayes was bitterly disappointed by the failure of this policy of conciliating white Southerners. Why did the Southerners fail to keep their promises? Had they ever intended to keep them?

C.V.W. Here again is this elusive question of motives. It is certainly true that the Redeemers, the conservatives, assured Hayes that they would protect Negro rights. But their motives were mixed and confused. I think they were guilty of less guile than critics have charged. It's a question, for one thing, of their conception of the Negroes' rights, which differed from that of the Radicals. The governors who negotiated individually with the President—Wade Hampton of South Carolina and Nicholas of Louisiana, both conservatives of the old order—were faithful in their own light to their promises. They handed out a remarkable amount of patronage to Negroes, and in some measure held in check local extremists. They had political reasons for so doing, since they stood to gain by Negro votes. The white supremacy element, motivated by vengeance and jealousy of the Negro, was also very resentful of upper-class conservative manipulation of the Negro vote. At the very start of the post-Reconstruction period, movements such as Martin W. Gary's South Carolina White Supremacy Party, opposed all "pampering" of the blacks. Put them in their place. Kick them out of political office. Keep them from voting.

I think we often don't realize the difference between the races in their perception of politics. To the Negro, politics was a means of gaining protection and jobs. Who had and could give those things? The conservatives. They had jobs to give, and they could, if they would, give some measure of protection. The Negroes were disappointed, mistreated, abused by the conservatives often, but the alliance was a real one, and it lasted a long time.

"This report is a picture of one nation, divided. It is a picture that derives its most devastating validity from the fact that it was drawn by representatives of the moderate and 'responsible' Establishment—not by black radicals, militant youth or even academic leftists. From it rises not merely a cry of outrage; it is also an expression of shocked intelligence and violated faith."—Tom Wicker (Introduction to the Report)

Report of the National Advisory Commission on Civil Disorders

Otto Kerner, Chairman

Summary Introduction

The summer of 1967 again brought racial disorders to American cities, and with them shock, fear and bewilderment to the nation.

The worst came during a two-week period in July, first in Newark and then in Detroit. Each set off a chain reaction in neighboring communities.

On July 28, 1967, the President of the United States established this Commission and directed us to answer three basic questions:

What happened?

Why did it happen?

What can be done to prevent it from happening again?

To respond to these questions, we have undertaken a broad range of studies and investigations. We have visited the riot cities; we have heard many witnesses; we have sought the counsel of experts across the country.

This is our basic conclusion: Our nation is moving toward two societies, one black, one white—separate and unequal.

Reaction to last summer's disorders has quickened the movement and deepened the division. Discrimination and segregation have long permeated much of American life; they now threaten the future of every American.

This deepening racial division is not inevitable. The movement apart can be reversed. Choice is still possible. Our principal task is to define that choice and to press for a national resolution.

To pursue our present course will involve the continuing polarization of the American community and, ultimately, the destruction of basic democratic values.

The alternative is not blind repression or capitulation to lawlessness. It is the realization of common opportunities for all within a single society.

This alternative will require a commitment to national action—compassionate, massive and sustained, backed by the resources of the most powerful and the richest nation on this earth. From every American it will require new attitudes, new understanding, and, above all, new will.

The vital needs of the nation must be met; hard choices must be made, and, if necessary, new taxes enacted.

Violence cannot build a better society. Disruption and disorder nourish repression, not justice. They strike at the freedom of every citizen. The community cannot—it will not—tolerate coercion and mob rule.

Violence and destruction must be ended—in the streets of the ghetto and in the lives of people.

Segregation and poverty have created in the racial ghetto a destructive environment totally unknown to most white Americans.

What white Americans have never fully understood—but what the Negro can never forget—is that white society is deeply implicated in the ghetto. White institutions created it, white institutions maintain it, and white society condones it.

It is time now to turn with all the purpose at our command to the major unfinished business of this nation. It is time to adopt strategies for action that will produce quick and visible progress. It is time to make good the promises of American democracy to all citizens—urban and rural, white and black, Spanish-surname, American Indian, and every minority group.

Our recommendations embrace three basic principles:

To mount programs on a scale equal to the dimension of the problems;

To aim these programs for high impact in the immediate future in order to close the gap between promise and performance;

To undertake new initiatives and experiments that can change the system of failure and frustration that now dominates the ghetto and weakens our society.

These programs will require unprecedented levels of funding and performance, but they neither probe deeper nor demand more than the problems which called them forth. There can be no higher priority for national action and no higher claim on the nation's conscience.

We issue this Report now, five months before the date called for by the President. Much remains that can be learned. Continued study is essential.

As Commissioners we have worked together with a sense of the greatest urgency and have sought to compose whatever differences exist among us. Some differences remain. But the gravity of the problem and the pressing need for action are too clear to allow further delay in the issuance of this Report. . . .

Why Did It Happen?

In addressing the question "Why did it happen?" we shift our focus from the local to the national scene, from the particular events of the summer of 1967 to the factors within the society at large that created a mood of violence among many urban Negroes.

These factors are complex and interacting; they vary significantly in their effect from city to city and from year to year; and the consequences of one disorder, generating new grievances and new demands, become the causes of the next. Thus was created the "thicket of tension, conflicting evidence and extreme opinions" cited by the President.

Despite these complexities, certain fundamental matters are clear. Of these, the most fundamental is the racial attitude and behavior of white Americans toward black Americans.

Race prejudice has shaped our history decisively; it now threatens to affect our future.

White racism is essentially responsible for the explosive mixture which has been accumulating in our cities since the end of World War II. Among the ingredients of this mixture are:

Pervasive discrimination and segregation in employment, education and housing, which have resulted in the continuing exclusion of great numbers of Negroes from the benefits of economic progress.

Black in-migration and white exodus, which have produced the massive and growing concentrations of impoverished Negroes in our major cities, creating a growing crisis of deteriorating facilities and services and unmet human needs.

The black ghettos where segregation and poverty converge on the young to destroy opportunity and enforce failure. Crime, drug addiction, dependency on welfare, and bitterness and resentment against society in general and white society in particular are the result.

At the same time, most whites and some Negroes outside the ghetto have prospered to a degree unparalleled in the history of civilization. Through television and other media, this affluence has been flaunted before the eyes of the Negro poor and the jobless ghetto youth.

Yet these facts alone cannot be said to have caused the disorders. Recently, other powerful ingredients have begun to catalyze the mixture:

Frustrated hopes are the residue of the unfulfilled expectations aroused by the great judicial and legislative victories of the Civil Rights Movement and the dramatic struggle for equal rights in the South.

A climate that tends toward approval and encouragement of violence as a form of protest has been created by white terrorism directed against nonviolent protest; by the open defiance of law and federal authority by state and local officials resisting desegregation; and by some protest groups engaging in civil disobedience who turn their backs on nonviolence, go beyond the constitutionally protected rights of petition and free assembly, and resort to violence to attempt to compel alteration of laws and policies with which they disagree.

The frustrations of powerlessness have led some Negroes to the conviction that there is no effective alternative to violence as a means of achieving redress of grievances, and of "moving the system." These frustrations are reflected in alienation and hostility toward the institutions of law and government and the white society which controls them, and in the reach toward racial consciousness and solidarity reflected in the slogan "Black Power."

A new mood has sprung up among Negroes, particularly among the young, in which self-esteem and enhanced racial pride are replacing apathy and submission to "the system."

The police are not merely a "spark" factor. To some Negroes police have come to symbolize white power, white racism and white repression. And the fact is that many police do reflect and express these white attitudes. The atmosphere of hostility and cynicism is reinforced by a widespread belief among Negroes in the existence of police brutality and in a "double standard" of justice and protection—one for Negroes and one for whites.

To this point, we have attempted to identify the prime components of the "explosive mixture." In the chapters that follow we seek to analyze them in the perspective of history. Their meaning, however, is clear:

In the summer of 1967, we have seen in our cities a chain reaction of racial violence. If we are heedless, none of us shall escape the consequences.

One of the editors of William F. Buckley's "National Review" suggests that
the nation is, indeed, divided and that the racial problem is not likely
to vanish from the American scene. Racial segregation is just as divisive
as geographic secession, yet some Americans of both black and white
complexion seem to be satisfied to maintain the cold war between the
two people—despite the ideals of the American Dream. Even though public
opinion polls indicate that most Americans of whatever color want to
come together into one nation; extremists, left and right, keep up the
agitation. America is as divided today as it was before, during, and
after the Civil War.

The Black Nation

James Burnham

In its September 22 [1970] issue *National Review* carried a brief review by J. D. Kirwan of Theodore Draper's *The Rediscovery of Black
Nationalism*. The reviewer finds in the author confirmation of his own
estimate of black nationalism: "hatesodden irrationalities"; "a fuzzy
abstraction [which] lends itself to all manner of slogan chanting and
heavy emotional hoopla"; "inherent contradictions stick out like guns
on a campus"; "basic false premise of racial collectivism"; "lost in a
web of esoteric confusion. . . ."

If black nationalism is analyzed as a theoretical concept, the
Draper-Kirwan finding of "irrationality-confusion-contradiction" is
no doubt valid, but we should not suppose that black nationalism as
an historical force can be laid to rest with this formal conclusion. If
only rational, clear, consistent concepts were operative in history,
nothing much would have happened.

A nation (and who can say exactly what a "nation" is?) does not
leap out fully formed from the forehead of time. Its birth may be a
very long agony. There now exist in the world 187 or 162 or something like that officially recognized nations, and there are several score
additional groups of human beings claiming to be nations. Are Nigeria,
Yemen, the Democratic Republic of Congo (Kinshasa), Kenya,
Mauritius, South Vietnam "really" nations? You can't answer just
yes or no. They, or some of them, are *becoming,* or may become, na-

From "The Black Nation" by James Burnham. Reprinted by permission from
the October 20, 1970, issue of *National Review,* 150 East 35th Street, New
York, N.Y. 10016.

tions. Nigeria is considerably more of a nation than fifteen years ago, and more by a quantum jump than before its civil war. Congo, looked at under one lens, is an aggregate of tribes, but it is also much more of a nation than before the Katanga war, the Stanleyville revolt and the expropriation of the big mining enterprises.

Draper states that black nationalist sentiment dates back at least to the beginning of the nineteenth century—time enough to prove pretty solid staying power. Until fifty years ago it usually expressed itself in Back-to-Africa form, as it still sometimes does, but beginning in the period between the two world wars attempts were made to locate it somehow or other within the geographical boundaries of the United States. The Communist Party doctrine of "Self-Determination for the Black Belt" was one of the best known variants in that period, though it never made much headway then in the black community.

Black is Black

It is in the past decade that black nationalism has been taking giant steps. Black is Beautiful, Black Studies, Afro Style, Black Poetry, Black Mathematics, Black Panther, Black Power—it's all "slogan chanting" no doubt, but the chanting is all to the nationalist tune. Crispus Attucks was probably an Indian and probably drunk on March 5, 1770 when a British bullet killed him, but this does not disqualify Attucks from being transformed into the Black Hero who was the first martyr in the American struggle for liberation. After all, George Washington may not really have chopped down that cherry tree or tossed the silver dollar quite all the way across the Delaware.

Actions, as always, are speaking louder than words. It is by act—by demonstrations and riots, organizing and disrupting, confrontations and non-negotiable demands, songs and novels and tracts, arson, looting, free breakfasts, takeovers, bombings and killings, international rounds of revolutionary capitals, their clothing (uniforms, rather), guns and hairdos—that the black activists are forging and shaping their nationalism. And [Frantz] Fanon is right in his facts about violence, however it may be about his evaluation. Of course violence is an indispensable part of a nationalism moving from idea to act. Whoever heard of a nationalism without violence?

There is a double irony. Integration's triumph in law coincides with its collapse in fact; black nationalism swells as integration deflates. Forced integration turns out to be the surest way to force blacks and whites apart—into a "resegregation" more complete than the initial segregation. No one (except in ceremonial talk) believes any longer that mass integration is possible; few that it is desirable. Integration has lost its historical dynamism—if it ever had any apart from the guilt-ridden fantasies of liberals. It is black nationalism that is presently dynamic, creative. To know that, we need only look and listen.

Where Is the Homeland?

But true nationalism must have a territorial base, acreage, a homeland? That does not seem essential. The Jews lacked acreage for nearly two thousand years, but remained (among other things) a nation. The gypsies are on principle without territorial root, and are a nation. There was never a nation of Algeria until, a few years ago, the revolutionary fellahin created it.

And is it true that the black nation has no territory? Ask a New York taxi driver who rules in Harlem, or a Chicago cop, who is in the Cabrini-Greene complex. The sovereign is he who controls the streets, the thoroughfares. Test it out.

It is in the cards that during the next decade the black nation will take control of several entire cities, with a few whites remaining, as in the black African nations, to carry out technical and administrative functions. Is it inconceivable that, in the decade following, the territory of the black nation might expand also to parts of the hinterland? Is it even certain that this would be so dreadful an outcome? Kirwan affirms it "symptomatic of the philosophic mess America is in today" that black nationalism should be considered "a viable alternative" by "congressmen and academicians." Black nationalism may not be the most attractive imaginable prospect, but as an "alternative" it is a damn sight more "viable" than integration.

Questions

1 Why was the House divided before the War for Southern Independence?

2 Can a House divided stand?

3 How might Lincoln have brought the House together had he lived longer?

4 Were the Southerners correct in standing for states' rights before and after the war? Explain.

5 Suppose the Southern Confederacy had won the war:
 a. What would have happened to the slaves?
 b. What would race relations there and in the

North be like today? In the South would they be similar to those in the Republic of South Africa today; that is, apartheid?

6 What are the fundamental causes of race conflict today?

7 Will the House continue to be divided?

8 Do we have any Radical Republicans today? If so, how do they differ from those in the 1860s and 1870s and how do they divide the nation?

9 Are there actually two "nations" in America today—one black and one white?

10 In his State of the Union address on January 22, 1971, President Richard M. Nixon admitted that the American Dream has not been realized for all: "For the black American, the Indian, the Mexican-American, and for those others in our land who have not had an equal chance, the nation has at last begun to confront the need to press open the door of full and equal opportunity, and of human dignity."

After reading of the many failures to achieve the ideals of the American Dream in the previous chapters, do you agree with Nixon's analysis in the excerpt that follows of the "nightmare" America has experienced? Do you feel that now we are ready—that now we must be ready—to leave strife and tension behind and to guarantee liberty and justice for all?

"In these troubled years just past, America has been going through a long nightmare of war and division, of crime and inflation. Even more deeply, we have gone through a long, dark night of the American spirit. But now that night is ending. Now we must let our spirits soar. Now we are ready for the life of a driving dream."

71 72 73 74   9 8 7 6 5 4 3 2 1